MW00441611

Advance Praise for Mort Zachter and *Red Holzman*:

"Mort Zachter's *Red Holzman* reads like a labor of love, using a lot of screen/roll writing to bring to life a man that led the Knicks to their two championship titles. There's a lot to it, as there was a lot to Red Holzman. Zachter gives the reader a glimpse of a man that would ask you to meet him in his office—the toilet stall—for a brief conference. Always done out of sight and off key. It was something he wanted you to know, about your demeanor or public statement, on the QT. Typical Red; always working, but not making it obvious. He was like a duck in water, and Mort captures a lot of what made Red Holzman great."

—Phil Jackson, Hall of Fame basketball coach

"In *Red Holzman*, Mort Zachter has written an affectionate and insightful biography of one of the truly great men in the history of basketball. He intimately captures the life and times of the coach I knew, the source I often relied on, and the friend I had for over 30 years. It deserves a wide readership.

—Ira Berkow, Pulitzer Prize–winning columnist and author of *To the Hoop: The Seasons of a Basketball Life*

"Before Mort Zachter's *Red Holzman*, most of what I knew about the legendary coach came from Phil Jackson, with whom I rarely had a conversation without him working tales about his beloved mentor. This biography afforded me the opportunity to dig in deeper into Holzman but also on many of the largely forgotten individuals who forged the early history of this game. The Knicks might not be doing so well, but their revered two-titled coach gets his due from Zachter."

—Jack McCallum, author of the best-selling *Dream Team*, *Seven Seconds or Less*, and *Golden Days*

"Zachter offers a comprehensive, if workmanlike, look at the life of New York Knicks coach Red Holzman (1920–1998), who guided the team to its only two NBA championships....NBA fans curious about the league in its earlier decades are most likely to find this solid biography of interest."

—*Publishers Weekly*

"Mort Zachter brought back to me a memorable picture of Red Holzman as I knew him. Red was a loyal man who possessed an incredible sense of humor; and an inordinate amount of humility who loved his privacy, family, friends, and players. Any success or accolades he received were channeled to his associates and his players. At the end of the day, Red just wanted to do his job and go home to Selma."

—Bill Raftery, award-winning basketball analyst

RED HOLZMAN

RED HOLZMAN

THE LIFE AND LEGACY OF A
HALL OF FAME BASKETBALL COACH

MORT ZACHTER

SPORTS
PUBLISHING

Sports Publishing books may be purchased in bulk at special discounts for sales promotion, corporate gifts, fund-raising, or educational purposes. Special editions can also be created to specifications. For details, contact the Special Sales Department, Sports Publishing, 307 West 36th Street, 11th Floor, New York, NY 10018 or sportspubbooks@skyhorsepublishing.com.

Sports Publishing® is a registered trademark of Skyhorse Publishing, Inc.®, a Delaware corporation.

Visit our website at www.sportspubbooks.com.

10 9 8 7 6 5 4 3 2 1

Library of Congress Cataloging-in-Publication Data is available on file.

Cover design by Qualcom
Cover photo credit: AP Images

Print ISBN: 978-1-68358-288-5
Ebook ISBN: 978-1-68358-289-2

Printed in the United States of America

"And the man Moses was a very humble man,
more so than any other man on the face of the earth."
—Numbers, 12:3

"I never really did anything spectacular or even really smart.
At best, a good job. . . . I'm just an ordinary man."
—Red Holzman

TABLE OF CONTENTS

PREFACE: FANFARE
FOR THE ORDINARY MAN

For me, Red Holzman was an easier interview dead than alive.

Beginning in the 1960s, to document the twentieth-century American-Jewish experience, in-depth interviews with well-known Jews from politicians like Golda Meir to playwrights like Arthur Miller were conducted. In 1978, an interview invitation was extended to Red Holzman, the most successful coach in the history of the NBA's New York Knickerbockers.

But Holzman hated being interviewed. He always told writers having dinner with him that when there was food on the table, everything was off the record. Manny Azenberg, a friend of Holzman, once sat in the back of a room where the coach was answering questions. Thinking Azenberg was a journalist, a writer new to covering the Knicks leaned over and asked, "Does this guy ever say anything you can use?"

Pulitzer Prize winner Dave Anderson wrote, "In the clamor over the Knicks players, Red Holzman often is forgotten. He prefers it that way. On the bench he is highly visible and highly vocal. But once the game is over, it's as if he vanishes. He hides behind innocuous phrases. He conceals himself under the camouflage of clichés. He never shares any strategic secrets. As a result, he is seldom quoted. But by not really saying anything, he is saying everything."

Remarkably, Holzman agreed to be interviewed. In 1978, for the first time in over a decade, he wasn't coaching the Knicks. He had been fired the year before, and Willis Reed, one of Red's best players, had taken over. But the former coach didn't agree to be interviewed just because he had time on his hands. Although Holzman would never admit it—and whether he viewed himself as a Jewish coach or a coach who happened to be Jewish—he understood his importance in basketball history. He not only played on an NBA championship team during the league's formative years, but helped bring a championship to New York, as Pete Axthelm wrote, when basketball was "The City Game."

In the spring of 1978, over the course of three sessions, Holzman was interviewed for a total of four hours. He never told anyone—not even his daughter—that he had done the interviews, and placed restrictions on their use. The agreement stated that they could not be used in any fashion until May 31, 1984, when his consulting contract with the Knicks ended. And during his lifetime, no one could use them without his written permission. The transcript of the interviews remained unread, in all likelihood, until I stumbled upon them in 2018—twenty years after Holzman's death. Even then, as per his written instructions, before I could see it, I had to convince the transcript's current guardians, the Dorot Jewish Division of the New York Public Library, that I was "a qualified scholar." I then spent hours sitting in the New York Public Library on 42nd Street reading the transcripts and feeling as if Holzman was alive and well and speaking just to me.

Sometimes I laughed. Sometimes I cried. Sometimes I needed coffee.

I'm not sure how scholarly Holzman would have found me. Unlike him, I have never attempted to complete the *New York Times* crossword puzzle, something he regularly enjoyed doing. And my goal is not to write an annotated version of his life, documenting precisely what he was doing and when. That approach wouldn't fit the subject. Instead, I've forsaken the individual trees and gone for the whole forest, focusing, wherever possible, on Holzman's unique voice and quirky sense of humor. For this, the transcript came in very handy. But I prefer to begin with a quotation which appeared on the first page of the *1998–99 New York Knicks Media Guide*, the year Holzman and his wife Selma both passed away. The guide was dedicated to their memory. It not only sums up Holzman's approach to life but provided me with a bit of guidance for my own.

"Look, the main thing in life is to enjoy yourself. You do your job the best you can and have a little fun."

—Mort Zachter
Princeton, New Jersey
June 2019

PROLOGUE:
ONE NIGHT IN SHREVEPORT

Red Holzman coached the New York Knicks to their only two championships.

If you wanted answers as to how he did it, Holzman was the last person you would have asked. He was, as the writer Mark Kriegel once said, "pathologically modest." During the Knicks' first championship season, when an out-of-town reporter was probing too deeply for the coach's taste, he responded, "Who cares about an *alter kocker* [Yiddish for old fart] like me?"

Fortunately, his players were more forthcoming. "There is not one player on this team who, when asked to explain its success, will not begin with Holzman," wrote Lawrence Shainberg in the *New York Times* in 1970. After the Knicks won their second championship in 1973, Dave DeBusschere, an invaluable player on both championship teams, said of Holzman, "He may well be one of the best coaches in the game, if not the best. There is more to the game of basketball than coaching or manipulating players, and this man has it. It's difficult to describe except to say he blends his coaching with every ingredient of life itself."

Holzman long possessed that inestimable trait. In the 1954–55 season, he was coaching the Milwaukee Hawks—one of the worst teams in the NBA. Ben Kerner, the financially strapped Hawks' owner, arranged for his team to play a three-game series against the Minneapolis Lakers in three different Louisiana cities to capitalize on the drawing power of their best player, Bob Pettit, a former college star at Louisiana State University (LSU). Unfortunately, Kerner didn't consider the fact that, in Louisiana, the Hawks only black player, Chuck Cooper—the first African American drafted in NBA history—would be playing in front of white crowds who had little to no experience with integrated team sports, a potentially incendiary situation. LSU did not have a black football player until 1971; a black basketball player until 1974.

On January 19, 1955, in New Orleans, Cooper played without incident, scoring six points. But the next night, in Shreveport, the crowd verbally abused him, repeatedly employing the N-word. Sixty-two years later, Bill Calhoun, one of Cooper's teammates, could still vividly recall, "It was the worst scene I've ever witnessed."

Holzman felt he had to remove Cooper from harm's way. He sat him down on the bench and the game continued. The Lakers were subsequently called for a technical foul. At the time, NBA rules allowed any player to shoot the free throw—even a player on the bench. Holzman, seizing an opportunity for Cooper to regain his dignity, had him shoot the free throw though other teammates were equally capable.

The coach knew how the crowd would respond, but he had

found a way for Cooper to rise above their bigotry. Cooper sank the free throw. Holzman's gesture shows the kind of man he was—savvy, humane, understated.

In 1998, shortly after Holzman's death, DeBusschere was again asked to comment on his former coach. "We were a great team," DeBusschere said, "but he made us great. He took people from diverse backgrounds—extremely diverse—and became the glue that put everyone together."

The question remains: How did Holzman, a native New Yorker, the son of immigrants, get the eight core players on his championship teams to all sing the same hymn?[1] Four were white: one, the son of a Detroit bar owner; another, a banker's boy from Missouri; the third, the pot-smoking son of two Pentecostal ministers from Montana; and the last, the greatest college basketball star in Ohio history, who, in his spare time, liked to memorize the phone book. Four were black: one, the son of a streetwise entrepreneur who ran a slice of the numbers racket in Atlanta; another, the product of a Gary, Indiana slum; the third, the proud grandson of an enterprising Louisiana farmer; and the last, one of the most entertaining offensive basketball players ever, out of rough-and-tumble south Philadelphia. Each was a star in his own right. So why did they give up their individuality and dedicate themselves to lifting each other up in a way that is rarely seen on a basketball court?

That story starts in Brooklyn with a schoolyard rat they called *Roita*.

---

1 Of the eight, five played on both championship teams, three on only the second.

CHAPTER ONE

"YOU SHOULD HAVE KNOWN MY FATHER."

A little over two miles from the site of the current Madison Square Garden, William Holzman was born in his parents' tenement apartment near First Avenue and First Street on August 10, 1920. Traversing those two miles to reach the pinnacle of his professional career would take him half a century. Along the way he paid his dues in long-forgotten basketball backwaters, from Sheboygan to Sunbury.

The journey began with his parents, Abraham and Sophie, two of the more than twenty million immigrants who arrived in the United States between 1890 and 1920. Holzman always said his father was from Poland but, according to census records, Abraham immigrated from Austria in 1901. At that time, a large portion of Poland was under the control of the Austrian Empire. "You know," Holzman would later say, using the homespun humor he favored to explain away controversy, negativity or, in this case, inconsistencies, "it was all mixed up at that time."

Abraham arrived in New York City at the age of eighteen and spent the rest of his life working as a tailor; his specialty was men's pants. Garment industry work was highly seasonal and, when Abraham was unemployed, he worried about supporting his family. He tried to conceal his anxieties behind a quirky sense of humor. Holzman once told Paul Horowitz, a writer for the long defunct *Newark News*, "Paul, you should have known my father. He was a great man. He said a lot of great things. He used to say: 'If I'm alive, we'll go Saturday. If not, we'll go Sunday.'"

Holzman also said his father was "happy with the simple things in life, the family, a good meal, a nice walk, a good nap. . . . He never worried about making too much money; whatever he made, my mother got."

In 1907, at the age of seventeen, Sophie immigrated from Romania. Four years later, she married Abraham. Their first child, Minnie, was born in 1912. A son, Julie, followed two years later. According to Red, Sophie was the backbone of the family. She was "a hard-working woman who always had time for everybody, always very pleasant, and had a lot of patience," he said. "She could get through with a whole days' work, put everybody to bed, and then go out and just take a walk or go to a movie or visit some friends, just to get away for an hour or so."

During the years he spent coaching under the intense gaze of the New York media, Holzman, like his mother, made sure to get away and decompress, whether at the racetrack, the movies, or a good restaurant.

Abraham's offbeat humor and ability to enjoy what he had, however pedestrian, was passed on to his son. In the 1960s, when people were first switching to color television sets, Holzman would ask, "What's wrong with black and white?" Though he could afford better as coach of the NBA champions, the modest house he purchased in Cedarhurst, Long Island, in the 1950s remained his home until the day he died. Red's daughter, Gail, remembers that, in the early 1970s, her mother was once sitting on the front porch of their home when a couple of kids rode by on their bicycles. One pointed at the house and said, "That's where Holzman lives."

The other kid replied, "No way. The coach of the Knicks would never live in a dump like that."

No matter how successful he became, Red always remained true to his humble roots. Manny Azenberg, who befriended him in the 1960s when they both worked at the Garden and who remained close with him for the rest of his life, said, "Red was the same through all the years I knew him—no pomposity."

At the height of the immigration wave that brought Abraham and Sophie to America, the Lower East Side of Manhattan was among the most densely populated places in the world. As subway lines expanded into Brooklyn in the early twentieth century, they served as escape routes for the congested masses. When Red was four, his family moved from Manhattan to the Ocean Hill-Brownsville section of Brooklyn. "Brooklyn was the country to us," Holzman later recalled. "They had some trees in those days. Not large, but they had some trees."

The third-floor walk-up apartment where they lived was a typical slice of working-class Brooklyn. Neighbors included Sam Kimerman, a milkman; Sam Foxx, a baker; and James Romano, who worked in the silver trade. Others in the building were taxi drivers, iron workers, and truck drivers. The Holzman home wasn't Kosher, but Sophie made challah and lit candles on Friday night before Shabbat. Family Passover Seders were "more a celebration than a religious thing," but Holzman attended enough Hebrew school to have a Bar Mitzvah upon turning thirteen.

At home, Abraham and Sophie spoke Yiddish, a mix of German and Hebrew that was common in Eastern Europe during their youth. Red cherished the language's unique phrasing and intonations for the rest of his life. As an adult, Holzman peppered his speech with the occasional endearing, but not necessarily positive, Yiddish word. When coaching the Knicks, he would call up the office of Freddie Klein, a longtime Knicks fan whom he felt close enough with to say, "Let me speak to the *putz* [fool]." And his parents called their red-headed son *Roita* [red].

Abraham could read and write English, but Sophie could not. She was, however, a superb cook. Her Romanian dishes left her youngest son with a lifelong passion for spicy foods. When Red was coaching the Knicks, their trainer, Danny Whelan, always kept a bottle of Tabasco sauce handy just in case he needed an extra "pop" to his meals. And assistant coach Butch Beard remembered his mentor was happiest the hotter the horseradish. "Red," Beard said, "liked to sweat."

In addition to Abraham, Sophie, and their children, the family unit included widowed Uncle Leon and his daughter Celia. Five years younger than his brother Abraham, Leon's purchase of a Brooklyn car repair shop had precipitated the family's move out of Manhattan. Luckily for Red, Leon had a more varied sports palate than Abraham, who was strictly a soccer fan. And, unlike Abraham, Leon had a car which he used to take Red to professional sports events. With Uncle Leon, the youngster attended New York Giants baseball games at the Polo Grounds in Upper

Manhattan and, closer to home, professional basketball games at Arcadia Hall on Halsey Street in the Bushwick section of Brooklyn. With his student ID card and 25 cents for admission, Holzman's love of basketball blossomed there.

In fact, in 1891, only a decade before the family had arrived in America, a Canadian physical education teacher named James Naismith had invented the game to keep his rowdier students occupied during the long New England winters. By the time Holzman began playing basketball in the 1920s, Naismith was still alive and espousing the view that the game was to be played "by passing the ball from one player to another until a player reaches an advantageous position to make a try for the basket." A straight line can be drawn from that concept, inherent in the first of the thirteen rules Naismith posted on the gym bulletin board at the YMCA Training School in Springfield, Massachusetts, to the words that became one of Red's coaching mantras: "Hit the open man."

Red's basketball career progressed in lockstep with the game's development. In the 1920s, professional basketball was often played in makeshift cages. It was a rough, low-scoring sport. Players would push each other up against the wire mesh that was set up along the length of the court to separate fans from those playing. By the end of games, players had scratches all over their bodies. There was also no three-second rule, and players stationed themselves close to the basket without limitation. Double-dribbling was permissible. (This allowed a player to dribble, stop, and then dribble again.) A jump ball followed every basket. With only one official assigned to each game and foul shots awarded only if the man in possession of the ball was fouled, professional basketball games often turned violent.

Unlike the basketball then played at the high school or college level—where Naismith's passing focus was the standard, and the game less physical—the pro game was more akin to football on hardwood.

> From an early age, Holzman was more comfortable in the schoolyard than the classroom. Red liked to joke that elementary school was "just to fill some time so we could go out and play ball. . . . I was not a great student. I think I became better later on, but I had to work very hard later because I hadn't acquired all the study habits that I should have had." In an era long before helicopter parents, Abraham and Sophie just assumed their son was going to do his homework. "And," Holzman said, "when I didn't and had problems, then they let me know about it . . . but you didn't want the shame of having to face your parents if you didn't do what you were supposed to be doing."

On the streets and schoolyards of Brooklyn, Red played touch football, softball, handball, soccer, stickball, punchball, and basketball, "whatever was current, whenever anybody had that type of a ball." During the Depression, in Ocean-Hill Brownsville, where putting food on the table could be a struggle, having a basketball was not always a given.

And, in a trend that would continue throughout his life, Holzman's childhood friends were of all ethnicities. "Mostly Jewish," he would later say, "but not all . . . there were a lot of Italian fellows and some Irish. Whoever was hanging around." Years later, when asked what were the differences between the various ethnic groups he interacted with as a child, Red responded by positively stating the obvious. "Basically," he said, "everybody was the same except for the religious aspect."

By the end of his time at PS 178, a combined elementary and junior high school just around the corner from where he lived, basketball was Holzman's best sport. He mostly played half-court, three-on-three games. "Basketball was very popular locally," Red recalled. "Kids were playing basketball everywhere. It was an easy game to play; you didn't need a lot of equipment."

As a child, no one taught Red the finer points of the game. With his father only knowing soccer, his brother Julie lacking any interest in sports, and his uncle busy repairing cars, Red learned the game in the school yards watching the better neighborhood players like Allie Lenowitz and George Newman, who later played for St. Francis College and Long Island University, respectively. But starting in high school, he was lucky to have two of the best basketball minds of the first half of the twentieth century teach him the game—and he was serious about learning. Decades later, Red summed up his approach this way: "If a player is ever going to be good—offensively or defensively—he's eventually got to study basketball the way he studies any subject in school."

Max Kinsbrunner, one of the players he saw at Arcadia Hall, was the star ball-handler of the Brooklyn Jewels. In college, Kinsbrunner played at St. John's, where he and his four starting teammates were called the "Wonder Five." When they graduated, all five were hired to form the Jewels and play professionally in the American Basketball League (ABL). By the early 1930s, with most professional leagues no longer playing in cages (and the double dribble banned), the basketball Red saw at Arcadia

Hall was closer to the more popular, faster-paced style played at the college level.

But professional basketball was still decades away from being entertaining enough to grow into a national sport. Other than layups, all shooting was limited to two-hand set shots and a jump ball still followed every basket. There was no requirement to bring the ball past midcourt within ten seconds. And with no 24-second clock, when a team had a lead, a master ballhandler like Kinsbrunner could ice the game by running out the clock dribbling up and down the entire court. Holzman was watching, dreaming of someday getting his chance.

In the early 1930s, when Holzman saw the Jewels play, professional basketball had a fly-by-the-seat-of-its-pants quality. Consider the entry into the professional game of Moe Goldman. A giant for his era at 6-foot-3, Goldman was the star of the same high school Red would later attend, Franklin K. Lane. With Goldman as the leader, Lane won the 1930 Public School Athletic League (PSAL) championship. Goldman then attended the City College of New York (CCNY). During Goldman's senior year, when CCNY traveled to Philadelphia for a matchup against Temple, Eddie Gottlieb, the owner of the ABL's Philadelphia team, the SPHAs (South Philadelphia Hebrew Association), offered Goldman a chance to play for $35 a game. Goldman accepted, and Gottlieb said he would reach out when his college career ended. That spring, Goldman played his final game for CCNY on a Saturday night. The following evening, he took a bus to Arcadia Hall, was introduced to his new teammates, given a SPHA's uniform, and started the game at center. For Goldman, like most players of the era, basketball was a part-time job. He played for the Jewels on weekends, for a team in Wilkes-Barre,

Pennsylvania, on weeknights, and worked full-time as a physical education teacher in the New York public schools.

In addition to the Jewels, Philadelphia SPAHS, and the Cleveland Rosenblums, another professional team Red saw play at Arcadia Hall was the all-black Harlem Renaissance Five. Their name came from the Renaissance Ballroom in Harlem where they originally played. The Rens were the best team of the era but were banned from playing in white leagues and had to barnstorm around the country. In 1933, they had an 88-game winning streak. From 1932 to 1936, their record was 497–58. In 1939, they won the World Tournament of Professional Basketball in Chicago, becoming the first all-black pro team to win a world title in any sport. The Rens focused on speed, passing, and pressing defense. "The Rens played so many games that they knew each other's moves instinctively. They played a switching man-to-man defense to save extra steps and conserve energy and emphasized team basketball and unselfishness," Holzman wrote in his autobiography. "Their style made a big impression on me and I filed it away for future reference."

Red recognized the injustice of such great players being banned from playing in white professional leagues. When he was in a position to exert his influence, first as a player and later as a scout and coach, his color-blind approach had its roots with the Rens. When I interviewed Dick Barnett, one of the black players on Holzman's championship Knicks teams, he made it a point to emphasize that Red ran the team without "any regard of color." All he cared about was a player's ability.

Despite being short for his age, Holzman was already devoted to basketball. Beginning in 1932, when he was twelve, he played in a league where no player above 4-foot-10 was allowed to participate. Following a growth spurt, Red eventually became the captain of the Franklin K. Lane High School basketball team. He also played on a team with the Workmen's Circle, a Jewish mutual-aid society located on the Lower East Side of Manhattan established to help immigrants adjust to American life. But, like many Jewish teenagers, Holzman joined the WC strictly to play basketball. He had no interest in the WC's political and religious activities.

For a brief period, the Franklin K. Lane team was coached by Red Sarachek, a seminal figure in New York basketball circles in the decades before and after World War II. Sarachek, who also coached at the WC, encouraged Holzman to play there and became his first basketball mentor.

From the 1940s through 1960s, Sarachek was the basketball coach at Yeshiva University, where his players' number-one priority was academics. If a player told Sarachek he had to study, that was reason enough for him to miss practice. In order to overcome a lack of quality players, he was forced to innovate. His motion offenses, trapping defenses, and in-bounds plays had young coaches from other teams attending Yeshiva practices to gain first-hand knowledge of Sarachek's methodology. Although his lifetime coaching record at Yeshiva was a losing one (202–263), it was still remarkable, considering that his typical teams featured pre-dental, pre-med, and rabbinical students.

In the 1930s, at the WC, Red became a devotee of Sarachek's unselfish, team-oriented style of basketball. He also discovered that the coach could be tough on his players, shouting at them when necessary. "I screamed at the kids so much," Sarachek later said, "that they were so nervous they couldn't miss the basket."

The WC wasn't just for young men; they had competitive athletics for young women as well. When the blue-eyed, lightly freckled Holzman was fifteen, he met a pretty, dark-haired, thirteen-year-old volleyball player named Selma Puretz. Red was interested in her immediately, but they didn't start dating right away because, as he would write in his autobiography, "I was pretty shy in those days."

Unlike Sarachek, Joe Calia, who coached both basketball and baseball at Franklin K. Lane, didn't have the luxury of focusing just on basketball. It was therefore exceedingly fortunate that Sarachek brought Holzman into the WC fold where he would make even more beneficial basketball connections.

When Holzman played for Lane from 1935 to 1938, the team was, in his own words, "lousy." Lane didn't have its own gym for most of Red's high school playing career. They used either their opponents' courts or makeshift venues such as the Central Methodist Episcopal Church. As a fifteen-year-old sophomore, Holzman was the team's sixth man. But, by his junior year, he was the team's best player and regularly led them in scoring.

During his senior year, foreshadowing his later coaching style, Holzman developed a reputation as a fierce defender; he was always assigned to guard the opponent's best scorer. In a December 16, 1937 game, Alexander Hamilton's coach Leo Merson had his leading scorer, Jim White, change uniform numbers with another player so Red wouldn't guard him. Holzman shut down his man, but White, who later became a star at St. John's, was the game's leading scorer; a game in which Hamilton won, 32–28.

During his senior year, despite being only 5-foot-10, Holzman was listed as a forward. At the time, the style of play featured

11

constant player and ball movement, so the difference between the guard and forward positions was nominal. With all players expected to be able to handle the ball and pass with authority, height was much less a factor in a team's success than it would become after World War II. In the 1930s, if a player stood over six feet tall, they would play at the center position.

Even if the Lane basketball team was "lousy," Red still got to experience playing on a championship team as a member of the school's handball team. One of his teammates was Ferdinand Alcindor, father of NBA great Kareem Abdul-Jabbar. Red had been playing handball in the schoolyard since he was a kid. Because he had been small for his age, he was not taken seriously by other players. Those who were foolish enough to play him—with 25 cents riding on the outcome—helped him pay his way into basketball games at Arcadia Hall.

As immigrants who were most comfortable speaking Yiddish, Red's parents had no frame of reference for understanding basketball. They referred to it as *narishkeit* (foolishness). In his autobiography, Holzman wrote, there were times he threw his gym gear out the back window of their third-floor flat and had to "fumble around in the dark in the courtyard searching for them" so his parents didn't think he was going out to play basketball. But, by the time he graduated from high school, his parents were supportive and even came to see him play. "They understood the game enough to know if you were winning or losing, and if you were getting any baskets. They didn't understand 'bad calls,'" he later remembered.

Although Abraham and Sophie would have preferred their son to spend more time hitting the books, they knew that in Ocean Hill-Brownsville, for kids who spent all their free time on the streets and in the schoolyards, staying focused on basketball was a good thing. It kept them clear of Murder Incorporated, a notorious band of Jewish and Italian hitmen whose base of operations was a candy store on the corner of Saratoga and Livonia Avenues not far from where Red lived.

Holzman graduated from high school in January 1938. He was missed. In the school's yearbook the following season, someone wrote, "It has been the tradition in Lane to turn out smart, fast squads with a brilliant display of defense ability and team work. It seems that this type of play left the school with the graduation of 'Red' Holzman."

Yet, despite being named to some all-city teams in his senior year, he was a mid-year graduate on a losing team, and not a single college recruited him. Red had a few tryouts with some local colleges, but no offers.

* * *

A few years before, another Brooklyn high school basketball player—also named Red—had participated in the tryout process with more positive results. Red Auerbach, three years older than Holzman, was also the son of Jewish immigrants from Eastern Europe. Auerbach grew up in the Williamsburg section of Brooklyn, about ten miles from Holzman's residence. But Auerbach received a basketball scholarship from a lesser basketball program, Seth Low Junior College in Brooklyn. Ironically, considering their similar backgrounds, the two Reds engaged in a fierce rivalry for the next half century. When Holzman's professional career ended, he had more victories than any other coach in NBA history except one: Red Auerbach.

The two Reds had very different personalities. As a coach, Holzman always tried to deflect attention away from himself and shift it where he felt it belonged—on his players. Auerbach, on the other hand, loved the limelight. At home games, when he was convinced his team, the Boston Celtics, would win, he would light up a victory cigar from the bench—even well before the final buzzer. Opposing coaches despised him for this. But when he lit up, all eyes—the fans and the opponents—were on him. The disparate demeanors of the two Reds had a genetic component. Abraham Holzman was comfortable as an employee; Hyman, Red's father, was a successful entrepreneur who ran his own drycleaning business. Holzman would evolve into the ultimate company man for a highly structured Knicks organization. In contrast, Auerbach was fortunate to eventually work for an owner, Walter Brown, who gave him carte blanche to run basketball operations as he saw fit. As a result, Auerbach effectively created the general manager position in the NBA.

When Auerbach and Holzman graduated from high school, college basketball was vastly more popular than the professional game. In New York City, beginning in 1934, doubleheaders involving the better local teams, such as St. John's, New York University (NYU), and Long Island University (LIU) were played before packed crowds at Madison Square Garden. Hosting college basketball doubleheaders in the Garden was the brainchild of a former newspaper sports reporter, Ned Irish. Running those games proved so lucrative that Irish gave up journalism and became a full-time promoter. By the late 1940s, Irish was not only a major force at Madison Square Garden, but also one of the most powerful executives in the NBA. And, by the late 1950s, he was Holzman's boss.

With the Depression still in full swing and no college scholarship available, Holzman was fortunate to get a full-time
job working in the garment industry. Someone active in the
Truckmen's Union Number 102, which ran one of the better
amateur teams in New York City as part of the International
Ladies' Garment Workers' Union League (ILGWU), saw Red
play on the Workmen's Circle team and recruited him. The
league was, according to Holzman, "pretty organized," with
scheduled games, uniforms, officials, timers, and scorekeepers,
and even charged a nominal admission fee.

Red's basketball skills had landed him a job that paid $29.50
a week pushing a handtruck through the Garment District
(between 34th and 42nd Street, with Seventh Avenue as its backbone). In the midst of the Great Depression, that was a very good
salary for an eighteen year old. In 1939, for example, Abraham
worked for only 26 weeks and made just $650. Holzman was
pleased to help his family out financially, but still dreamed of
getting a basketball scholarship and going to college. Thanks to
a basketball referee, he got his chance.

CHAPTER TWO

"YOU EVEN SAW THE LIBRARY ONCE IN A WHILE."

In 1939, Red was still playing for the Truckmen's Union when Phil Fox, a referee who called games in the ILGWU League, recommended him for a basketball scholarship at the University of Baltimore. After World War II, Fox's theatrical foul calling as an NBA referee earned him an invitation to tour with the Harlem Globetrotters. Luckily, Fox appreciated Holzman's solid—but far from flashy—defensive abilities.

The university hoped to improve the quality of its basketball program in order to entice top college teams from out west to play in Baltimore. With Ned Irish's soldout doubleheaders at Madison Square Garden as the template, Baltimore wanted its share of college basketball's expanding economic riches. Abraham and Sophie were initially upset that their youngest child was leaving New York, but the opportunity to be the first Holzman to attend college outweighed their concerns.

For the 1939–40 season, Holzman, along with two other freshman players who also happened to be Jewish, Ozzie Schaeffer and Nat Winitsky, became starters on the University of Baltimore Bees. Of the fifteen players on the squad, only seven were over six feet tall. Red was listed as 5-foot-10 and weighing 170 pounds. Schaeffer, at 6-foot-3, was one of the team's tallest players. Their coach was Bucky Miller, a former star college football player. Holzman would later call Miller "a good coach." That wasn't a rave review by Red's standards since he would have never publicly said anyone was a bad coach. As it turned out, Miller's coaching abilities wouldn't matter much; Red would be back in New York before the basketball season ended.

The Bees won their season opener against Georgetown on December 2, 1939. The game was played at the Baltimore Coliseum, and even the mayor of Baltimore was on hand to welcome the crowd of 1,200 fans. Team captain Mike Pellino led the Bees in scoring that night but, by the end of January, Holzman was the team's leading scorer.

Early in the season, the Bees had a four-game winning streak against less formidable opponents like Western Maryland. But on December 19, the Bees lost at home to the defending NCAA champions, the University of Oregon, 45–40. Oregon had won the very first NCAA tournament that past spring. While the Bees had quicker players, Oregon utilized its height advantage to gain victory.

A week later, on December 26, playing at home, the Bees lost in overtime to Stanford, 45–43. The Bees again had the faster players; their nationally-ranked opponent, the taller players.

Holzman was the high scorer in the game with 15 points. In a sign of how important defense was considered in that era, the box score, in addition to showing field goals and foul shots made by each player, listed the total number of interceptions by each team.

Red once again led the team in scoring, this time against Washington College, on New Year's Day, 1940. But, by the end of January, he was off the team. The Bees played visiting Michigan State on January 29, 1940, but, according to the *Baltimore Sun*, "at the insistence of the Spartans' athletic authorities," the Bees three freshman starters, Holzman, Winitsky, and Schaeffer, were disqualified from playing. No reason was given. But a week later, just prior to a February 9 game against Wake Forrest, the *Sun* reported that Red and Winitsky "had departed because of academic deficiencies," and that Schaeffer was "suffering from a nasal condition and was not likely to see much action."

In his biography, Holzman would explain his sudden return to New York: "I was determined to go home, so that was it, I went. The food in Baltimore was foreign—not like the soul food my mother made. There wasn't much of it either, and I was always hungry. I missed my folks. I missed Selma." No doubt he was homesick. But considering how well both Red and his team were playing (the Bees' record was 10–4 prior to his departure), it's doubtful he would have left prior to the end of the basketball season if academics were not an issue.

Upon his return to New York, Holzman was a hot ticket. Clair Bee, the coach of LIU, one of the best basketball programs in the city, wanted Red to come play for him. But he instead transferred to the City College of New York (CCNY) where the man who ran the basketball program was not only one of the greatest basketball players of the first half of the twentieth century, but one of the nation's most successful college coaches: Nat Holman.

In the 1920s, few professional basketball teams remained together long enough to focus on passing and team play. The original Celtics were the most notable exception. Although the team was founded by Irish players from the Chelsea section of New York City, and though a shamrock was prominently featured on their jersey, Nat Holman, the son of Russian Jewish immigrants, was their most famous player.

Born on October 16, 1896, the fourth of ten children, Nat Holman grew up on the Lower East Side of Manhattan. His parents owned a grocery store on Norfolk Street, and a strong work ethic was drilled into him early on. But, like so many children of Jewish immigrants growing up in that neighborhood (where there were few, if any, baseball fields available), basketball became Nat's game of choice. By age twelve, Holman was such a good player that he competed against adults at the University Settlement House, a Jewish version of the YMCA. The court there was small, only 70-by-40 feet, and inspired him to become a master of constant motion, deception, and subtlety to create good shots. These tactics later became the trademarks of the teams he would coach. Holman attended the Savage School for Physical Education, which eventually became part of NYU. While still in college, Holman began his professional basketball career. Playing for six dollars a game, he soon had more offers to play than there were nights in the week.

After serving in the Navy during World War I, Holman became a star on a team called the New York Whirlwinds. In 1921, the Whirlwinds and the original Celtics were scheduled to play a three-game series to determine the best team in the New York metropolitan area. After splitting the first two games, the third was never played because gamblers attempted to fix the outcome. Ironically, a gambling-based scandal later put a shadow on Holman's coaching career.

Holman, who stood 5-foot-11, played so well against the Celtics that their manager hired him and teammate Chris Leonard to play exclusively for his team. Holman and Leonard would form a starting five—with Johnny Beckman, Dutch Dehnert, and Joe Lapchick—that would become one of the few entire teams inducted into the Basketball Hall of Fame. Holman was the highest paid at $12,500 per season— the equivalent of almost $190,000 today.

A few years earlier, in 1919, Holman had become the coach of the CCNY Beavers and somehow managed to juggle college coaching and playing professionally until he retired in the 1930s; his coaching career continued until the 1950s.

Although the Celtics had no coach—few, if any professional teams in that era did—the familiarity the players developed with one another over the years played a role in the evolution of several fundamental concepts of team basketball: the give-and-go play (one player passes the ball to his teammate and immediately cuts to the basket to receive a return pass), the pivot play (a player sets up in a stationary position at or near the foul line and, after receiving the ball, becomes the center point of what Holman would call the "offensive orbit"), and a switching man-to-man defense (defenders did not just guard their man, but switched to defend other opponents when blocked by an opposing player). Many of the fundamentals Holman drilled into his CCNY players were mainstays of Celtics play, especially a focus on ball possession and passing to insure a high-percentage shot, preferably a layup.

At the height of their fame, the Celtics barnstormed all over the country and became the best-known team of the era. When most professional basketball games were still being played in high school gyms and dance halls, the Celtics were drawing 9,000 fans to a game in Chattanooga, 10,000 to Madison Square Garden, and 12,000 to see them play a February 22, 1922, doubleheader in Cleveland. Although basketball was the least popular professional team sport at the time, Holman developed a national reputation. In the 1920s, what Babe Ruth was to baseball, Jack Dempsey to boxing, and Red Grange to football, Holman was to basketball.

Along with his reputation, Holman's opinion of himself swelled. In a piece published in *Collier's* magazine in 1950—at the height of Holman's coaching fame—Stanley Frank, a CCNY alumnus who had served as the sports editor of the campus newspaper, wrote, "Holman does not discuss basketball with coaches, players, or officials. He lectures them." Later, in the same piece, to soften his take, Frank added, "Based on a quarter century of close-up observation, we offer this appraisal of Holman: What appears to be a presumptuous, even pompous attitude on his part where basketball is concerned simply is an expression of Holman's pride. He firmly believes his name and the words 'Mr. Basketball' are interchangeable. Any unfavorable reflection on the game, therefore, is an affront to his personal pride."

During his first 20 seasons coaching CCNY (1919 to 1939), his record was a staggering 230–61 (a .790 winning percentage). Holman's success was remarkable considering that CCNY was a commuter school without dorms and had strict academic requirements for admission (a high school average of 81 or higher was required). In large part, CCNY's success was due to Holman's coaching abilities—but also to his fame. He made CCNY a desirable landing spot for talented New York City basketball players whose skills were just below a level that would enable them to get a scholarship at a private college, but whose priority was getting a good academic education. CCNY was referred to as the poor man's Harvard: a tuition-free school that provided an outstanding education to those who were bright enough to gain admission. Nat Holman did not often land a player such as Red Holzman's fellow Franklin K. Lane alumnus, Moe Goldman, one of the best players in the entire country when he played at CCNY. But Holman had a steady flow of quality players who considered themselves first and foremost, students. Some of Red's teammates became doctors, school principals, and investment bankers. As Red would later say when asked to explain the reasons for Holman's success, "He got a lot of good players."

But, in the 1939–40 season, immediately prior to Red's arrival, the CCNY Beavers didn't have enough good players. They finished 8–8, the worst season of Holman's coaching career to date. None of his previous teams had ever lost more than six games. As a result, in the spring of 1940, Holman must have been pleased to land Holzman, a player who had already competed against the best college basketball teams in the country. Although Red's grade point average at the University of Baltimore may have been below 81, because he was a transfer student, academic requirements appear to have been less vigorously applied. After passing the CCNY entrance exam, he joined the basketball team beginning in the fall of 1940. For the next two seasons, Red became CCNY's on-court leader.

In 1978, when asked to describe a typical day at CCNY, Holzman said, "Come to school, go to class, go to practice, and then an hour train ride home, so you did your studying on the train, and then maybe when you got home. Usually you were tired. The team had a training table where we could have our meals and sometimes maybe we'd eat there and then go home." Holzman joked that, during his free time in between classes, "You even saw the library once in a while."

Nat Holman cared about his players' grades, "because how were you going to stay in school if you didn't get by," and tutors were available if a player had a problem with a specific subject. Red received a financial stipend while attending CCNY. As he later recalled, "there was some kind of help. I forget what they called it in those days where you were allowed to do some work to make a few bucks to sustain yourself."

Holzman's responses during his Dorot interviews shows the challenges he created for interviewers. He was a master at answering a question by not answering it. For example, during the interview, after Red stated he majored in economics at CCNY, the interviewer asked, "Besides economics, what other subjects did you have to study?"

Holzman's reply: "Oh gee, I don't know. English, took some German at school. Name it, I don't know. Normal."

On the other hand, in his autobiography, Red is clear in describing Nat Holman's demeanor with his players. He called it "distant nearness," friendly but with a solid demarcation between himself and his players. "Most coaches," he would later write, "are not that chummy with their players . . . especially in college. They might make sure they know what they're doing and take care of them properly, but socially I don't think there's that much togetherness." In his 1950 piece on Nat Holman, Stanley Frank noted that although all of his players had enormous respect for his abilities, "Bill [Red] Holzman . . . was not on chummy terms with Holman when he played for him."

But Red appreciated Holman's coaching skills. In 1978, he said his coach was "an excellent, great coach. He knew how to impart his knowledge to you, and he knew what was important, and he knew what he wanted you to do, and of course he was stressing the team aspect of the game."

Nat Holman's strong suit was not during games but during practice. "That's where he was really great," Holzman said, "where he taught you the game." Practice started promptly at four and, for the next two hours, there was no talking. "You don't talk in biology class—don't talk in my class," Holman would say. He taught his student-players the importance of ball control, passing with care, taking only open shots, never holding the ball, and constant movement. In a further evolution of the pivot play from his Celtics days, Holman called this five moving pivots: each player looking to set up one of his teammates with a pass.

The coach also expected you to learn your lessons. If you didn't, he'd let you know about it. "He yelled at his players," Red would say years later, adding, "All coaches have to yell at times. He didn't like mistakes. He put on his coach's frown if you got a little too fancy. He wasn't happy about that."

"I have no patience with mediocrity," Holman told Frank. "I'll string along a sophomore, but a boy has had a full year of my teaching, I want a passing grade, just like the teacher of mathematics or history. As the French say, by dint of great hammering one becomes a blacksmith. You correct mistakes by pounding at them."

When Red became the Knicks' coach, he took numerous pages from his college coach's playbook. In particular, he pounded away at the anvil of team defense. In fact, he was so focused on defense that he'd repeat the axiom Holman had drilled into him: "If you have to relax, do so while your team has the ball. Never relax while on defense." Yet, the most important lesson Holman would teach him was creating rules that produced fundamentally sound play without rigidly controlling his players.

During Red's first winter playing at CCNY, in a speech to the Metropolitan Basketball Writers, Holman said, "There are five essential factors for winning basketball. Emotional maturity, which comes with experience; the will to win; good fellowship; leadership; and alertness make up those five. The boys are now playing the type of basketball I try to teach, and I guess that accounts for our recent showings. They know our offense and they know our defense. There is nothing fixed in my system—everything is spontaneous."

Like Holman, Holzman's coaching system would focus on just a few, crucial rules which allowed his players the freedom to improvise based upon the specific opponent and game circumstances.

The seasons Red played for CCNY were among the most successful of Holman's coaching career. The Beavers not only went undefeated against all other schools in the metropolitan region, but also played in the National Invitational Tournament (NIT) for the first time (it was then the preeminent postseason college basketball tournament). Holzman's play was a major factor. For the 1940–41 season, the sports section of the CCNY yearbook *Microcosm* read, "At the first practice session, Coach Holman took the wraps off a red-headed newcomer, a transfer from Baltimore University. This fellow, who looked deceptively unlike a basketball player, soon had the metropolitan press sitting up and taking notice." A few weeks before the start of the Beavers' 1940–41 season, Holman said of Holzman, "Here is the fellow who should spark the team. He is rugged, a great playmaker, brilliant defender, and as good an all-around man as there is in the city."

It didn't take Red long to live up to his coach's expectations. After winning their home opener, in their second game of the season (a win over St. Francis), Holzman led all scorers with 21 points. Following that game, a description in the *New York Times* read, "Holzman, a magnificently coordinated athlete, also principally engineered the second-half uprising that turned a close contest into a runaway."

Although he now "looked" like a basketball player, CCNY lost their next three games against opponents from outside the New York City area: Oklahoma A&M, Niagara, and Santa Clara. With 18 points, Red was CCNY's leading scorer in the game against Santa Clara. But, as was the case in Baltimore, despite his best efforts, CCNY was a shade below the top national basketball powers. Following the three losses, the team would lose only one more game the rest of the season (to Loyola) prior to the NIT.

Red's play was crucial to victories over CCNY's three major local rivals: St. John's, Fordham, and NYU. In their annual game for New York City bragging rights against a St. John's team coached by Holman's former Celtics teammate, Joe Lapchick, Holzman bottled up St. John's best player, Jack "Dutch" Garfinkel. As in high school, because he exerted maximum effort on both ends of the court, defense was his forte. In his own words, he "hounded" his man. As a result, Holman always had Red guard the opponents' best offensive player even if they were significantly taller.

In CCNY's final regular-season game, with the metropolitan basketball championship and an invitation to the NIT on the line, Holzman was the game's leading scorer with 14 points as the Beavers defeated NYU, 47–43.

That winter, Coach Holman's accolades regarding Holzman reached a new peak when speaking before a meeting of the Metropolitan Basketball Writers Association. "Bill Holzman is proving himself the inspirational leader of the outfit and, of course, Red Phillips is a great sparkplug."

Along with Holzman, Claude "Red" Phillips was CCNY's other top scorer. Unlike Holzman, Phillips decided not to pursue a professional basketball career after college. As a married man with a family to support, he wanted a steady paycheck and became a policeman. In 1995, when Phillips died, Holzman ranked him among the game's great backcourt players. He even favorably compared Phillips to two of his former professional teammates, Bob Davies and Bobby Wanzer, both of whom ended up in the Hall of Fame.

The words *inspirational leader* merit examination. As the team's primary ball handler, Red was never focused on scoring for himself but on making sure his teammates got open shots. When describing Claude Phillips, Holzman said, "I was the passer, and he was the shooter." As a college player, he was already living the motto he would become best known for as a coach: "The sign of a great player is not how much he scores, but how much he lifts his teammates' performance."

In CCNY's first appearance in the NIT, they easily defeated Virginia in the opening round, 64–35. But a record- setting crowd of 18,357 at the Garden saw Ohio University knock CCNY out of the tournament in the semifinal round, 45–43. Red not only led CCNY in scoring but, as *New York Times'* Arthur Daley wrote, "[Holzman] covered Frank Baumholtz of the Bobcats like an overcoat, roughed him steadily but escaped with only two personals." Normally Ohio's top scorer, Baumholtz was held to 12 points. He would later become an outstanding outfielder for the Chicago Cubs. LIU beat Ohio for the NIT championship, though CCNY defeated Seton Hall in the consolation game for a third-place finish and 15–5 record for the season.

During Red's two seasons at CCNY, Uncle Leon would drive Abraham and Sophie to see their son play. His parents no longer referred to basketball as *nonsense.* Sophie was so impressed by the Garden that she dreamed of her son getting married there.

Norm Drucker, who became a well-regarded NBA referee, joined Red at CCNY for the 1941–42 season. Norm's son, Jim, told me that his father held Red in high regard, saying "Holzman was the star of the team." In addition, the 1941–42 CCNY team's best players were Phillips, who was back for his junior year, and Sonny Hertzberg, who was good enough to later play professionally for the Knicks. CCNY was once again the best team in the metropolitan area, defeating all their local opposition (including St. John's, NYU, and St. Francis). Their 50–34 victory over St. Francis was particularly memorable. Just before the first half ended, Holzman scored on a set-shot from behind the midcourt line.

That March, CCNY again qualified for the NIT tournament. Although favored to win, they were upset by Western Kentucky in the opening round, 49–46. According to the 1941–42 CCNY yearbook, Holzman played a great defensive game (to go along with 17 points), but unfortunately could "only handle one man at a time." With the United States actively engaged in fighting World War II, CCNY added one more game to their season to raise funds for the Army Relief Fund. Their opponent was LIU, and Red did an excellent job guarding their best player, Hank Beenders, who was 6-foot-4. In order to compensate for being six inches shorter than his opponent, he fronted Beenders and denied him the ball. Normally, on defense, a player stands behind his opponent blocking his path to the basket. When a player fronts his opponent, he attempts to deny them the ball by blocking the passing lane. Holman said that Holzman was one of the first players he ever saw guard an opponent by fronting them. They would win the game, 42–34, and the team finished the 1941–42 season with a 15–3 record.

Red's outstanding play, and the resulting newspaper clippings, brought him a taste of fame. Decades later, when he was asked about the notoriety, he downplayed it, saying, "I think locally around my neighborhood I was somewhat of a celebrity during the basketball season. But you know, they get used to you. And after a while, you're not that much of a celebrity." For years afterwards, his fame continued in the Brooklyn and Long Beach schoolyards when he would continue to play pickup basketball. "You were treated rougher," Holzman said. "They knew if they did well against you, that meant that they were achieving something."

But that was a small price to pay for learning what it was like to have sellout crowds at the Garden screaming your name. Decades later, as Knicks coach, this gave him a unique understanding of the rush his players were feeling. And, in his day, Holzman was a fan favorite.

During World War II, George Reynolds, a fan who attended games at the Garden during Holzman's years at CCNY, wrote a letter to the *New York Times* saying he missed seeing "court magicians" capable of running "a matchless floor game" like "Red Holzman."

During his college years, Red would spend his summers playing basketball in the Adirondack Mountains of upstate New York, where he worked as a busboy at the Scaroon Manor hotel. At the time, it was common for hotels in the area to hire college basketball players to work as waiters or busboys and have them play against other hotels in the evening as entertainment for their guests. That is where Holzman befriended Fuzzy Levane, another basketball player from Brooklyn. Levane, whose father was a musician in the Metropolitan Opera orchestra, had won a PSAL championship at James Madison High School and was a star at St. John's University. Levane worked as a waiter, with Red as his busboy. Holzman joked that the gregarious and outgoing Levane was such a sloppy waiter you could tell what he served from the stains on his white jacket. Levane, in turn, liked to poke fun at Red. "The only time I saw him was on Friday," Levane said, "when he came around to collect the tips." The two men remained close friends for the rest of their lives. When one needed help, the other was there for him. Holzman later wrote that Levane was "connected to me like my hip bone is to my leg bone."

After the 1941–42 season, Holzman was again named to the All-Metro team and awarded the first Walter Williamson Trophy as "the athlete who has done the most for the college during the year by outstanding performance and sportsmanship." According to *Microcosm*, Red someday hoped to play for the Brooklyn Jewels, the team he had watched as a boy at Arcadia Hall. But, with the United States already engaged in World War II, he would instead be utilizing his basketball skills to benefit his country.

With so many young men in the armed forces, Nat Holman's CCNY teams had losing records. But after the war, CCNY basketball reached its apex. Holman's 1949–50 team is the only one in college basketball history to win both the NCAA and NIT tournament in the same season. Since teams can no longer play in both tournaments in the same season, CCNY will forever remain the only team to accomplish that feat.

Unfortunately, seven players on that team were found to have engaged in a point shaving scandal. The classic example of point-shaving is when a player whose team is, for example, favored to win by five or more points, intentionally misses a shot near the end of the game to make sure his team wins by only four (or less) points. The player is then compensated for his efforts by the gamblers who arranged the fix and placed large bets on the opposing team.

Nat Holman denied having any knowledge of his players' misdeeds, but neither Holman nor the CCNY basketball program ever recovered, with the coach losing his job. Although he was eventually reinstated, CCNY went from playing at the Garden against the best teams in the country to never again competing at a Division I level. The question of whether Holman should have known of the point shaving hung over him for the rest of his life.

Nat Holman was far from naïve. He had seen gambling corrupt basketball games as far back as 1921 when he played for the Whirlwinds. He also knew Madison Square Garden was a hotbed of gambling. Fans would be screaming at players at the end of games to score, or not score, based upon the point spreads which were published in all the local newspapers. Even before the 1949–50 scandal, Holman's CCNY players had already been approached by gamblers to either throw games or shave points. In February 1945, the *New York Times* reported that, as part of a New York City investigation into instances of "corruption of players," then-team captain William Levine said he had recently been approached prior to a CCNY-Syracuse game to manipulate the score. "Levine testified that he had heard from Red Holzman, City College 1941–42 captain, that the latter had been approached with a proposition to 'throw' a game and that in each instance the gamblers' offers had been rejected."

In 1970, a young, well-meaning writer by the name of Mike Shatzkin was blissfully unaware that Holzman had been approached by gamblers during his college career and made the mistake of asking Red if his Knicks players were aware of the point spreads. Shatzkin had brought up a sore point, one that had cost Red's beloved CCNY Beavers dearly. As documented in Shatzkin's book, *The View From Section 111*, Red said, "No, I have never heard of any gambling by players, or interest in it, and I don't want to degrade myself by discussing it."

CHAPTER THREE

"THE BEST THING I EVER DID IN MY LIFE."

When the United States entered World War II, Holzman decided that, rather than waiting to be drafted, he'd control his destiny by joining a military branch of his own choosing. As a result, in the summer of 1942, Red enlisted in the Navy.

More than thirty-five years later, with respect to his military service, Stephen Steiner naively asked Holzman, "Did you yearn to see battle?"

"To be honest with you, no," he replied. "I didn't yearn to see battle. No. I don't think there were too many people that yearned to see battles."

From that perspective, Holzman made the right choice. Although he served in the Navy until the end of the war, he never left the United States. What he was fortunate enough to do was play basketball. On enlisting, Seaman First Class William

Holzman was sent to the naval base in Norfolk, Virginia, and was assigned to play for the Norfolk basketball team. Over the next three years, in part due to his basketball skills, the Norfolk team was rated among the best in the nation.

Steiner later asked, "When you told people you were playing basketball in the Navy, did they look at you as if to say, 'aren't there better things to do in the Navy?'"

"No," Holzman responded, "they probably looked at me and were envious. In other words, I didn't give myself the orders to play basketball in the Navy. They gave me the orders to play in the Navy. They knew I was a basketball player; they wanted me to play there; they ordered me to play there, and that's what I did."

Red's attitude toward how he spent his time in the Navy provides a good example of his straightforward, no-nonsense demeanor. He generally acted in a manner he deemed appropriate and didn't feel a need to justify his behavior to anyone. Interestingly, one exception was when he was a coach and had to cut a player. His former players would joke that Holzman praised their abilities with such vigor they wondered why he was letting them go.

Initially, Red was the only sailor playing on a team with chief petty officers. The team's coach, a career Navy man by the name of Gary Brodie, motivated the players by threatening them. "Get your ass moving," he would say, "or you'll be on a ship to the Pacific tomorrow." The team won thirty-one games and lost only two. Holzman filed away Brodie's motivational technique, as he liked to say, for future reference. It would later come in handy while coaching the Milwaukee Hawks.

Red's Navy team played against other branches of the service whose rosters were also composed of players from all over the United States. When the war ended, Holzman was convinced he could play basketball professionally after excelling against such top-notch national competition. He also saw that sports served as a morale booster for sailors preparing to ship off to active duty. Red later said the basketball games were "entertainment for the men and an identification with the Navy and with pride. We were a winning team, and the guys who used to come and see us play would root like hell for us and had a great time."

At some point during the early portion of his military service, Holzman attended physical training school, most likely at the Great Lakes Naval Training Station in Chicago. After returning to Norfolk, he was promoted to the rank of chief petty officer. In addition to playing basketball, he was assigned to the morale unit where his primarily focus was teaching first aid, leading exercise training, and helping to maintain the recreational facilities.

In 1978, he was asked three consecutive questions—all dealing with the same issue. Since he was the only Jewish player on his Navy basketball team, did he ever hear any anti-Semitic comments:

1. on the court,
2. off-the-court, or
3. from his superior officers?

Word for word, his response was the same: "No. I never had any problem with that." The third time he added, "I don't know if it was because I played basketball and played fairly well, but I didn't seem to have any problem with it." After not getting the answer he was looking for, Steiner took a different approach, asking if any of his friends who didn't play basketball encountered anti-Semitism. At that point, frustrated by Steiner's continued line of narrowly focused questioning, Red responded, "No. You know, I never sought that type of thing out. I never looked for that. I think people that look for that really find that. I know it exists at various places, but I never really sought that out."

According to Robert Peterson's book, *Cages to Jump Shots: Pro Basketball's Early Years*, anti-Semitic incidents "may have been more flagrant in basketball's earlier period [1920s and '30s]." But, Peterson wrote, though "bias against Jews was widespread in society" during World War II, in professional leagues immediately thereafter, "anti-Semitism was occasionally manifested on the basketball court, but it was not very intense, according to the Jewish players who were interviewed for this book."

Holzman's comments about the level of anti-Semitism he experienced in his playing career were consistent with Peterson's conclusions. Red must have dealt with it at some point, but didn't want to discuss the particulars. In another interview, when his NBA career was discussed, Steiner once again brought up the topic, asking if he "ran up against anti-Semitism playing in the league" or comments "from a fan, especially on a road game?" "I haven't run . . . you know, that always keeps coming up, but no, I haven't had any of those problems," Holzman said. "I didn't listen to the fans because I was busy playing basketball. I don't know if they were in love with me, but . . . [Red laughed at this point] I don't know."

Red Auerbach's basketball skills also brought him to the Navy base in Norfolk. He had used his stay at Seth Low Junior College to get a scholarship offer from George Washington University (GW). After graduating from GW, Auerbach was coaching high school basketball when the United States entered World War II. Red's coach at GW, Bill Reinhart, made sure Auerbach ended up in the Navy. Like Holzman, Auerbach went to physical training school and was then promoted to the rank of chief petty officer. On his return, he was "put in charge of all recreational activities on the base."

Great entrepreneur that he was, he even managed to create a side business while still in military service. On several Sundays, usually an offday at the Norfolk base, Auerbach would bring a team of Navy basketball players to Washington, DC, to play against a local professional team, the Lichtman Bears. He arranged the games, played in them, *and* served as coach—all while earning some cash for himself and his players.

Interestingly, in their autobiographies, neither Red mentioned that the other was also stationed at the Norfolk Naval base. Holzman's secretary with the Knicks, Gwynne Bloomfield, said that Red told her he knew Auerbach when they served in Norfolk. In fact, they both mention befriending the New York Yankees star shortstop Phil Rizzuto, who was also stationed at Norfolk. According to Holzman, he and Rizzuto "became pretty friendly."

In 1942, after Rizzuto and Holzman both got a weekend pass, they were driving back to New York City together when Red stopped to phone Selma. They had continued to date during his college days at CCNY and she often attended games. According to his autobiography, Selma told him that her parents had arranged for them to get married at Garfein's, a banquet hall on East Houston Street in Manhattan. And that weekend, before eighty friends and family, with the groom dressed in his Navy uniform, Selma and Red were married.

Rizzuto didn't attend Holzman's wedding, but when Selma and Red moved into a Norfolk apartment off the base, they invited him over for a three-course meal of tomato juice, a tomato-filled Spanish omelet, and tomato soup. Rizzuto, a very polite dinner guest, expressed only a faint hope that dessert wasn't tomato pie.

In Selma, Red had found not only his life partner but also his equal. Like her husband, she was witty but self-effacing. As his longtime friend, Manny Azenberg, said of Selma, "She was a girl from Brooklyn without any pretenses."

The marriage lasted for fifty-five years until Selma's death. Ernie Grunfeld, the Knicks' general manager in the 1990s said, "They were a devoted sharing team. He was dependent on her." Spending so much time on the road, Red had to delegate a great deal of responsibility to his wife. "Even to this day my wife manages most of our money . . . maintaining the household and things like that, that's her problem," he said in 1978. "She handles that, and there were days when she had less and she managed, and there were days when she had more and she's managed."

In the 1980s and '90s, the *New York Times* Pulitzer Prize–winning writer Ira Berkow came to know Holzman and Selma well. Berkow wrote of Selma, "She was loving, kind, thoughtful, generous, genuine, funny, and interesting. She could see right through phonies, and didn't suffer fools. Didn't suffer referees, either."

Selma loved basketball as much as her husband. When he became the coach of the Knicks, she kept a scorecard of every game she attended. After games, when they stopped for dinner on their way home to Cedarhurst, Selma often questioned him about a coaching move she didn't like. "Red," she would ask, "why did you play that guy for so long?" Holzman would reply, "I didn't play him that long." To which Selma would say, "You played him for an hour."

Asked if he listened to Selma's basketball advice, Red said, "Most of the time."

And, unlike Red, who tended to be guarded in what he said publicly, Selma spoke her mind. And, like her husband, she did it with a sense of humor. Mary Saul, the wife of Pep Saul, one of Holzman's teammates on the Rochester Royals, told me, "Selma was very funny." In the 1990s, when Selma and Red were once out to dinner at a restaurant with Berkow and his wife Dolly, the presentation of the check started a disagreement. The two couples always alternated who paid. Holzman insisted it was their turn to pay, but Dolly disagreed. She kept a written record of who paid each time they went out, and it was their turn. Red responded by saying he also kept a record of who paid, and it was their turn to pay. At this point, Selma decided the matter. Shooting a look at her husband and then Berkow, Selma told Dolly, "What do you want to pay for? Let these two *zhlubs* (bumpkins) pay."

As this story shows, Holzman was never one to have tight pockets. When he and Selma attended Broadway shows that were produced by their friend, Manny Azenberg, Red always insisted on paying for his own tickets.

Selma was not just funny, but also compassionate. If she learned one of her husband's Knicks players had a cold, she prepared her homemade chicken soup for him.

As coach of the Knicks, Holzman took negatives written about him with a grain of salt. But Selma's feelings mattered greatly to him. After his coaching career ended, he usually attended Knicks home games with her. They always sat in the same seats. One night, Selma couldn't attend the game, and Holzman invited Dolly Berkow to use her ticket. During this particular game, Berkow was sitting with the press at courtside. At some point, the camera panned to what the Madison Square Garden announcer thought would be an image of Mr. and Mrs. Holzman sitting side by side. He began to say, "Red and Selma," but caught himself when he saw a younger woman he didn't recognize, and the camera quickly panned away. After the game, Holzman, Dolly, and Ira were having a drink at the Garden in Room 200, a restaurant frequented by upper management and VIPs. The Garden announcer came over to Red and apologized for his slipup. Holzman said only, "It's okay." Although Dolly was sitting next to him, he didn't bother to say who she was or make it clear that nothing inappropriate was going on. Dolly asked Red why he didn't clear the air. He replied, "As long as Selma knows, what anyone else thinks doesn't matter."

"Marrying Selma," Holzman wrote in his autobiography, "was the best thing I ever did in my life."

* * *

In some ways, for Holzman, life in the Navy had not changed that much from his CCNY days. On the night of February 15, 1943, before a crowd of over 12,000, the Norfolk Training Center team easily defeated LIU in a game at Madison Square Garden. Norfolk was effectively an all-star team featuring several former college stars. In addition to Red, there was Ralph Bishop (who had played at the University of Washington), Matt Zunic of GW, and Bob Feerick (a star at Santa Clara who played professionally after the war). But as Louis Effrat reported in the *New York Times*, "this was more of an all-round outfit, every man helping set up scoring plays. Holzman, an old Garden favorite, was as brilliant as ever, but he did not steal the spot light, so good were his teammates."

Playing on the Norfolk team gave Red another lesson he stored away—a group of stars who played team basketball on both ends of the court were practically unbeatable.

Near the end of World War II, Holzman was reassigned to the Treasure Island Navy Base near San Francisco. To get there, Red and Selma drove across the country, with Selma keeping a journal of their trip. Already acting as family money manager, in it, she kept track of all their expenses, as well as noting places along the way they found of interest. Red found it helpful that the Treasure Island base had a field house with basketball courts where he could practice. Although he had joined the Navy prior to completing his degree at CCNY, he didn't return to college full-time after the war. "I was married then," he later said, "and I felt that I should make a living, and there was an opportunity for me to make some money playing basketball."

After he was discharged from the Navy in November 1945, Red had good reason to be optimistic regarding his basketball prospects. He was selected as one of the forty all-time best armed-services basketball players. Other players on the team included Hall of Fame players like his future teammate, Bob Davies. Holzman was twenty-five years old when discharged, and at the peak of his physical abilities. Luckily for him, professional basketball was still maturing and the best players were no longer paid on a per-game basis. The only question was whether he was good enough to play in one of those leagues.

In 1978, he was asked, "If basketball had not worked out, what would your alternative have been?"

"I would have had to get involved with something else and probably gotten into it," he said. "I had already been to school; maybe I could have gotten into teaching or things of that nature. But I never had to face that problem, so I didn't face it."

This response gives insight into his approach—not just to basketball, but to staying confident. Holzman avoided the negative as if it were the plague; his approach was also to never worry about things beyond his control. Keeping his gaze firmly fixed on living his basketball dreams worked, but he did hedge his bets. After the war, taking classes over the summer, Red completed his undergraduate degree in 1947.

CHAPTER FOUR
"LIKE BEING IN HEAVEN."

***

In November 1945, Holzman was discharged from the Navy and returned to New York to begin his professional basketball career. Initially, the only option available was playing as a free-lancer. One weekend, Red played in five games for five different teams on five different courts. But Fuzzy Levane threw him a lifeline. The toss came at the urging of Les Harrison, one of the most innovative entrepreneurs in the formative years of the NBA.

Les Harrison was born and raised in Rochester, New York. His father had died when he was eighteen years old, which forced him into his father's business selling fruit and vegetables from the back of a truck. But ever since 1923, when he graduated from high school, his passion was promoting professional basketball. By the start of World War II, Harrison had assembled an outstanding team jointly sponsored by the Seagram Liquor Company and Eber Bros., a fruit and vegetable wholesaler. The team played under the name Eber, as newspapers in Rochester wouldn't accept liquor advertising. In 1945, Harrison purchased a franchise in the National Basketball League (NBL) for $25,000. This made Rochester the eastern-most franchise in a league whose best teams were located in small, Midwest cities such as Sheboygan and Fort Wayne. But the NBL was the only league in the country with a paid commissioner, a balanced schedule, and, most significantly, players under seasonal contracts paid on a monthly basis.

Although Harrison called it "a glorified warehouse," the city-owned 4,200-seat Edgerton Park Sports Arena was where the newly christened Rochester Royals (today, the NBA's Sacramento Kings) would play their home games. Through the years, attending a Royals game became a popular night out, and Edgerton—the largest indoor arena in Rochester—was often sold out. But Edgerton had its oddities. When configured for basketball, just a few feet behind the endlines of the court were several sets of doors that, on one end led to a concession area and, at the other, went directly outside. As a result, with one good push a player driving to the basket could end up in the snow.

With a playing facility set, Harrison needed players. One of the first he brought in was Fuzzy Levane. Although Levane had been an outstanding player at St. John's, his appeal to Harrison was as a *shtick* (gimmick); a player of a specific ethnic group who would draw *his* people. Harrison thought Levane would be his Jewish draw. But there was one issue: Levane was Italian. When Harrison realized his mistake, he told Levane to get him a Jewish player. And so he brought in two: his former St. John's teammate, Dutch Garfinkel, and Red Holzman. Garfinkel only briefly played for the Royals before spending most of his career with the Boston Celtics.

But Holzman soon showed he was more than a mere *shtick*. After signing a contract for the 1945–46 season for $400 a month, Red took a seat on the bench since the Royals were particularly strong in the backcourt. Their starters were Al Cervi, who was so good he skipped college and started playing professionally straight out of high school; and Bob Davies, an All-American at Seton Hall. Both were future Hall of Famers. Holzman hedged his bets and kept playing a couple of games a week for a team in Troy, New York. But in a game against Sheboygan, with the Royals trailing by a sizable amount, Levane convinced Harrison to give Red some playing time. Much to Harrison's surprise, Holzman helped the Royals come from behind and win the game. After that, Harrison moved him into the starting lineup and switched Davies up front to give the Royals a three-guard offense.

The top big men on that first Royals team were George "The Blind Bomber" Glamack, a 6-foot-6 All-American at the University of North Carolina who, despite poor vision in one eye, was fond of taking 15-foot hook shots with either hand; and 6-foot-8 center John Mahnken. Other players on that team included Otto Graham, who became a Hall of Fame quarterback for the Cleveland Browns; Del Rice, who had a lengthy career as a catcher with the St. Louis Cardinals; and Chuck Connors, the star of one of the first westerns on television, *The Rifleman*.

A gifted athlete, Davies was one of the first professional players to utilize the behind-the-back dribble during games. He played his entire 10-year career in Rochester, and would be the team's best player and biggest drawing card. Interestingly, neither Harrison nor Holzman were thrilled with Davies using the behind-the-back dribble during games. They considered it a form of showboating that embarrassed opposing players. Yet Red would later say that Davies was one of the few players of that generation who could have played in the modern-era NBA.

Davies understood what a wonderful team Harrison had put together. "That 1945–46 team," Davies said, "was the best I ever played with. We had speed and drive. We ran our opponents into the ground." The Royals finished second in the Eastern Division of the NBL, two games behind the defending champions, the Fort Wayne Zollner Pistons.

The Pistons were owned by Fred Zollner, who ran a successful piston manufacturing plant in Fort Wayne. Much like the Trucker's Union team Holzman had played on, Zollner employed his players on a full-time basis in his plant. He even segregated all basketball receipts and, after paying his direct expenses, divided the balance among his players. Such largesse helped draw the best professional players to Fort Wayne and provided a secure foundation for a team that eventually become the NBA's Detroit Pistons.

In what has become a legendary basketball travel story, the only way the Royals players could get to Fort Wayne was by catching an evening train from Rochester to Chicago. The next morning, at 5 a.m., the train would make an unscheduled stop in the middle of an Indiana prairie where there was only an uncovered wooden platform. The players would get off and, carrying their suitcases, walk about a mile—often in below freezing temperatures—toward a blinking yellow light at an intersection of a half dozen two-story buildings. There, one of the players with the best aim would throw pebbles at the second-story window of the Green Parrot Café. Eventually, the proprietress of the coffee shop would come down and serve the tired and hungry players breakfast. Decades later, Holzman could still taste the fresh coffee, the bacon and eggs, and maple syrup–covered griddle cakes. After breakfast, four or five cars would drive the players the 40 miles to Fort Wayne. There, the players checked into their hotel and slept until game time.

Following such a long and strange trip, it was no surprise that the Royals, shooting only 16 percent from the field, lost their opening game in the first round of the 1946 NBL playoffs in Fort Wayne, 54–44. But the Royals came back to win the series and advance to the finals against Sheboygan, the top team in the Western Conference.

In the first game of the series with Sheboygan, played in Edgerton Arena, Holzman scored 10 points in the third quarter to turn the momentum of the game around and give the Royals the victory. After taking Game Two, the Royals won the third game to sweep the best three-of-five series and win the championship. Red often said that winning on the road in those days was tough, even more difficult than when he was coaching in the NBA. The last game of the championship series, played in the Sheboygan Armory, was a good example why. The *Rochester Democrat and Chronicle* reported that in the Armory, some 300 kids seated on bleachers erected on a stage, "bombarded the Royals, sitting in front of them with chewing gum, folded newspapers, buttons, pebbles, tinfoil balls, and match boxes."

The Royals won the championship with team-first play, balanced scoring, and speed. Nate Messinger, who refereed all three games, said, "Those guys were a bunch of wildcats. I thought the Illinois Whiz Kids were fast, but Davies, Cervi, Holzman, and Mahnken would have left those kids standing still. There is no offense like the fast break when you have the men who can make it tick—and this Rochester bunch was tailored to order for the lightning break."

In the very first year of their existence, the Royals were league champions . . . but that didn't mean they were the best team in the country. There were also the two great black teams of the era, the Harlem Globetrotters and New York Rens. After the playoffs ended, Les Harrison, always in need of funds to meet payroll, arranged games against both squads, to be played in Schenectady. The Royals played the Globetrotters on March 26, 1946. Playing a serious game, without the comedic routines that would later characterize their play, the Globetrotters defeated the Royals, 57–55. The outcome may have been different if the Royals best player, Bob Davies, had played. Unfortunately, he was in his offseason job as the coach of the baseball team at Seton Hall University. A few weeks later, with Davies back with the team, the Royals, playing under the name "Schenectady Pros," wearing uniforms that read, "Schd'ty," defeated the Rens, 73–59.

Harrison was an outstanding judge of talent. But he had too many roles—general manager, scout, travel coordinator, and even, when needed, equipment manager—to be an effective coach. Instead, former professional basketball player Eddie Malanowicz served as the team's coach. But due to his responsibilities as a public school principal, Malanowicz was not always available for road games. As a result, Royals players often made suggestions to Harrison as to what plays they thought would work. And he was open to the players' ideas. Harrison had played basketball in high school but never got a chance to attend college and learn from a great coach (like Red did from Nat Holman).

When Holzman coached the Knicks to their two championships, he was fortunate to have a group of extremely intelligent players and, like Harrison, Red elicited feedback from them. Manny Azenberg recalled Holzman telling him, "I can't teach them anything. They're smarter than I am."

In many respects, the 1945–46 season was the high point of Holzman's playing career. In his first year in the league, he had proved himself to be one of the league's best players. He won the NBL's Rookie of the Year Award and was named to the All-NBL first team. For Red, it was the fulfillment of a lifelong dream. In 1978, he said, "Playing basketball and getting paid for it was like being in heaven."

And Holzman's timing could not have been better. In 1946, a new league, the Basketball Association of America (BAA), intended to rival the NBL, came into existence. The BAA was established by managers of National Hockey League (NHL) arenas who hoped to keep their seats filled on nights when there were no hockey games, boxing matches, or ice-skating shows. The BAA established franchises in major cities such as Boston, Philadelphia, Washington, DC, Toronto, Chicago, St. Louis, Cleveland, Detroit, Pittsburgh, and New York.

Walter Brown, the president of Boston Garden, was one of the leading proponents of the BAA. He wisely selected his team's name, Celtics, not only for its association with the Original Celtics of the 1920s, but for its appeal to the city's large Irish population. In addition, in 1950, Brown hired Red Auerbach to be the Celtics' coach and general manager. Brown knew he was a novice when it came to running a basketball team and wisely gave Auerbach autonomy in making all player personnel decisions. By then, Auerbach had already coached two other BAA franchises, one in Washington DC, and the other, called Tri-Cities, which represented three small towns in Illinois and Iowa.

In contrast, in New York, Ned Irish didn't feel a compelling financial need to bring professional basketball there. Between college basketball, hockey, track meets, the circus, and rodeos, Madison Square Garden had a full schedule. Yet, Irish knew that without a New York franchise, the BAA would be less likely to survive. He eventually agreed to participate, but for several years the Knickerbockers played many of their games at the 69th Regiment Armory on Lexington Avenue—not the Garden. More significantly, because Irish had so successfully made college basketball a revenue generator for the Garden, he did not hesitate to take a hands-on approach with the Knicks player personnel decisions even though he was a promoter, not a basketball expert. For decades, player personnel decisions were often made based upon fan appeal rather than ability. To some extent, this was why the Knicks' very first team started five Jewish players. The exception occurred when Irish's influence was offset by a strong basketball professional such as Joe Lapchick, the former Original Celtic who was the Knicks' coach from 1947 to 1956.

The contrasting approaches of Brown and Irish set the long-term tone for the only two original NBA franchises that still play in the same city in which they began in 1946. As a direct result, the Celtics have won more championships than any other NBA team, 17; the Knicks, only two.

The BAA had the best venues; but the NBL had the better players. And the establishment of the BAA created additional demand for the services of the best NBL players. Nowhere was that demand greater than in New York, where the Knicks were about to start their inaugural season.

Ned Irish was well aware of Holzman's popularity when he played for CCNY. Representing Madison Square Garden's interests as the BAA began operations, Irish asked the Knicks' first coach, Neil Cohalan, to offer Red a contract to play for the Knicks. But Holzman remained loyal to Harrison and gave him an opportunity to match the offer. Harrison exceeded it, and Red signed a contract for the 1946–47 season which paid him nearly $12,000. It was, as Holzman would later say, "a heck of a lot of money." The salary was so large that he was able to stop playing for the Troy team. In later years, as his skills diminished and he became the first guard off the Royals bench, Red referred to himself as "the best paid substitute in basketball."

As a player, Holzman's most notable contribution to the long-term success of professional basketball may have taken place off the court. According to official NBA records, which date back to 1946 when the BAA was created, the NBA didn't have black players until the 1950–51 season. But the official records ignored the fact that, in the fall of 1946, Les Harrison signed a thirty-year-old black player, William "Dolly" King, to play for the Royals. King, who grew up in Brooklyn, had been a college star at LIU.

The signing was historically significant. Jackie Robinson would not integrate Major League Baseball until the spring of 1947. Wendell Smith, the sports editor of the black newspaper the *Pittsburgh Courier* wrote a letter to Harrison congratulating him on "signing a player without regard to race, creed, or color. It is another democratic step in the field of sports, and I am sure your liberal attitude will be appreciated by thousands of basketball fans throughout the country."

During the 1946–47 season, Red Holzman, Fuzzy Levane, and Dolly King shared a room at the Hotel Seneca in downtown

Rochester. On the road, if King was refused service because of his race, Levane, Holzman, and King would all walk out and eat in their hotel room. In Fort Wayne, when a hotel denied King accommodations, the entire Royals team left and stayed in another hotel. The solidarity of the three basketball players is impressive considering the time period. Beginning in 1947, when Jackie Robinson first began playing for the Brooklyn Dodgers—and throughout his entire playing career which ended in 1956—he never had a white roommate. On April 15, 1947, the same day Robinson began his major-league career, Nat Holman, the featured speaker at a dinner in Rochester celebrating the Royals, spoke out against racial discrimination in sports and praised Harrison's signing of Dolly King.

Nat Militzok, another Jewish basketball player from New York City who played for the Knicks the same season Holzman, Levane, and King were teammates in Rochester, expressed what Holzman surely felt. "There is really love between teammates on a successful, happy team," Militzok told Robert Peterson, the author of *Cages to Jump Shots*, the definitive book about pro basketball's early years. "We were one big family. There were no blacks, no Jews, no Italians—they were just our friends. And we loved to be together. I wouldn't trade that experience for anything in the world."

Neither Dolly King, nor Pop Gates—another black player in the NBL during the 1946–47 season—were re-signed for the following season. Instead, they both ended up joining the Rens. Holzman would later say of King, "A hell of a player, and a hell of nice guy. Dolly King hardly ever talked about racial issues. He just went about his business of playing basketball."

The Royals finished the 1946–47 season with the best record

in the NBL, and were awarded the Naismith Memorial Trophy. It was also a good season for Holzman, who averaged a career-high 12 points per game and was a second-team All-Star.

But in the playoffs, in what would become an unfortunate trend, the Royals lost in the championship round to a team led by George Mikan, basketball's first dominant big man. Yet, just as Mikan's Chicago American Gears won the series-deciding game in Chicago that April, good news arrived from New York. Selma had given birth to a daughter, Gail Donnie, weighing 8 pounds, 7 ounces. Red passed out cigars to his Rochester teammates upon hearing the news.

After the Gears folded at the end of the 1946–47 season, Mikan began playing for the Minneapolis Lakers. However good the Royals were, the results would shortly be the same. They invariably were just a shade below Mikan's team. From 1948 to 1954, the Lakers won only one more regular-season game than the Royals (267 to 266), but the Lakers won five championships; the Royals, only one.

Mikan was the difference. He was *the* dominant player of the late 1940s and early '50s. When the Lakers played the Knicks in New York, the marquee at Madison Square Garden did not read KNICKS V/S LAKERS but rather GEO MIKAN V/S KNICKS. At 6-foot-10 and 240 pounds, Mikan was not just taller and broader than most players of the era, he was determined. Neither fast nor the best leaper, Mikan would set himself up close enough to the basket for a hook shot he had perfected to the point of being very difficult to defend. Prior to the 1951–52 season, the lane was widened from 6 to 12 feet to limit his dominance.

If there was one team Holzman's Knicks teams tried to emulate, it was the Rochester Royals. Leonard Koppett, who wrote the definitive account of the early years of the NBA, *24 Seconds to Shoot*, called the Royals "the most perfect team" of that era. Hall of Fame guard Bobby Wanzer, who eventually replaced Al Cervi on those Royals teams, noted, "There weren't any egos on the team. We respected one another and we wanted to win. The team came first. We were evenly balanced and everybody did his job very competently. You never knew who would be the high-scorer. We moved the ball to whoever had a good shot and was hot. We protected the ball because there was no 24-second rule and we might not get the ball back right away. Winning was everything."

In the early years of Holzman's career with the Royals, he was an iron man. From the 1945–46 season through 1949–50, Red never missed a regular-season game. And, once he played, he was rarely tossed. "It was in Moline two years ago," Holzman told writer George Beahon of the *Democrat and Chronicle* in March 1950, "only time I ever was tossed out of a game. The official called one I thought should have been exactly the reverse. I handed him the ball and, believe me, this is exactly what I said: 'You are the world's BEST referee.' He must have been listening to fourteen other people, because he thumbed me out immediately. I protested, until he mentioned a $50 fine if I didn't scram in 30 seconds. When he threatened the fine, I said: 'Brother, don't look now, but I just left.' The fans thought we were cutting up each other's ancestry."

During his first season with the Royals, Red and Selma lived with Fuzzy Levane and his family in Rochester. Holzman described Rochester as "a very nice lovely town to play in, nice people." After Gail was born, Selma and Red rented their own apartment in Rochester for the season, but left for the summer months to spend time on the beach in Long Island. Holzman was later asked if he gave his daughter "what you would call a Jewish upbringing." His response shows he was more concerned about what kind of person Gail would become, rather than her level of religious observance. "Well I think she had a good liberal upbringing. We like to feel that she was as Jewish as anybody, she was brought up with Jewish people, but thankfully she was [also] brought up with enough other people to give her a broad outlook on people and I think that was nice."

The Royals' strength was in their backcourt, consisting of four players who would eventually become NBA coaches: Al Cervi, Red Holzman, Fuzzy Levane, and Bobby Wanzer. A fifth, Bob Davies, coached at Seton Hall. But no matter how talented and smart these players were, without more help up front they would never be able to beat a Mikan-led team in the playoffs. As a result, in the middle of the 1947–48 season, Harrison purchased the contract of 6-foot-9 center Arnie Risen from the Indianapolis Kautskys for $25,000. Just a few years before, Harrison had paid that much to purchase the entire Rochester franchise. Risen, who had played his college ball at Ohio State, was an outstanding all-around player who could score, rebound, and play solid defense. Unfortunately, Risen only weighed about 200 pounds, which put him at a disadvantage trying to muscle Mikan away from the basket. But with the addition of two forwards, Arnie Johnson and Jack Coleman, the Royals had enough bulk up front to compete with the Lakers. However, to complement Mikan, the Lakers responded by adding two future Hall of Famers to their frontline, Vern Mikkelsen and Jim Pollard, and Slater Martin to their backcourt.

The 1947–48 NBL season ended with the Royals winning the Eastern Division with the best record at 44–16. Mikan's Lakers finished with a record of 43–17 to win the Western Division. In the playoffs, the Royals defeated Fort Wayne and then the Anderson Duffy Packers to advance to the championship against the Lakers. Unfortunately, in the final game against Anderson, an elbow from their center, Howard Schultz, broke Arnie Risen's jaw, and he was unable to play in the championship. The Royals lost to the Lakers, three games to one.

While the Royals continued to play team basketball and spreading the floor, Mikan, who led the league in scoring with 21.3 points a game, proved unstoppable. Holzman could take some solace in the fact that he, along with his backcourt mate Al Cervi, were selected to the NBL All-Star team.

For the 1948–49 season, the Royals and Lakers, as well as Fort Wayne and Indianapolis, left the NBL and joined the BAA. Because the Royals and Lakers were the two best teams in the BAA, they were both placed in the Western Division so at least one team from the original BAA teams would play in the championship round. And that's how things played out. The Royals finished with the best record in the league, 45–15, one game better than the Lakers, 44–16. But after the Royals defeated St. Louis in the opening round, they played the Lakers in the Western Division finals. With Bob Davies suffering from the flu, the Lakers took the best-of-three series in two straight games.

The BAA was renamed the NBA the following season, and expanded from 12 to 17 teams. The Royals and Lakers were again placed in the same division, the Central. The Royals lost only one home game all season but still finished in a regular-season tie with the Lakers at 51–17. The teams would have to play a one-game playoff to determine the Central Division champion. With two minutes left in that game, the score was tied. In what was the standard strategy of that era, the Lakers stalled and held the ball until the final seconds of the game. With just three seconds left, Tony Jaros, one of the worst shooters on the Lakers, hit a 40-foot shot to give them a two-point victory. The loss had the Royals playing, and losing to, a very physical Fort Wayne team in the first round of the playoffs. The Lakers won the championship, defeating Syracuse.

If the Royals had the lead late in that one-game playoff, they would have utilized the stall as well. Holzman and Fran Curran, who played at Notre Dame, were the two players Harrison put into games for just that purpose. They were referred to as "firemen." As Red later said, "We'd [Holzman and Curran] go in at the end of the game, and if we had a three-or-four-point lead, everybody would head for the exits because we'd just freeze it out. And if you were fouled, you could take the ball out of bounds, so you'd retain possession. You wouldn't shoot the foul. You could either shoot the foul or take it out of bounds, so you'd just keep taking it out of bounds. And we made very, very few mistakes. I mean everybody would get out of the way. He'd [Curran] take it for a while, then I'd take it, and I guess it must have been very boring to a lot of people, but going down to the end [of a game], we'd do a lot of that."

The Royals luck would change in the 1950–51 season when they won their first and only NBA championship. That season, with six franchises folding, the NBA was reduced to 11 teams. The Lakers won the Western Division with a league-best record of 44–24. The Royals finished right behind them in the West with the second-best record at 41–27.

The Royals' most memorable regular-season game was a two-point loss to the Indianapolis Olympians in Rochester on January

6, 1951. The game, which took six overtimes to complete, was one of the motivators behind the establishment of the 24-second clock. During each five-minute overtime period, each team held onto the ball hoping for a last-second shot to win. Tedium reigned. In the fourth overtime, neither team took a shot. Many Rochester fans walked out while the game was still being played. With four seconds left in the sixth overtime, after the Royals had held the ball for nearly three and a half minutes, Arnie Risen missed a desperation shot. The Olympians gained possession and scored the winning basket as the buzzer sounded. Holzman set what could very well be an NBA record for most minutes played in one game. Years later, Red would say that when he was young he could run all night. The six-overtime game against Indianapolis proved him right. He played 75 of the game's 78 minutes.

After defeating Fort Wayne in the first round of the playoffs, the Royals faced the Lakers in a best-of-five series for the Western Division crown. Although the Lakers would have home-court advantage, luck was on the Royals side—Mikan had suffered a hairline fracture of his ankle in the last game of the regular season. In order to give Mikan extra rest prior to the opening game of the series, the NBA allowed a one-day postponement, causing Les Harrison to have what was kindly described as a "meltdown."

After an 18-hour train trip, even with Mikan limited by his injured ankle, the Royals lost the opening game in Minneapolis, 76–73, playing an uncharacteristically sloppy, turnover-riddled game.

For the second game in Minneapolis, Les Harrison decided to start Holzman in place of Bobby Wanzer. It was an unusual move, as Red had come off the bench for almost the entire season. But since he started and led the Royals to their only regular-season victory in Minneapolis that season, Harrison thought he would again be a steadying influence.

The decision made Harrison look like a genius, as the Royals won, 70–66. Red was the top scorer in the game with 23 points, hitting 10 of 13 shots from the field and three of four free throws. He also played outstanding defense, holding the Lakers' backcourt star, Slater Martin, to one basket. Most important, in the fourth quarter, Holzman intentionally avoided taking a shot and focused on avoiding turnovers and protecting the Royals' lead. Red took control of the game with five minutes left and the Royals holding a two-point lead. He called a timeout with four minutes left so Bobby Wanzer could be brought into the game to help freeze it out. Holzman played all 48 minutes.

The Royals' win in Game Two changed the momentum of the series. Both teams flew together on the same chartered DC-4 to Rochester. On the flight, in an amazing display of good sportsmanship, the Royals' Jack Coleman told Mikan that spraying ethyl chloride on his ankle would help him. Mikan tried it. It helped, but not enough. The Royals easily won Game Three, 83–70, and closed out the series two nights later with an 80–75 victory before a capacity crowd of 4,260 at Edgerton Arena.

With Mikan and the Lakers defeated, the Royals had a good chance of winning a championship since they held the home-court advantage against the Eastern Division champion New York Knicks. The Royals won the first two games of the series in Rochester with ease. In New York, playing at the 69th Regiment Armory (because the circus was booked at the Garden), the Royals won the third game, 78–71. But it was far from over, as the Knicks went on to win the next three games to tie the series.

In the seventh and deciding game back in Edgerton Park, the Royals, led by Bob Davies and Arnie Risen, defeated the Knicks, 79–75, to win their first NBA championship. With 44 seconds left, Davies broke a 75–75 tie by sinking two free throws. The Royals controlled the tap following the second free throw. Holzman then dribbled the ball until the final seconds when he fed Jack Coleman, who scored the final basket of the game.

* * *

In the next two seasons, Holzman's playing time decreased. Red would joke that he knew his career was almost over when he saw members of the Harlem Globetrotters, looking for a few easy minutes on defense, argue over who would guard him. As his playing career neared its end, he spent more time on the bench, where he sat next to Harrison and recommended substitutions and game strategy. Harrison called Holzman, "the smartest basketball player in the game."

As a footnote to his years in Rochester, Holzman loved telling his friend Manny Azenberg the following story. According to Azenberg, at the core of their friendship was the fact that he was "a nice Jewish boy from the Bronx," and Red was "a nice Jewish boy from Brooklyn." Like Holzman, Azenberg was fluent in Yiddish, and Red always told the story in Yiddish.

One Saturday morning during his years in Rochester, as Holzman joked, "when I had nothing better to do," he attended synagogue. Since both Abraham and Sophie died in the early 1950s, it's possible Red had gone to synagogue, not because he had "nothing better to do," but because he wanted to say Kaddish, the Jewish memorial prayer, for his parents.

As Red told it, when he walked into the tiny synagogue, there were about "twenty old Russian Jews all about 5-foot-2" praying. To them, Holzman, at 5-foot-10, was a giant, and everyone turned to look him over. He took a seat in the last row of the synagogue. The *shamash*, the person who maintains the synagogue (the equivalent of a sexton in a church), walked down the aisle to speak with him. The *shamash* wished Holzman a "Good Shabbat" and he answered him in Yiddish. The *shamash* returned to the front of the synagogue and told the rabbi, "The giant speaks Yiddish."

The *shamash* was instructed to find out more about the red-headed visitor. He walked back down the aisle and asked, "What's your name?"

Red told him, "Velvel," his Yiddish name.

"What do you do, Velvel?"

Holzman didn't know the Yiddish word for basketball, so he described throwing a ball into a basket.

The *shamash* responded, "From this you can make a living?"

CHAPTER FIVE

"THE END OF THE WORLD."

After the 1952–53 season ended, Harrison gave Holzman his unconditional release. Although Red's physical abilities had faded, the ever-loyal Fuzzy Levane, who was then coaching the Milwaukee Hawks, offered him a job as a backup guard. In the 1953–54 season, despite being the oldest player on the Hawks, Red played in more games and scored more points than he had the previous season in Rochester.

But for Holzman, Milwaukee was far from heaven. The Hawks might as well have been invisible for all the attention they received. Milwaukee was enthralled with their new major-league baseball franchise, the Braves, who had relocated from Boston. In 1953, the Braves set a National League attendance record. Their stars included future Hall of Famers Eddie Mathews, Warren Spahn, and, beginning in 1954, Hank Aaron. Even in the dead of winter, Milwaukee fans were more interested in whether or not a Braves player caught anything while ice fishing rather than the outcome of a Hawks game. And the Hawks usually lost. In each of their four seasons in Milwaukee (1951 to 1955) they finished last in the Western Division.

Contrast that to Rochester. The Royals had been one of basketball's best teams, their fans adored them, and they had a monopoly as the only major-league sports franchise in the city. Holzman would always feel a sense of pride in knowing he helped bring Rochester its one and only major-league championship.

Worse yet, from a family perspective, Milwaukee was a never-ending road trip. In Rochester, when Red came home during the basketball season he could spend time with Selma and Gail. But they remained in New York and never lived in Milwaukee or St. Louis, where the Hawks eventually moved.

Besides being away from his family, Holzman soon faced a new challenge. After winning just 11 of their first 46 games to start the 1953–54 season, Hawks owner Ben Kerner fired Levane and offered Red the team's coaching job. Asked about the transition, he later said, "It was one of those things where you come there with the guy who's a good friend of yours, but the owner says, 'Look, I'd like you to become the coach, but if you don't become the coach, it's not changing a thing, the coach is going to be fired and I'm going to get someone else.'"

So, at age thirty-three, Holzman was an NBA coach. Things may have progressed faster than he anticipated, but Red becoming a coach was not a surprise to anyone who knew him. From the first time seeing Max Kinsbrunner at Arcadia Hall, he wanted to make his career in basketball. And with his playing career over, coaching was the next logical step. Bill Calhoun, Red's teammate on the Royals, told me, "Holzman was coaching even when he was playing." Fran Curran, Holzman's backcourt partner in

Rochester, said, "I never played with a smarter ballplayer in all my life."

The question was not whether Holzman would coach, only when. In early March 1950, when a "Red Holzman Night" was held at Edgerton Arena, George Beahon, who covered the Royals for the *Rochester Democrat & Chronicle* reported, "As for coaching, he's been rumored in connection with the CCNY job . . . coaching is definitely in his future." But it's highly unlikely Holzman had any interest in coaching at CCNY after the point-shaving scandal devastated the program. For Red, his only option was the NBA.

But, in the insular world that was the nine-team NBA in 1953, he must have known what he was getting into coaching a team run by Kerner, known to be among the most mercurial of NBA owners. One of Kerner's veteran players, Bob Harrison, who had previously played on the Lakers' championship teams, told me, "Kerner was a tough owner. If you played well for him, he patted you on the back. If not, you could expect a foot somewhere."

In 1946, Kerner had been running a printing business in upstate New York that sold advertising for sporting event programs. One of his clients was a basketball team in Buffalo that owed him money. That debt resulted in Kerner acquiring the NBL's Buffalo Bisons. To stay afloat, he moved the franchise west. The newly named Tri-City Blackhawks played their home games alternating between Moline and Rock Island, Illinois, and Davenport, Iowa. Despite the move, the team continued to struggle financially. In five seasons, 1946 through 1951, they went through six coaches with Red Auerbach being the best of the bunch. And the interactions between those two established a pattern that would continue for all of Kerner's subsequent coaches.

By the time Auerbach arrived in Tri-Cities for the 1949–50 season, he had already successfully coached one of the original NBA franchises, the Washington Caps, and was used to making his own personnel decisions. But so was Kerner, and a conflict was inevitable. At one point, Kerner wanted to trade center John Mahnken for Celtics forward Gene Englund. Auerbach convinced Kerner the trade would leave the team without depth at the center position. But, on the Blackhawks next road trip, Auerbach received a telegram from Kerner informing him that he'd made the trade. Auerbach immediately decided he needed to find a new job. As luck would have it, the very next season, the Boston Celtics needed a new coach. Celtics owner Walter Brown called Kerner, who was more than happy to get rid of his strong-willed coach. With Auerbach now with the Celtics, the Blackhawks kept losing and Kerner moved them to Milwaukee and shortened their name to the Hawks. In his entire 20-year professional coaching career, Auerbach had only one losing season—the one year with Tri-City.

Unlike Auerbach, Holzman never got a chance to work for a hands-off owner like Brown. Instead, his coaching inauguration was following in Auerbach's footsteps working with Kerner. In the four years after Auerbach's departure, the team had gone through five different coaches—with Holzman being the sixth. When Red became the Milwaukee coach in the middle of the 1953–54 season, they already had one of the better centers in the league, the 6-foot-11, 245-pound Charlie Share, an All-American out of Bowling Green, who became the first core player Red utilized to build a winning squad.

The next key piece came in the 1954 NBA Draft. Picking second, the Hawks selected Bob Pettit, a 6-foot-9, 205-pound

All-American center from LSU. Pettit not only become the Hawks' best player, but one of the best in NBA history. In September 1954, when Pettit arrived at Wayne University in Detroit for his first professional training camp, he was used to playing with his back to the basket. Holzman took one look at his thin frame and told him he would never make it as a center in the NBA. Pettit wrote in his autobiography, "Red Holzman was the coach and I will always be grateful to him because he made me a forward." Pettit was a determined, hard worker, and he retooled his game by learning how to free himself for jump shots, with his coach assisting in the development. "I spent long hours teaching Bob to shoot facing the basket instead of with his back to it," Holzman wrote in his autobiography, "and his shooting got better and better as he developed confidence."

The Detroit training camp was the first for Holzman as a head coach. In contrast to his practices with the Knicks, where defense would be his primary focus, the Hawks' training was evenly divided between offense and defense. Although he was learning on the job, Bob Harrison, the Hawks' top backcourt player that season, told me Holzman was already "a great coach" and he "learned a lot from him."

From his years in Rochester, Red knew veterans tested rookies by physically challenging them. In the early days of the NBA, with many of the original owners coming from hockey backgrounds, the belief was that rough play and the occasional fight put fans in the seats. As a result, referees "let them play" and were less likely to call fouls. Joe Lapchick, who then coached the New York Knicks, put it this way: "They ask you the question right away and, if you don't give the right answer, you're in trouble."

The veterans wasted no time working Pettit over to see if he had "the right answer." In his very first professional game, a preseason exhibition against the Minneapolis Lakers, Pettit was matched up against the 6-foot-7, 225-pound Vern Mikkelsen, who had a reputation for rough play. Pettit described that game in his autobiography: "For the first half I might as well not have been on the floor; I didn't do a thing. The Lakers just beat me to death. I had no idea of the physical contact that went on under the basket."

At halftime, Holzman approached Pettit and asked him if he liked playing professional basketball. Pettit thought it was a strange question but said that he did. Taking a page from the playbook of his Navy coach, Gary Bodie, Red told Pettit, "If you don't go out there and hit the first guy you see coming at you, I'm going to ship you back to Baton Rouge tomorrow."

Caught off guard, Pettit asked if his coach was serious. "Yes," he shouted. "The first guy who comes close to you in the second half, I want you to hit with an elbow. You have to get a little aggressive and get these guys off you."

So on the first play of the second half, Bob Harrison threw a pass to Pettit in the high post and ran past him trying to use Pettit to pick off his man, the 5-foot-10, 170-pound Slater Martin. Pettit swung the ball around to elbow the diminutive Martin, but missed and ended up elbowing Mikkelsen. As Pettit wrote, "I just stood there looking at him and watching him look down at me and I felt he could . . . crush me like an ant if he wanted to and so I said the only thing I could think of, 'Please excuse me, Mr. Mikkelsen.'"

After that, Pettit understood what was at stake. Over the next few years he added weight and grew stronger. Pettit evolved into one of the top scorers and rebounders in the league, eventually becoming the first NBA player to score 20,000 career points. Pettit was his era's version of Larry Bird, an excellent shooting forward whose intelligence, court awareness, and dedication to the game enabled him to excel. Bob Harrison told me, "Pettit was a typical southern gentleman. You couldn't dislike him. He was one of the finest men I've ever known."

Even with Pettit establishing himself as the team's second foundation player, the Hawks finished the 1954–55 season in last place in the Western Division with a record of 26–46. Though they had six losing streaks of four games or more (including dropping eight in a row), it was still a five-game improvement over the previous season. The slight turnaround was also due to the addition of another rookie, Frank Selvy. In the 1954 draft, before the Hawks had taken Pettit with the second overall selection, the Baltimore Bullets had picked Selvy, a college star at Furman, with the first overall pick. In his senior year, Selvy averaged over 40 points a game and set an NCAA record by scoring 100 points in a single game. But the Bullets went out of business, and the NBA held a dispersal draft for their players. The Hawks, who had the worst record in the NBA the prior season, had the first pick and took Selvy. In the 1954–55 season, Pettit averaged over 20 points per game, Selvy averaged 19 (splitting time between the two clubs), and Holzman had found his third foundation player.

The two rookies were the fourth- and fifth-highest scorers in the league that season and earned an invitation to the NBA All-Star Game, which was played in New York City on January 18, 1955. Holzman initially didn't want Pettit and Selvy attending the game, most likely because the Hawks began their three-game swing through Louisiana against the Lakers the very next night. However, they very much wanted to attend, and Red ultimately let them go. In his autobiography, Pettit noted that Holzman was so concerned about the two rookies traveling from Milwaukee to New York, with an overnight stopover in Chicago, that he explained the travel plans to the two twenty-two-year-old college graduates in very specific detail. Pettit later wrote, "He [Holzman] figured we were a couple of small-town hicks too dumb to get to New York by ourselves."

In addition, there was a mismatching between Pettit's expectations of how a coach should act and Red's low-key style. Pettit wrote that, in one game in high school, he had a poor first half and his team was losing. At halftime, his coach, Kenner Day, "walked into the dressing room, picked up a towel, wet it, and hit me as hard as he could across the head with the wet towel. 'You get out there and show me something this half,' he said." In the second half, Pettit scored 20 points and led his team to victory.

Holzman was not the type to hit one of his players in the head—let alone with a wet towel. When Red won championships with the Knicks, Hall of Famer Bill Bradley referred to Holzman as "the right man, in the right place, at the right time." For the Hawks, he was the wrong man, in the wrong place, at the wrong time. With Kerner as owner and Pettit as their leading player, the Hawks needed a hard-edged, emotional coach to bring them a championship. Local St. Louis newspapers described Holzman as "little," or "not a demonstrative man," or "the soft-spoken leader of the Hawks." Eventually, a highly aggressive coach, Alex Hannum, turned out to be the right man for the job. "Hannum," Pettit wrote, "went on to become one of the top coaches in the game."[2]

With the Hawks, even Holzman's nomenclature was out of place. Consider something as simple as how Pettit and Red each utilized the word *handle*. According to Pettit, "The most important thing a coach must have is the ability to handle players and I don't think you acquire this. I think this is innate." In 1978, Holzman was asked if he could "handle" Wilt Chamberlain, one of the greatest offensive players in NBA history but a man with a reputation as being hard to coach. "You don't mean could I have handled him. You mean could we have gotten along and got any contribution from him. I think you handle dogs, you don't handle people."

In May 1955, despite the Hawks' poor record, Kerner announced that Holzman would be retained for the 1955–56 season. The Hawks had a nucleus of players to build from: Pettit and Share up front; Selvy and Harrison in the backcourt, complemented by the addition of two rookies, Dick Ricketts (a 6-foot-7 forward from Duquesne) and Al Ferrari (a 6-foot-2 guard from Michigan State).

In the summer of 1955, Ben Kerner moved the Hawks to St. Louis. In Milwaukee, no matter how creative Kerner was in trying to draw fans—with promotions such as giving an 89-cent pound of coffee with each $1.25 ticket purchase—nothing boosted attendance. But St. Louis had potential, having recently lost the St. Louis Browns, their American League baseball franchise that had moved to Baltimore (becoming the Orioles).

---

2   With Hannum as their coach, the Hawks won the 1957–58 NBA championship. He would later coach the Philadelphia 76ers to a title.

In St. Louis, Red did what he could to promote the franchise. In May 1955, Holzman showed up at Busch Stadium with Bob Pettit for a photo-op with the St. Louis Cardinals' vice president prior to a game against the Brooklyn Dodgers.

That fall, Red was back in St. Louis for the opening of training camp. Jack Rice, a reporter for the *St. Louis Post-Dispatch*, attended one of those practices. He noticed that Red's style was subdued but that he got his points across when his players made mistakes or needed encouragement to stay focused. Holzman seldom raised his voice or used his whistle, but his remarks were "sharp," and his tone "conversational, not sarcastic." To one player, who was holding the ball on offense for more than a few seconds, he said, in the finest tradition of Nat Holman, "Let's quit visiting, let's go now." After Holzman blew his whistle and said, "Shoot baskets," his players formed groups to shoot free throws. At the other end of the court, a man in street clothes "wheedled" a ball from one of the players and started to shoot. Red, who was a stickler for closed practices with only his players present, gave the interloper loud advice, "Get out." And he did. "Sunday shooters—they'll take over if you let 'em," Holzman said.

Later, during a scrimmage, after deciding that things had started poorly, Red stopped play and made a simple observation. "That's the one thing you want to work on here, ball handling and possession of the ball. If you throw it away, you're not going to get a shot at the basket."

At that point in training camp, Holzman planned on having five players—Pettit, Ricketts, Selvy, Ferrari, and Jack Stephens—all twenty-two years old or younger, work together as a unit in the hope that, with experience, they would form a cohesive team. This solid nucleus of young players gave the coach confidence for the upcoming season. In early October 1955, at an Ad Club lunch honoring the new St. Louis basketball team, Red stuck his neck out further than he ever would during his tenure in New York. "Coaches shouldn't be making this kind of prediction," he said, "but I think we should finish no worse than second in the league this year and maybe we could take it all." Holzman quickly qualified the statement by saying that the team would have to bear out his prediction on the court. Ironically, at the same press conference, Alex Hannum, the Hawks' most seasoned veteran (and later the team's head coach), did not equivocate.

"We're going to make you like us," said Hannum. "We'll be out to win."

The Hawks usually played their home games in the Kiel Auditorium, which could seat approximately 9,300. With a goal of attracting as many fans as possible, Kerner charged a low admission fee and offered fans an occasional show after games featuring such acts as the Count Basie Orchestra, Duke Ellington, and Emmett Kelly, then the world's most famous clown. But, in their first season in St. Louis, the Hawks suffered a setback when Frank Selvy had to fulfill his Army service and played only 17 games. He wouldn't return for another two seasons.

During the 1955–56 season, the Hawks traded rookie Dick Ricketts to Rochester for two veteran players: forward Jack Coleman and guard Jack McMahon. Coleman, standing at 6-foot-7, became the team's third-leading scorer and rebounder behind Pettit and Share. McMahon shared backcourt duties alongside Bob Harrison. Although Kerner made all the trades, he no doubt had input from Holzman in acquiring two of his former Rochester teammates. And listening to his coach showed immediate dividends. In the Hawks' final 33 games, they went

20–13 and Red's prediction for the season proved accurate. The team finished with a 33–39 record, tied with the Minneapolis Lakers for second place in the Western Division.

Pettit led the league in scoring and rebounding and was named league MVP. With Pettit logging the most minutes on the team, Holzman had taken unusual steps to keep him fresh at the end of games. For example, in a game against the Lakers on November 30, 1955, Pettit not only didn't start, but didn't enter the game until the second quarter. But Red's unorthodox strategy somehow worked and the Hawks came from behind to win the game.

But things did not seem to be working out as planned for rookie guard Al Ferrari. Kerner called him into his office and told him he was cutting his salary in half because he wasn't scoring. Ferrari complained that he couldn't score if he didn't play, but Kerner didn't care. Somehow, the fact that Ferrari had signed a contract to be paid $5,000 for the season was of no consequence. Ferrari came to Holzman and explained the situation. Red then started Ferrari in a game, and he played well. This allowed Ferrari to go back to Kerner and successfully lobby to get paid in full. Ferrari's increased playing time proved beneficial during the playoffs.

Since the Hawks and Lakers finished the season with identical records, they played a one-game tiebreaker to determine who had the home-court advantage in their best-of-three opening playoff round. The Hawks lost the tiebreaker, which gave the Lakers home-court advantage.

Dealing with the defeat against the Lakers, the Hawks had to go back out there the following night against the same foe. While the Hawks overcame a 19-point deficit to take Game

One, they were blown out in Game Two, 133–75. After such a one-sided game, Holzman tried to rally his troops. "Fortunately, this game only counts as one win and one loss, and we'll regroup by the tip off of game three. After all, the Lakers beat us in the second-place playoff game and we came back and won the very next night. Why can't we do it again even up here in Minneapolis?"

The Lakers, who had won three of the last four NBA titles and had never lost in the first round of the playoffs, were solid favorites to win the deciding game. But the Hawks took Red's advice and, behind 41 points from Pettit and Ferrari scoring the tying and winning points on two free throws, the Hawks edged the Lakers, 116–115.

But there was no time for celebration, as the Hawks headed to Ft. Wayne for the first game in a best-of-five series with the Pistons for the Western Division crown. After splitting the first four games, the series came down to the deciding game. Pettit, who had averaged nearly 26 points a game during the regular season, had been held to just 7, 16, 19, and 15 points in the first four games of the series. Before the fifth game, Red said, "We promise to have some interesting surprises offensively and maybe something on defense as well for this game. We naturally want to try to increase the scoring output of Pettit in order to win. He is our main weapon and with our backs to the wall, we have to go to our bread-and-butter guy."

Holzman's surprise was another unorthodox move. Shortly after the opening tip-off, Red pulled Pettit and Ferrari out of the game with the hope of confusing the Pistons. While he hoped such a move would give him a mental advantage and jolt Pettit out of his scoring slump, it didn't work. Although the Hawks briefly had a five-point lead in the third quarter, they eventually lost, 102–97.

While it's tough to see positives in losing, despite being defeated the Hawks had improved dramatically over the course of the season. In the playoffs, an empowered Al Ferrari had been the team's second-leading scorer behind Pettit.

That season, prior to a game against the Syracuse Nationals (the defending NBA champions), Holzman's comments reveal how he believed a championship basketball team should be constructed: "Teamwork does the trick for Syracuse. The Nats have a wonderful nucleus of men who have played and worked together for the last four or five years. Players know each other's moves and anticipate spurts by teammates with sharp, spot passes." But this approach couldn't happen overnight. It required finding the right players and sticking with them until they jelled as a team. Later, in New York, Red would have a chance to put this approach into practice. That wouldn't be the case in St. Louis.

After the Hawks' playoff run, Kerner signed Holzman to a one-year contract estimated to be between $9,000 and $10,000 to coach the team for the 1956–57 season. After a successful first season in St. Louis, Red was under considerable pressure to produce a championship. This was especially true in light of one of the most famous trades in NBA history: a trade that made Auerbach's career but had Holzman out of basketball before the season ended.

In the six years since Auerbach started coaching in Boston, the Celtics had become one of the best teams in the NBA. But, prior to the 1956–57 season, they had yet to win a championship in their first decade of existence. The Celtics had three great offensive players in Bob Cousy, Bill Sharman, and Ed Macauley, but lacked an equally talented rebounder and defender who could initiate the fast-break offense Auerbach favored. Before the 1956 NBA Draft, Auerbach's college coach, Bill Reinhart, told him that if he drafted Bill Russell, the All-American center from the University of San Francisco, the Celtics would become a championship team.

Russell was the most gifted rebounder and defender of his era. He didn't just dominate the game—he changed the way it was played. At a time when players were taught never to leave their feet on defense, Russell was leaping to block shots. Due to his dominance and unique abilities, the NCAA committee widened the lane from 6 to 12 feet and instituted a goaltending rule. And he was *still* a winner. With Russell leading them, the SF Dons set an NCAA record with 60 consecutive wins. Auerbach trusted Reinhart implicitly and decided he would do whatever was necessary to acquire Russell.

But the Celtics didn't have the first overall pick. That sat with the Rochester Royals , with the St. Louis Hawks picking second. After confirming that Les Harrison—who already had a strong rebounder and defensive player in Maurice Stokes—would not be selecting Russell for the Royals, Auerbach contacted Ben Kerner and proposed a trade. The Celtics would send the Hawks Ed Macauley, a 6-foot-8 former college star at St. Louis University—who would be an immediate box-office draw for Kerner—in exchange for Russell, whom the Hawks would select with their number two pick. Kerner must have been overjoyed. As the only NBA city below the Mason-Dixon line, it was an open question how the St. Louis fans would respond to having a black man—especially one as forthright as Russell—as their star player. But Kerner was a smart poker player. In addition to Macauley, he demanded Auerbach trade him a second player, the All-American forward out of Kentucky, Cliff Hagan. Auerbach agreed. Russell showed what one transcendent defensive player can accomplish, and the Celtics won eleven of the next thirteen NBA championships.

The Hawks entered the 1956–57 season with too many front-court players and not enough backcourt men. Holzman had to find playing time for returning veterans Pettit, Coleman, and Share, as well as Ed Macauley and outstanding rookie Willie Naulls, who had been an All-American at UCLA. With Frank Selvy and Al Ferrari lost for the year due to military duty, Holzman attempted to move Cliff Hagan to the backcourt. With Share at center, Pettit and Macauley at forward, and Coleman the first forward off the bench, there was no regular spot in the rotation for Hagan up front. There was no way that the rookie would start ahead of Pettit, one of the best players in the league, or Macauley, who was not just an all-star but a fan favorite who grew up in the St. Louis area. An "Ed Macauley Night" was even held when the Hawks opened up their season with a Saturday night game against the Lakers.

The problem was that Hagan was a poor ballhandler. Despite standing only 6-foot-4, Hagan had been an outstanding center in college and rarely put the ball on the floor for more than a dribble or two. That season, Norm Stewart, who later became a successful college basketball coach at Missouri, was a rookie with the Hawks. "Cliff Hagan," Stewart told me, "had as much of a chance of being a guard as I did of making the team."

Stewart, who played in only five games for the Hawks before being released, recalled an intersquad scrimmage when he and another rookie, Bob Schafer, were matched up in the backcourt against Hagan and the veteran guard Jack McMahon. After Hagan literally ran over McMahon as he was bringing the ball up the court, Schafer said to Stewart, "If we can't beat these guys, we shouldn't be out here."

Despite what seemed obvious to everyone, Holzman was quoted in the *St. Louis Dispatch* as saying, "Hagan is fitting in real nice as a back-court player. He has good basketball hands, handles the ball well, and when he's in sound physical shape, he can move with the swiftest."

Red tried to motivate Hagan to play guard, telling him that his former teammate at Kentucky, Frank Ramsay, was the same height and playing in the backcourt for Boston. But Hagan simply couldn't handle the ball as well as Ramsay.

Jack Levitt, who then ran the 24-second clock at Kiel Arena and later worked for the Hawks in numerous capacities, told me it was Kerner, not Holzman, who insisted Hagan play in the backcourt. No matter who made the decision, the Hawks desperately needed a top backcourt player and more playing time for Hagan up front. "If Hagan got the ball down low on the right side," Stewart told me, "it was two points."

Knowing how high expectations were for the 1956–57 season, Holzman ran a tough preseason camp. Stewart recalls that Red's focus was on "sound basketball," which meant take good shots, guard your man, make your free throws, "and get the ball to Pettit." During one practice, Holzman saw that Jack Coleman, the second-oldest player on the team, was not in shape. Red kept Coleman on the court so much that day that, after he intercepted a pass and started to dribble down the court on a fast break, his dribble kept getting higher as he was sinking lower. At midcourt, Coleman's dribble was up to his waist; by the time he hit the foul line it was up to his shoulder. Finally, Coleman's legs went out from under him as he fell and turned the ball over. Holzman stopped play and walked up to Coleman, who was still lying on the floor. "Jack," Red asked, "what wrong?"

"Damn it, Red," Coleman replied, "I'm tired."

That fall's preseason camp, held at Knox College in Illinois, was tough for everyone—especially the younger players. "Holzman would run our butts off," Cliff Hagan told me. "We all had blisters on our feet."

This was Pettit's third season in the league, and teams continued to get physical when guarding him. In one game against the Lakers, Clyde Lovellette committed a hard foul on Pettit. Charlie Share, who acted as the Hawks' enforcer, punched Lovellette, and the two men started to go at it. The Lakers' Ed Kalafat, who was 6-foot-6, 245 pounds, and the most feared fighter in the league, stepped in to break up the scuffle. But then someone accidently punched Kalafat, and the fight immediately stopped. No one wanted to get Kalafat upset. "Kalafat," Stewart told me, "was stronger than goat's milk."

The early portion of the season didn't go well for the Hawks. The team lost six straight games from November 27 until December 8, leaving them with an 8–11 record. According to Stewart, even before the losing streak, "Kerner tried to fire Red after every game." That December, Holzman's actions didn't match the grace under pressure he would show later in his coaching career.

Red had good reason to be fearful. Uncharacteristically, Kerner planned on making a major trade without Holzman's input. Slater Martin, the All-Star guard who had led the Lakers to four championships with his ball handling and outstanding defense, was having contract problems. Seeing retirement as a possibility, he opened a sporting goods store. But Martin got a call from a sportswriter asking if he would be willing to play in St. Louis. Martin said he would, but only if Kerner met his salary demands. The problem was that Minneapolis would never trade Martin to another team in the division—especially one they'd had a strong rivalry with. But Kerner, working in concert with his friend Ned Irish, the Knicks' president, came up with a plan. New York signed Martin, and he played for them for approximately a month, just long enough to create the impression they wanted him as a Knick. Then Kerner traded forward Willie Naulls to New York for Martin. When Martin was playing for the Knicks, only three people knew what was going on: Kerner, Irish, and Martin. But rumors spread quickly.

When word got to Holzman, he knew that unless the Hawks started to win consistently, he would soon be out of a job. Decades later, Hawks center Charlie Share told Terry Pluto, who was writing a history of the early days of the NBA, "Towards the end, Holzman gave us a pep talk where he pulled out pictures of his wife and kid and asked us—pleaded with us—to win so that he could keep his job and feed his family. We knew that he was in real trouble."

Red had lost Kerner's support and, with it, the support of his players. It was no coincidence that the Hawks six-game losing streak ended on December 11, 1956—Martin's first game playing for the Hawks. Ironically, the game was against the Knicks at the Garden. Before the game, Kerner told the press that Holzman's job was in danger. "It's a game of emotion. If we don't start winning soon, I'll be forced to make a change," he said to the *St. Louis Post-Dispatch*. "And I've talked that over with Red and he understands it." Holzman took a clipping of Kerner's comments and posted it up in the Hawks locker room. His pregame speech that night consisted of two words, "Let's go."

The Hawks defeated the Knicks, 137–128, setting, what was at the time, an NBA record for most combined points scored in a game. After the victory, Red was asked what had changed. "I didn't do anything different. I try to do the same things all the time, win or lose. We just try to do things I think will work best. Tonight, we cleared the boards better and faster than ever, and we made our shots. That's all."

On December 22, in a nationally televised game against the Celtics played at the Boston Garden, Holzman watched the Hawks blow a 14-point fourth quarter lead. With 10 seconds left, Bob Cousy threw an overhand bullet pass to Tommy Heinsohn, who scored to tie the game. Then, with eight seconds left, Ed Macauley took a desperation heave from 70 feet away from the basket. The shot missed badly, and Boston gained possession and called timeout. Bill Sharman then scored on a jump shot to give the Celtics a 95–93 victory.

After the game, which drew national attention because it was Bill Russell's NBA debut, Holzman told the press that he had fined Macauley $50 for "two plays you couldn't condone if a rookie made them." He said that Macauley not only let Heinsohn get away from him for the tying basket but should have called timeout to set up a final shot with eight seconds remaining. Holzman's public reprimand of Macauley, who was far more popular in St. Louis than the coach, was big news. The Associated Press ran the story nationwide.

Red's uncharacteristically public criticism of a player showed the stress he was under. It also briefly motivated his players, as the Hawks ended December with a four-game winning streak. But instead of starting the new year on a high note, it began with four consecutive losses. The fourth was in St. Louis on Sunday, January 6, and left the Hawks with a 14–19 record.

The next day, Holzman was relieved as head coach. "I believe the club is better than its record would indicate," Kerner said after the decision had been made. The owner wanted "the right man . . . one with a little fire." Two days later, on January 8, Slater Martin was named the team's interim coach. Afterward, he felt that Red was "a little cool" to him because he'd believed that Martin was brought to St. Louis to replace him. But he didn't want to coach, and told Kerner that if he wanted a championship he could get him one, but only as a player. For Martin, coaching was a distraction. Less than two weeks later, Alex Hannum was named to replace him as the Hawks' coach.

Cliff Hagan told me that Hannum was a "natural leader." He was so strong willed that the players called him "iron-head." But, for the Hawks, the 6-foot-7 Hannum was exactly what they needed: the kind of leader who, if he thought it would help, would hit a player over the head with a wet towel.

By the end of the season, as Holzman had predicted, the team began to jell. In February, Bob Pettit broke his arm and Hannum was forced to put Hagan into the starting lineup, where he excelled. When Pettit returned, Hannum moved Macauley to the bench and kept Hagan on the floor. As a result, the team that would dominate the Western Division for the next few seasons was set: Share at center; two future Hall of fame players, Pettit and Hagan, at forward; and Martin and McMahon in the back-court. Luck wasn't on Holzman's side, as it seems he was fired a month too soon.

As Red had predicted, give the right players enough time to play together and you'll get results. The Hawks peaked just as the regular season ended. In the playoffs they advanced to the championship round but lost to the Celtics in a series that wasn't decided until the final seconds of double overtime in the seventh game.

During the championship series, Red Auerbach and Ben Kerner renewed their long-standing distrust for one another. In St. Louis, as the Celtics warmed up prior to the third game of the series, Bob Cousy told Auerbach he thought the basket the Celtics were shooting at was not regulation height. Auerbach demanded that the basket be measured. Thinking the coach was trying to show him up, Kerner ran onto the court screaming obscenities. Auerbach coldcocked Kerner, knocking him back-wards. NBA Commissioner Maurice Podoloff was not impressed with Auerbach's justification for hitting Kerner. "He called me a bunch of bad names," Auerbach said, "and I just didn't want to hear him anymore." Podoloff fined the Celtics coach $300.

The basket turned out to be at regulation height.

The following season, 1957–58, Slater Martin accomplished what he had promised. The Hawks, coached by Hannum, defeated the Celtics in the NBA Finals to win their first and only championship. Bill Russell sprained his ankle in the third game of the series. Ed Macauley later said that had Russell been healthy, he didn't think the Hawks would have won. Following the championship, Hannum requested a raise. Negotiations ended with Kerner firing him. By 1968, after going through a half-dozen more coaches, Kerner sold the Hawks to a Georgia real estate developer who moved the team to Atlanta.

Until St. Louis, Holzman had handled professional basketball's ups and downs with equanimity. "But when I was fired by Ben Kerner in 1957," Red later wrote, "it was the end of the world." He was then not only out of basketball for an extended period of time, but felt the pressures he had seen weigh down his father: "I had my wife, Selma, and daughter, Gail, to support. I was on a dead-end street. That's when I made up my mind never to coach again."

But he would. As Butch Beard, Holzman's assistant coach with the Knicks, told me, "You have to fail to learn how to succeed."

That spring, Red made ends meet working in various sales jobs. He sold life insurance for Cy Block, who had leveraged his brief major-league baseball career into a thriving business. He also worked trying to solicit clients for a freight business run by Arthur Brown, who owned the New Jersey Americans, a semipro basketball team. Red even had a third part-time job with Gimbels Department Store selling food plans that could be purchased when a customer bought a refrigerator. Years later, he told his son-in-law, Charlie Papelian, that he enjoyed making small talk with potential customers but had a problem "closing the deal."

Red was no salesman. Luckily, Fuzzy Levane again come to his rescue. After being fired by the Hawks, Levane had worked in Milwaukee for the Schlitz Brewing Company. They would end up transferring him back to New York, where he reconnected with Holzman and they both ended up selling insurance for Cy Block. Levane was also working as a part-time scout for the Knicks. And, in early April 1958, when Knicks coach Vince Boryla was promoted to general manager, Levane replaced him as coach and began lobbying for Red to be given his scouting job.

CHAPTER SIX

"KID, YOU'RE GOING TO DO PRETTY WELL IN THIS GAME."

Knicks president Ned Irish wasn't in favor of hiring Holzman. In fact, he preferred Sonny Hertzberg, who was the other candidate for the scouting job. Irish was more familiar with Hertzberg, the Knicks' leading scorer in their inaugural season. But, at Fuzzy Levane's insistence, general manager Vince Boryla convinced Irish to hire Red. "He [Boryla] didn't realize how badly I wanted and needed that job," Red would later write in his book.

Boryla's decision paid long-term dividends for the Knicks, as Red scouted every one of the 1970 championship team's starting players during their college careers: Willis Reed, Dave DeBusschere, Bill Bradley, Walt Frazier, and Dick Barnett; as well as their most effective players off the bench: Cazzie Russell, Dave Stallworth, and Mike Riordan. Reed later said, "The one thing that Red had that no one else had, was the luxury of being involved in drafting and being involved in acquiring all the players on the team in trades. So he knew a lot more about them—their temperament, their basketball ability—than anyone else. That gave him a tremendous advantage when he became the coach, and he used it very well."

In April 1958, after taking the scouting job, Red's pay was $2,500 a year. Today, adjusted for inflation, that is the equivalent of less than $22,000 a year. No doubt, those were the days when Selma did her part by managing the household "with less." But Holzman proved his value and eventually built the part-time scouting position into a full-time job.

Upon joining the Knicks, Ned Irish still had enormous influence on the team's draft selections. This had been the case since 1947, when the Knicks selected Wat Misaka, a 5-foot-7, 150-pound guard from Utah. In that year's NIT final, the Garden crowd was enthralled by Misaka, who led Utah to an upset victory over Kentucky. Irish gave Misaka a guaranteed $3,000 contract without first consulting with coach Joe Lapchick. Shortly after the 1947–48 season began, Lapchick concluded that Misaka could not physically compete in the NBA and cut him from the team. Irish, to his credit, paid Misaka in full. But a precedent had been set. Beginning with Misaka, the first player ever drafted by the Knicks, Irish would be influenced by a player's potential gate appeal—over the advice of his basketball professionals.

Yet, the Knicks' draft picks in 1948—forward Harry Gallatin, and, in 1949, guard Dick McGuire—worked out well. Gallatin was a relative unknown, having played at North East Missouri State Teachers College. McGuire was a locally familiar figure, having been an All-American at St. John's. Gallatin and McGuire became Hall of Fame players. But, in the 1950s, prior to Holzman being hired, in all but one case (Ken Sears, the team's first-round pick in 1955, who had six productive seasons with the team) the Knicks' first-round draft picks had little to no impact. As a result, after making the playoffs in each of their first ten years of existence (1946 to 1956), the Knicks fell into a fallow period (1957 to 1966) in which they made the playoffs only once.[1]

Holzman quickly learned that Irish called the shots regarding the team's draft picks, but was not afraid to speak his mind if he disagreed. This was never clearer than at a 1961 team draft meeting attended by Holzman, Irish, Boryla, and first-year coach Carl Braun, who tested Holzman to see if he would stand up to Irish.

The Knicks were trying to decide which one of two potential backcourt players they would select with their second pick: Johnny Egan of Providence or Whitey Martin of St. Bonaventure. Braun preferred Egan, while Irish and Boryla preferred Martin. Throughout the entire discussion between the three men, Red stayed quiet. He just sat there, until Braun asked for his opinion.

Holzman didn't hesitate or waste words, "Egan without a doubt."

Red hadn't previously said anything because he knew he'd be wasting his breath; Irish was going to do what he wanted. With their second-round choice, the tenth selection in the 1961 draft, the Knicks picked Whitey Martin. Two picks later, the Detroit Pistons selected Johnny Egan.

After one lackluster season for the Knicks, Martin's NBA career was over. Egan, on the other hand, played in the NBA for

---

1   In their first ten seasons, the Knicks had a record of 368–286 (.563). In their following ten seasons, they had a record of 292–478 (.379).

11 productive seasons—including three seasons with the Knicks after they acquired him in a 1963 trade. And in the 1970s, after his playing career ended, Egan coached the Houston Rockets for four seasons. In 2018, when I spoke to Egan, he was unaware that Holzman had wanted the Knicks to select him in the 1961 draft. Egan told me that didn't surprise him. "Red," Egan said, "was a silent assassin."

* * *

In the early 1960s, the Knicks were a terrible team.[3] Braun was soon fired as Knicks coach. The Knicks would then go through another three coaches, Eddie Donovan, Harry Gallatin, and Dick McGuire; all while Holzman was inconspicuously scouting for the club. In 1970, Carl Braun told writer Phil Berger, "Red is as dumb as he wants you to think he is. He's dumb like a fox. Red is the type of guy who . . . I always get the feeling looking in Red's eyes that he's right on top of everything, but he's not saying anything."

But Red could also be genuinely disarming when he wanted to be. In the mid-1960s, decades before he became the general manager of the Chicago Bulls, Jerry Krause was a scout for the Baltimore Bullets. The two knew of each other from their scouting rounds, and one night, Krause was in Oklahoma City to see Flynn Robinson play for the visiting Wyoming team. That same evening, there was a game being played in Wichita, Kansas, with

---

3   In the eight seasons before Holzman became head coach (1959–60 through 1966–67), the Knicks were a combined 217–418 (.341 winning percentage) with their best finish being the 1964–65 season, where they finished 31–49, 18 games under .500.

another prospective talent. At 4:30 the next morning, Krause arrived at the Kansas City airport and saw Holzman sitting there waiting for a flight.

"Where have you been?" Red asked Krause.

Krause, who was, in later years, well known for being secretive, said, "Down the road."

"Son," Holzman answered, "I want to tell you something. I know where you've been and if you got any brains in your head, you know where I've been, so let's cut the bullshit and let's be friends."

They did. And, as a result, Krause learned a great deal about the art of scouting. Krause explained Holzman's methodology this way, "Red never scouted from the motel. See, you go into a town, what do you do? Let's say you get there early in the morning. Got a game that night. A lot of times, if you're smart, you go out to the college and you say to the coach, 'Look, if you got a room with a projector and some of your game film.' You sit there and you watch for five or six hours; you're not in the motel sitting on your ass. You're out working and you're getting a little extra than the other scouts in the league. You're stealing a little. That's the way Red was. Our coach at Chicago, Dick Motta— used to coach at Weber State College—he said Red was the only scout to come to a practice. Red would go to see a guy, and if he'd like him, he'd keep going back. He wanted to see him in as many different situations as he could."

Krause and Holzman were once seated next to each other on a flight when it became clear the plane would be delayed. "Red hauls the little airline-book out—the little book with all the schedules—gets all the alternate schedules out and asks the stewardess, 'Will you please check on these other flights for me?'

He was all prepared to get us to this other place because he was the only scout in the game who had the airline book with him. He never made a show of it, he just did his job."

Today, Red's scouting methods seem quaint, but, when the profession was in its infancy, he was breaking new ground. And the countless hours of travel during the college basketball season didn't bother him as he looked forward to having the summers off and being home with Selma and Gail. Scouting gave him a chance to be his own boss while utilizing his skills in evaluating players. He went where he wanted and when he wanted while answering to no one. And, unlike coaching, Red did his work anonymously. There was no press to contend with. As a scout, all that mattered was the quality of his evaluations.

In this regard, Holzman was outstanding. Although he would always say that the Knicks' draft picks were the product of a "we"—himself, the coach, the general manager, and, in the years prior to 1964, Ned Irish—ultimately, whether his advice was followed or not, it was Red's initial impression of a college player as documented in his one-page written reports (which Selma typed for him) that was the touchstone for all personnel decisions.

The 1959 draft was the first Holzman worked on for the Knicks. That year they took Johnny Green of Michigan State with the fifth pick of the first round. It turned out to be a fine choice as Green, a 6-foot-5 forward with incredible leaping ability, played with the Knicks for six seasons and was a three-time All-Star. But in that draft, Red was hoping to select Dick Barnett as the long-term replacement for Carl Braun, the team's thirty-one-year-old guard. Barnett had led Tennessee A&I to three consecutive NAIA national championships playing for the legendary Hall of Fame coach John McLendon. But the Syracuse

Nationals (today's Philadelphia 76ers) beat them to Barnett, selecting him with the fourth pick. Holzman later wrote in his book, "I had scouted Barnett at Tennessee State [previously called Tennessee A&I]. I knew he was a good shooter and a fine defensive player."

It wasn't just that Red saw Barnett's on-court potential, but he identified with his journey. Barnett grew up in a poor neighborhood in Gary, Indiana, where his love of basketball motivated him to practice his shot every day of the year—even if it meant having to shovel snow off the court. He played two seasons for the Syracuse Nationals before leaving the NBA to play for McLendon, who had taken a job coaching the Cleveland Pipers of the American Basketball League (ABL). But the Pipers, who were owned by Cleveland businessman and future New York Yankees owner George Steinbrenner, folded in 1962. Barnett then returned to the NBA to play for the Lakers, where he had the misfortune of playing third fiddle to two of the greatest players in NBA history: Elgin Baylor and Jerry West. As a result, Barnett never received the acclaim a player of his abilities deserved. But Holzman knew Dick's potential. In 1965, with Red's encouragement, the Knicks traded Bob Boozer for Barnett.

By 1960, Holzman had become a full-time scout traveling over 20,000 miles a season looking for potential talent in the college ranks. That year, picking third in the draft, the Knicks selected Darrall Imhoff, a 6-foot-10 center from California. The Knicks didn't get a chance to select either one of the two players Red wanted, Oscar Robertson or Jerry West. The Cincinnati Royals picked Robertson first; the Lakers took West second.

Prior to the 1960 draft, Irish's preference was to draft a center. "It is not hopeless," Irish was quoted as saying in March 1960.

"In fact, the outlook is on the bright side. We do not need too much in the way of playing personnel. Perhaps a good tall man to back up Charlie Tyra and a good corner man behind Ken Sears and Johnny Green—not much more."

Holzman's preference was to select a backcourt player. In an AP piece published on February 25, 1960—well before that year's draft—Red was quoted as saying that Robertson and West were the best professional prospects, but Imhoff was a question mark. "Imhoff isn't much of a shooter," said Holzman. "He's big enough and is good on defense, but to make it in the NBA you have to be able to score. That's where Robertson and West really stand out. Robertson reminds me a lot of Elgin Baylor. He can do everything. West also is excellent on defense. He may be a little small to be used up front in our league, but he'd make a whale of a backcourt man."

Robertson, like West, became one of the greatest players in NBA history. Imhoff played only two seasons for the Knicks before they traded him to Detroit. Based upon his pre-draft comments, it's unlikely Red suggested the Knicks take a center when they still needed a guard to replace their player-coach, Carl Braun, then entering his final playing season. Irish picked who he wanted—Imhoff. This despite the fact that Irish said, "The others [Boryla, Braun, and Holzman] will submit a list of fifteen names to me. These will be in the order of their preference. I, of course, will accept their recommendations."

In a 1960 AP article, Holzman said the qualities he looked for in a player were: offensive potential, strength, defensive ability, and good character. "A boy can be a fine player, but if we think he's not dependable or might not get along with the other members of the team we start looking for someone else." Based upon his preferences and perception of the team's needs, if Red had the final say that year he would have selected Providence back-court star Lenny Wilkens. Holzman knew all about Wilkens, who grew up in Brooklyn and was an outstanding high school player at Boy's High. Wilkens was not just a great player but a man of impeccable character. St. Louis selected Wilkens two picks after the Knicks chose Imhoff. Wilkens was elected to the Hall of Fame as a player (1989) and as a coach (1998).

To see his recommendations ignored must have frustrated Holzman. But he prided himself on staying even and managing his emotions. As Red told Robert Lipsyte of the *New York Times* a few years later, "I just try to stay cool. I never thought getting an ulcer made you a more dedicated man. Is a fighter better if he has a cauliflower ear?"

In 1978, when asked about the life of an NBA scout, he said, "Well, it can be lonely, but if you're working for a good organization like the Knicks you always went first class and you usually had a lot of free rein in what you were doing and you set your own schedule, so that was good. It made you work harder too because [laugh] you didn't want to miss anything or any place, and it wasn't bad. You know, it kept you very, very busy. There's a lot of statistical work that you could always be doing, and really work that only you could do because you know what you had to do. But I enjoyed it. I thought I'd be doing that for a long time."

Despite the tedium, Red approached his scouting job with a positive attitude. But others in the coaching profession found seeing Holzman alone and constantly on the road disturbing. In the winter of 1963, Red crossed paths with an acquaintance from New York, Roy Rubin, who was then the coach of LIU. It was on a Saturday night outside a diner in the town of

Sunbury in central Pennsylvania. Red was scouting a Sunbury Mercuries Eastern League game. Rubin's LIU team had just lost to Susquehanna University. After Holzman left, Rubin shook his head and said something his team's student-manager, Edward Hershey, would long remember. "Red is one of the good guys," Rubin said. "But he was an NBA coach and look where he is now. The pro game can eat you alive."

* * *

In May 1961, the Knicks hired Eddie Donovan to replace Carl Braun as their coach. Donovan had been a successful coach at St. Bonaventure University. That year, the Knicks selected one of Donovan's players—forward Tom Stith—with the second overall pick of the draft. Unfortunately, Stith contracted tuberculosis, which limited him to only one season in the NBA. In the 1961 draft, everyone's top pick was Walt Bellamy, a 6-foot-10 center from Indiana. The Knicks had finished the previous season with the worst record in the NBA and had the first pick. Irish assumed the Knicks would select Bellamy. However, a new NBA franchise, the Chicago Packers, were awarded the top pick and selected Bellamy. It would take several years, but the Knicks eventually acquired Bellamy in a trade.

In preparation for the 1961 NBA Draft, seeking a possible alternative to Bellamy, Holzman left no stone unturned—even local stones. That season, he made a trip to the 69th Regiment Armory in Manhattan to see the star center of the Hunter College team, Charley Rosen, in a game against St. Francis of Brooklyn. As Rosen wrote in his book, *The Chosen Game*, Red took a seat in the first row of the bleachers directly under Hunter's basket.

Near the end of the game, following a long downcourt pass, Rosen got the ball about 15 feet away from the basket. Dunking was then frowned upon in the college ranks, especially if it was done to embarrass a defending player. But with an open path to the basket, Rosen decided he was going to dunk. Wearing a brace on his left knee due to a cartilage tear, Rosen dribbled to the basket and tried to jump off his left foot. He ended up missing the dunk, slamming the ball on the underside of the rim, and falling to the floor. Neither the Knicks, nor any other NBA team, drafted Rosen.

The first two players selected in the 1962 draft were Jerry Lucas and Dave DeBusschere. Lucas, a nationally recognized star at Ohio State, was selected by the Cincinnati Royals. DeBusschere, who attended the University of Detroit, was chosen by the Detroit Pistons. Holzman had scouted both players. As in the case of Barnett, Holzman had hoped the Knicks would have the chance to draft DeBusschere. Ultimately, DeBusschere and Lucas would both play for the Knicks.

With the second overall pick in the 1962 draft, the Knicks selected Paul Hogue, a 6-foot-9 center from the University of Cincinnati. Knicks coach Eddie Donovan said that Hogue, "was our number one pick from the outset." Irish, no doubt, had seen Hogue win the MVP Award during the Holiday Festival held in Madison Square Garden that past December. But Hogue lasted only one full season with the Knicks and was out of the NBA the following year. Instead of Hogue, the Knicks could have selected Zelmo Beaty, another center who became an All-Star with the Hawks.

The 1963 draft was the final one in which Irish had a strong influence. Beginning in 1964, focused on plans for building a new Madison Square Garden, Irish delegated decision-making authority to Donovan. But in that 1963 draft, the Knicks selected 6-foot-5 Art Heyman. A three-time All-American and the college player of the year, Heyman led Duke to the Final Four in his senior year. The pick was no surprise. According to Michael Strauss in the *New York Times*, Knicks officials had been talking about Heyman since the previous winter, "as though he were already wearing one of their uniforms." Heyman did well in his rookie season. But, by his own admission, he rubbed people the wrong way and ended up with a nomadic professional career playing for seven different teams.

The Knicks priority should have been taking a big man, especially after Paul Hogue proved to be a bust. By taking Heyman, who had the box-office appeal Irish wanted because he was Jewish and from Long Island, the Knicks passed on center Nate Thurmond, a future Hall of Fame player.

One of the Knicks late-round picks was guard Bill Raftery from La Salle. Raftery didn't have much of a chance to make the team, but Holzman was pulling for him. He was the kind of player—hardworking and smart—that Red was always looking for. Raftery was good enough to make it through the team's rookie summer camp. But after a morning workout during a preseason practice, Raftery was cut at lunch time. When Holzman, who was attending practices in his role as assistant coach, came back from lunch, he asked Pete Carusso, a basketball coach at Kings Point College who served as referee during Knicks practices, "Where's Billy?"[4]

---

4   Raftery never played in the NBA. He became a basketball coach at Fairleigh Dickinson University and, later, at Seton Hall. Raftery jokes that his best recruit at Fairleigh Dickinson was Red's daughter, Gail, who went to college there. He has since become a popular network television commentator, working at CBS Sports and ESPN, and FOX over thirty-plus years.

Beginning with the 1964 draft, with Irish less involved and Eddie Donovan the chief decision maker, Holzman's input became meaningful. The timing was crucial. The team still needed a center, and there were three highly rated big men in that year's draft: Jim Barnes of Texas Western, Luke Jackson of Pan American, and Willis Reed of Grambling. Barnes was viewed as the most athletic; Jackson as the most likely to contribute immediately; and Reed as having the greatest long-term potential. The Knicks had them rated equally, but selected Barnes with the first overall pick. Philadelphia took Jackson with the fourth pick. The Celtics had the final pick of the first round, but Red Auerbach selected Mel Counts, a seven-foot center from Oregon State. Holzman and Donovan were amazed that every other team in the first round had passed on Reed, and the Knicks selected him in the second round.

Holzman had traveled down to Louisiana on numerous occasions to see Reed play. In 1978, Red was asked about his impressions the first time he saw him play in college. "He was a big, strong kid that could shoot," Holzman said. "He was still crude, at that point, but he looked like he had tremendous talent. We always felt he was one of the three best players in the country."

As was his habit with a player he was interested in, Holzman made sure to see Reed play on numerous occasions. The first time Reed saw Holzman, he was standing in the office of Grambling football coach Eddie Robinson, which had a glass window that looked out to the gym. Red was wearing a gray pinstriped suit and holding a tan raincoat over his arm and talking with basketball coach Fred Hobdy. Reed had impressed Hobdy with his leadership skills. When the Grambling team needed motivating—and

101

without any prodding from Hobdy—Reed often took the initiative and spoke to his teammates.

That day, Hobdy introduced the two. This was an unusual occurrence. As a general rule, prior the draft, Red rarely had any interactions with the players he was recruiting. At some point, Holzman measured Reed, concluding he was 6-foot-8 and not the 6-foot-10 he was listed at. Red could measure height, but not heart. Reed came from a good Louisiana family where his grandfather (who was a farmer) and parents taught him the importance of hard work. Reed grew up picking cotton for four dollars a day—until he was strong enough to haul hay for five dollars a day. And being passed over in the first round motivated Reed to work even harder than he usually did. The result was a Hall of Fame playing career.

In New York, used to being *the star* at Texas Western, Jim Barnes was unable to adjust to sharing the spotlight with Reed. Barnes lasted only one full season with the Knicks and spent most of his career bouncing from team to team. Barnes's greatest value to the Knicks was being one of the three players the Knicks traded to acquire Walt Bellamy. The others were Holzman favorites Johnny Green and Johnny Egan. Beginning in 1964, Holzman's increased involvement in the Knicks draft selections was obvious. That year, in stark contrast to almost all of their previous drafts, even their late round draft picks such as Fred Crawford (fourth round) and Emmette Bryant (seventh round) had several productive seasons for the Knicks.

But Red could make mistakes. In the mid-'60s, during a training camp practice, he noticed that a rookie he had strongly recommended was having problems fighting through screens set to his left. Holzman hadn't noticed this before. During a break, he counseled the player to look out the corner of his left eye and fight through the screen.

"I can't look out the corner of my eye," replied the player, whose name has been lost to the sands of time.

"You can't?" Holzman said. "What's so hard?"

"I'm blind in my left eye."

The 1965 draft was the last to have territorial picks which allowed teams to forgo their first-round pick in exchange for the right to select a specific player from a local college team. After Ned Irish convinced everyone that New York City was closer to Princeton than Philadelphia, the Knicks selected Bill Bradley of Princeton University with their territorial pick. The son of a banker, Bradley was born in Crystal City, Missouri, and grew up a fan of the St. Louis Hawks. He even attended a basketball camp run by the Hawks' Ed Macauley. A three-time All-American, Bradley almost single-handedly drove Princeton to the NCAA semifinals (where they lost to a Michigan team led by Bradley's future Knicks teammate, Cazzie Russell). The fact that Princeton, which did not offer athletic scholarships, could advance so far in the NCAA tournament was a testament to his determination and skill. There also was some risk involved in selecting Bradley. He had accepted a Rhodes Scholarship and would spend two years at Oxford. But Red knew he would be worth the wait. In his autobiography, Holzman wrote, "After seeing Bradley just once in college I never went out of my way to scout him again . . . . He was just great."

In addition to Bradley, the Knicks' next three picks in that year's draft all went on to have long NBA careers. They selected Dave Stallworth from Wichita State in the first round. But, after suffering a heart attack, he was forced to sit out two seasons until he was cleared to continue his playing career. Stallworth would make an invaluable contribution to the Knicks' first championship team. In the second round, the Knicks selected 6-foot-5 Dick Van Arsdale of Indiana. Van Arsdale played for the Knicks for three seasons. In 1968, Phoenix selected him in the expansion draft and he played for them for nine seasons and was a three-time All-Star. Holzman even did well with the Knicks' third-round draft pick, Barry Clemens, a 6-foot-6 forward from Ohio Wesleyan. Clemens played for the Knicks for one season before being selected by Chicago in the 1966 expansion draft. An outstanding shooter, Clemens went on to have an 11-year NBA career.

Holzman scouted Clemens on the Ohio Wesleyan campus in Delaware, Ohio. Before the game, Clemens's friends noticed a strange face in the crowd. It wasn't hard for them to figure out that Holzman was there to scout Clemens, the team's best player and the leading scorer in school history. Clemens's friends changed seats and sat all around Red as Clemens began to practice his jump shot. He hit 25 straight as his friends counted them out for Holzman's benefit. Red was a good sport about it.

Michigan star Cazzie Russell was the leading scorer in the nation during his senior season, and the Knicks grabbed him with their first pick in the 1966 draft. Russell and Bill Bradley were both 6-foot-5, and in the NBA they would be most effective playing small forward. After Bradley returned from Oxford, he and Russell engaged in a fierce competition for the starting position.

In 1966, when the Chicago Bulls were in their inaugural season, their chief scout was a twenty-six-year-old from Chicago Heights, Jerry Colangelo. It was his first job in professional sports. Colangelo had played college basketball at Illinois. In one of his first scouting trips, he traveled to Kansas City to see the National Association of Intercollegiate Athletics (NAIA) tournament which featured the smaller college basketball programs.

During the tournament, scouts would watch eight games a day from ten in the morning until eleven at night. For their late-night dinners, Colangelo joined the four veteran scouts who were also attending: Marty Blake of the St. Louis Hawks, Buddy Jeannette of the Baltimore Bullets, Pepper Wilson of the Cincinnati Royals, and Holzman. The group would always defer the choice of restaurant to Red. In Kansas City, he favored an Italian restaurant around the corner from the Muehlebach Hotel where they stayed.

At those dinners, Colangelo said little. He just sat and listened to the other scouts talk basketball. On the third night, Holzman turned to Colangelo and said, "Kid, you're going to do pretty well in this game."

"Why's that, Red?"

"Because you don't know anything," Red said. "Because you keep your mouth shut."

Colangelo took Holzman's comment as it had been intended—as a compliment. For the rest of his professional sports career, Colangelo would impart the same wisdom to young people he encountered: whenever possible, get down in the trenches and surround yourself with voices of experience and absorb everything you can before deciding on a course of action. Colangelo did well with that approach, eventually becoming the owner of two professional sports franchises: the Phoenix Suns and baseball's Arizona Diamondbacks.

Colangelo and Holzman "developed a close relationship in a short period of time." Until December 1967, Red and Colangelo would arrange their schedules to travel together to the same college games and tournaments. "He took me under his wing," Colangelo told me. Holzman offered Colangelo advice on how to maximize his time while traveling. He also expanded Colangelo's circle of contacts and introduced him to many college coaches. Holzman would continue to offer Colangelo "invaluable advice" for many years, especially in the early 1970s when he was coaching the Phoenix Suns.

Shortly before the 1967 draft, Colangelo reciprocated.

It was the last draft that Holzman fully participated in as a scout. And, in typical fashion, Red kept his opinions to himself. There were four highly rated backcourt players coming out of college that year: Jimmy Walker, Earl Monroe, Walt Frazier, and Clem Haskins. Unfortunately, the Knicks had the fifth pick in the draft and could possibility miss out on all four players. The first pick belonged to Detroit, who early on made it clear they were focused on Walker, signing him to a long-term contract the day before the draft. Walker would go on to have several All-Star seasons, but never reached the level of success expected of a number one draft pick. Baltimore had the second pick. They also tipped off their hand early making it clear that Monroe, already a South Philadelphia legend, was their man.

Chicago had the third pick. Colangelo had seen Monroe play thirteen times and "absolutely loved him." His boss in Chicago must have somehow known that Baltimore was locked into Monroe because he asked Colangelo, "Who is your number two?"

Colangelo wanted Walt Frazier. He had seen Frazier and his Southern Illinois Salukis play against Kentucky Wesleyan. Decades later, Colangelo was still excited about that game when he told me about it. "Southern Illinois won, 52–51," Colangelo said. "In some way, Frazier was involved in every play: points, rebounds, assists, intercepted passes. He dominated the game. I later saw Larry Bird do it as well."

Unfortunately for Colangelo, after Chicago ownership contacted Frazier's representative, he was deemed too expensive. Instead, the team selected Clem Haskins, who had a solid NBA career but never developed into a Hall of Fame player like Monroe or Frazier. The fourth pick belonged to Detroit. They already had a future Hall of Fame guard, Dave Bing, to pair with Walker, and didn't need another backcourt player. Instead, Detroit drafted Sonny Dove, a forward from St. John's.

From their travels together, Colangelo sensed Holzman "loved Frazier." Prior to the draft, Colangelo called Red and told him that Chicago would be passing on Frazier. "I don't know if Red played cards," Colangelo told me, "but he would have been a great poker player. He never showed anything. All he said was, 'Okay.'"

Knowing they had no other competition, the Knicks never bothered to contact Frazier or his representative before the draft. Holzman wasn't the only member of the Knicks organization who wanted Frazier. Ned Irish had seen him win MVP honors leading Southern Illinois to the 1967 NIT title. Although Irish was then giving Donovan and Red the final say, the owner made it clear he preferred Frazier. The Knicks selected Frazier and signed him to a three-year, $100,000 contract. Holzman's scouting report on Frazier read in part:

> "Very few weaknesses . . . Good size, strength and weight for guard position . . . good jumper and rebounder for his position . . . Hands and ball-handling steady . . . Gets the big basket and steal . . . Good leader . . . Team goes to him in the clutch . . . Seems to have good knowledge of the game . . . Might even be tougher in the freelance game . . . Could be great defensive man in NBA."

Walt Frazier Jr. grew up in Atlanta, Georgia. As a kid, he saw how popular his father was when running a piece of the local numbers racket and how quickly the good times ended when he fell out of favor. As a result, Frazier wanted to take control of his financial future and never depend on the whims of others. After the 1967 NIT, Frazier felt he had the talent to play in the NBA and dedicated himself to fully developing those talents. He would become one of the best backcourt men in NBA history.

For their 12th-round pick, the Knicks selected Mike Riordan of Providence. In preparation for the draft, while scouting Jimmy Walker, Holzman took notice of his teammate Riordan, a 6-foot-4 forward who was the Friars' second-leading scorer. Red saw a bit of himself in Riordan, a tough New York City kid who grew up with a photo of the Knicks backcourt star, Richie Guerin, on his wall. The 128th player selected in the draft,

Riordan played a crucial role as a substitute on the Knicks' first championship team.

In between the selections of Frazier and Riordan, the Knicks selected a player whom Baltimore Bullets scout Jerry Krause felt had potential. Like Krause, Holzman saw something in Phil Jackson, a 6-foot-8 forward from North Dakota State, that merited close consideration. Krause assumed Jackson would last until the third round, but Red made Jackson what he would later refer to as "one of our sneaky picks," selecting him in the second round. Krause would have to wait many years to hire Jackson. And, when he did, it wasn't as a player but as an assistant coach for the Chicago Bulls.

CHAPTER SEVEN

"I COACH WITHOUT A CLIPBOARD."

While Holzman was mostly on the road during the college basketball season, the summer did not have as many work-related responsibilities. As such, he enjoyed spending time with Selma and Gail at the beach. Each summer, they took out a membership at the Sands in Atlantic Beach, which was a short drive from their Cedarhurst home.

In addition to scouting, Holzman served as an assistant coach each fall during the Knicks' preseason games. This helped satisfy his coaching itch, but only in part. In Milwaukee and St. Louis, Red may have been at Ben Kerner's beck and call, but he ran his own practices and utilized his own game strategies. It was therefore no surprise that in 1963, when Holzman's friend Dick Isaacs, whose family had been doing business in Puerto Rico for many years, told him about a possible summer head coaching position there, Red expressed interest. A bonus was that the basketball season in Puerto Rico ran from June until September and wouldn't impact his scouting duties. He also knew that some well-known college coaches, such as Tex Winter, had gained invaluable experience coaching in Puerto Rico.

After following his standard procedure of discussing all major decisions with Selma, Holzman took the job. The decision resulted in an all-expense-paid education—not just in coaching basketball under international rules, but in life lived to the fullest.

Beginning in 1963, Holzman spent four summers as the coach of the Leones de Ponce (Ponce Lions), one of the better teams in the Baloncesto Superior Nacional (BSN), Puerto Rico's top-tier professional basketball league. According to Red, Ponce played at a level equivalent to a good small-college team. Their players ranged in age from students to businessmen. Ponce's main star was a veteran point guard, Juan "Pachin" Vicens, who had previously excelled in numerous international tournaments.

Upon his arrival, the first challenge Holzman faced was communication. Red did not speak Spanish. Over time, he learned the key words and phrases needed to instruct his players. But he had two things going for him. First, his players spoke more English than he spoke Spanish—more than enough for them to communicate with him. And Red was not afraid to make mistakes as he learned the language. In this regard, his sense of humor transcended the language barrier. He always got a laugh out of his players when he asked them, "Do I have an accent when I speak Spanish?" Holzman and his players communicated well enough for him to have them prepared for any situation that might come up in a game. Ed Rush, the long-time NBA referee who called games in Puerto

Rico in the 1960s, told me, "Holzman was the perfect fit for that group."

Games were played in outdoor stadiums and held in the early evening due to the heat. The fans in Puerto Rico loved basketball and, unlike Red, they held nothing back. Team owners were especially passionate. "The owners were crazy," Rush said. "It was the most emotional atmosphere I'd ever seen. I never experienced anything like that again in my career. It was all fueled by emotion, betting, and Bacardi."

Sometimes, after the end of a game, visiting teams had to wait at center court for an hour—surrounded by police—until the fans calmed down. The referees even needed police escorts to get to the games. And, during games, fans threw eggs and tomatoes onto the court. In order to cut down on this—and keep the fans separated from the players—some teams installed a fishnet wall around their home court. On some courts, players and referees entered and exited through a trap door that led to a tunnel. After games, a police van would be parked at the end of the tunnel to take players away. In such a crazed environment, the coach of the home team could literally, if he wished, put opposing coaches in harm's way. But not Holzman. He prided himself on staying even no matter how stressful the situation. "Red had a calming effect," said Rush.

It must have reminded him of the cages that existed in the early days of professional basketball. Coaching in such an intense environment left the usually even-keeled Holzman capable of later handling whatever the New York fans dished out during the course of an NBA game.

> In one game during his first season coaching the Knicks, a fan berated him for not utilizing swingman and fan favorite Dick Van Arsdale, who normally logged a significant chunk of playing time. During a timeout, the fan started cursing at Holzman, who turned around and shouted back, "He's sick, you stupid shmuck."

If they didn't have a game, the Ponce team would practice most evenings on a basketball court laid out on the infield of the local baseball stadium. Not all the players showed up for every practice, but Red worked with those who did. In his autobiography, Holzman wrote about getting "an eerie feeling" during these practices. When he looked into the stands, all he saw was the glow from the cigarettes or cigars of fans sitting silently in the darkness, watching practice.

The first summer Holzman coached in Puerto Rico, Ponce lost several games in a row. Willie Vicens, the team's general manager and a major figure in Puerto Rican basketball asked Red to see him. Willie's brother, Juan, was the team's best player. Vicens told Holzman the fans wanted him fired because he didn't use a clipboard. No one had ever seen a coach work without one before. Holzman explained that he never used a clipboard, preferring always to keep his focus on the game. Satisfied with Red's response, Vicens told the fans that Holzman, as a former NBA coach, should be given a chance to show what he could do.

Red might not have used a clipboard, but he could get emotional during games. When he began coaching in Ponce, he would always wear wristwatches. During games he would wave his arms so rigorously that his watch would fly off his wrist. After going through numerous watches, he went to a jewelry store and bought a Bull's Eye pocket watch with a white face and black numbers. "I loved that ticker," he wrote in his autobiography.

His love for the pocket watch grew over the years. Not only was it a nice memory of his summers coaching in Puerto Rico, but he would use it as the official time clock when fining players who were late for practice. The fact that it only cost three dollars, and that some of the players he was fining had the fanciest, most expensive, jewel-encrusted timepieces, made Red appreciate that Bull's Eye all the more.

Unlike some of his players, he was never a slave to conspicuous consumption. In the 1960s, he ordered his suits from Brooks Brothers, dressing well but never flashy. His suits were all the same color. When asked about this, he said, "Who's looking?" An interesting response from a man who later made his living in front of 19,500 fans at Madison Square Garden. Despite becoming a recognizable public figure, Red always kept a low profile. For example, in order not to make it obvious that he had purchased a new car, he would buy them in the same make, model, and color. No matter how successful he eventually became, Red remained more at ease on the New York City subway than in a chauffeur-driven limo.

By the end of the 1963 season, Ponce made it all the way to the championship game against a team coached by Lou Rossini, then the coach of NYU. Rossini would later coach the Puerto Rican national team in the 1964 and 1968 Olympics. The BSN championship game was played in San Juan at the 18,000-seat Bithorn Stadium, which was normally used for baseball games. Winning in San Juan, located on the northern coast of Puerto Rico where sudden rainstorms were common, was never easy for

Ponce. If the home team was behind and the court needed to be dried off so play could continue, the fans would run onto the court, take off their shirts, and use them to dry it off. If Ponce was winning, however, the mop-up crew was nowhere to be found.

Holzman's center, a 6-foot-2 engineering student named Cesar Bocachica, missed the 1963 championship game because his flight was cancelled due to a tropical rainstorm (a game in which Ponce lost). But despite this, Vicens must have thought Red was a good coach and hired him to return the following summer. With Holzman coaching, Ponce won the BSN championship in each of the next three seasons (1964 to 1966). As he pointed out in his autobiography, leaving on a high note was the right way to end his stay.

The Holzman family spent their summers living at the Hotel el Ponce International, which was located on a mountain on the southern coast of Puerto Rico not far from where the team practiced and played their home games. Many guests worked for the Maidenform Bra and Girdle Corporation, which had a factory nearby.

During the day, the American coaches and referees would spend time at the beach talking basketball. "We learned a lot about each other [coaches from referees and vice versa]," Ed Rush said, "The guys who were there had an authentic respect for the profession."

In his four summers on the island, Gail told me that her father "took his Puerto Rican experience to heart. He embraced the culture, examining other aspects of what was happening in Puerto Rico, and learned a lot about the people."

But Holzman didn't just learn about coaching under all

types of conditions with players who were culturally far different from himself. He also made several lifelong friendships, as he and Willie Vicens stayed in touch for the rest of their lives.

After each of those three championships there was a large party. Bill Raftery, Holzman's late-round draft pick whom the Knicks cut, happened to be in Puerto Rico for one of those summers. Raftery, who by then had started his college coaching career at Farleigh Dickenson, found himself celebrating with Red. "Pete Carusso [the basketball coach at Kings Point]," Raftery told me, "was the only guy who could keep Red out late and Selma wouldn't get on him."

As part of the post-championship celebration, a much-revered local physician, Dr. Victor Perez, insisted on taking Holzman out. In contrast to the acrimonious atmosphere the fans created during games, when the fans met one of the successful coaches from the summer league away from the court, he was treated like a celebrity. That evening, Red, Raftery, and Dr. Perez had dinner at a restaurant owned by Hall of Fame baseball player and Puerto Rican hero Roberto Clemente. Decades later, Raftery still had a distinct memory of their group ending up at the home of Dr. Perez late one evening and Holzman standing in the driveway teaching Perez's son how to shoot free throws.

"A lot of people in Puerto Rico knew Red," Rush said. "He was a highly respected figure. They knew he was real."

Following Holzman's final season coaching in Puerto Rico, his Ponce players wrote him a letter signed by all the players on the team. It read as follows:

Dear Red,

There is no need to mention how much your coaching and friendship has meant to all of us. But anyway, we have tremendous hope that the future brings us together again.

Thanks a million, coach. Our best to your wife and daughter.

We shall have a few "whiskeys" in your name.

Will always remember you.

Edwin L. Loubriel	Cesar Bocachica
Piro Guzman	Tomas Gutierrez
Pedro Rodriguez	Angel Garcia
Wichy Correa	Tomas Serrano
	Feo Cordova
	S. Dijois
	Pachin Vicens

In the summer of 1967, Holzman decided not to return to Puerto Rico to coach Ponce. As a result, he was available to play a part in the signing of the player who would become his most successful coaching protégé, Phil Jackson.

In 1967, Holzman's role as assistant coach and chief scout included playing chauffeur. When Jackson flew to New York to discuss contract terms with general manager Eddie Donovan, Red and Selma picked him up at John F. Kennedy International Airport. Their Cedarhurst home was only a 10-minute drive from the airport. In fact, they lived so close that when a plane flew over the house, the noise was sometimes so loud that conversations had to momentarily stop. In later years, when a visitor to the house found the recurring noise annoying, Holzman told him that living beneath the flight path of the low-flying jets had its benefits. "It gives me time to think," Red said, "before I answer."

It was Jackson's first time in New York, and he developed an immediate appreciation for Holzman. Having scouted Jackson, Red knew him by sight, so, when Jackson walked into the terminal, he and Selma immediately approached him. Never seeing him before, all Jackson knew was that Red was a former NBA player, so he was looking for someone tall. "Instead," Jackson wrote in his book, "I found a stocky, balding 5-foot-9 individual who looked about as tough as I ever imagined anyone his age could ever look." Jackson described Selma as "a cherub-faced woman who was unexpectedly warm."

Selma had her own first impression of Jackson, who stood 6-foot-8, weighed 220 pounds, and had shoulders that appeared to form 90-degree angles with arms that were so long he could open both front doors of a VW Beetle while sitting in the back seat. Selma saw humor in Jackson's unique appearance, later telling her husband, "Red, he forgot to take the hanger out."

After introductions, Holzman said, "Get your luggage and we'll drive you to your hotel." This was the kind of straightforward approach Jackson would later learn typified Red.

They drove to Manhattan in Holzman's Chevy. Jackson sat in the front. Selma was in the back seat next to two lampshades that needed to be fixed. Red indicated that they were going to drop the lampshades off at a repair shop downtown. "We're going into the city anyway," he said, "we might as well get a number of jobs done."

Driving through Queens, they went under a pedestrian over-pass. Jackson looked up and saw a group of teenagers leaning over and laughing. One threw a rock at them. It hit the wind-shield and shattered it. Holzman, outraged, grimaced, but kept driving. Red told Jackson, "New York has a lot of issues. You got to deal with it." Jackson had no clue how to respond. Nothing like that ever happened in Montana, where he was born, or in North Dakota, where he came of age as the son of two Pentecostal ministers.

Holzman dropped Selma off first at the lampshade store and then left Jackson off at his hotel. Jackson's negotiations with Knicks general manager Eddie Donovan didn't result in an agree-ment and, after a couple days in New York, he returned to North Dakota unsigned. He had also been drafted by the Minnesota Muskies of the upstart American Basketball Association, who offered him a two-year, no-cut contract. Red appreciated Jackson's intelligence and defensive focus and wanted him to play for the Knicks. Eventually, the Knicks offered him a one-year, no-cut contract for $13,500 and a $5,000 bonus, to which he gave his oral acceptance. Leaving nothing to chance, Holzman flew out to North Dakota to meet Jackson and get him to sign the contract.

Jackson was in Fargo serving as a chaplain at the annual gathering of Boys State, an American Legion sponsored week of leadership training for high-school students entering their senior year. Politics and Boys State were a tight fit. A few years earlier, future president Bill Clinton had been a Boys State rep-resentative to Washington DC, where he got a chance to shake hands with President Kennedy. In the summer of 1967, a man who had his own presidential aspirations, New York City mayor John Lindsay, was in Fargo to address the group on the same day

Holzman arrived. He pointed this out to Jackson. "The mayor of New York is here, and everybody knows it," Red said. "And you're here getting signed and nobody knows it."

Jackson must have been impressed with the comment. In his book *Eleven Rings*, Jackson wrote, "That's when I knew I'd found my mentor."

As Jackson wrote in his first book, *Maverick*, Red didn't try to impress him with "New York glamour." When Jackson said he wasn't sure if he wanted to be a minister or a basketball player, Holzman told him that playing professional basketball would give him time to figure out what he really wanted to do in the long term and begin preparing for it. He let Jackson know that, if he had any challenges dealing with New York, he would be there for him. Holzman's greatest concern wasn't if Jackson could play in the NBA, but how the son of two ministers would adjust to life in the Big Apple.

Red also sensed that he had found a coaching apprentice; someone who was a student of the game, verbally well-skilled, empathetic, and intelligent. Jackson's lifestyle in New York proved to be far from ministerial, however. In later years, Holzman would tease the pot-smoking, long-haired Jackson how, sitting there in his dorm room in Fargo in the midst of the Boys State convention, he had envisioned himself becoming a preacher.

In 1967, shortly before ensuring that Jackson's NBA career started with the Knicks, Bill Raftery decided he wanted to broaden his experience and coach in Puerto Rico. For a young guy like Raftery, the money wasn't bad either: $3,000 for a summer's work.

After he stopped coaching in Puerto Rico, Holzman was still revered there. So much so that, with his recommendation, Raftery was able to land a head coaching job in the BSN. Although he wasn't coaching Ponce, he felt the pressure of great expectations since he was perceived as Holzman's protégé.

"It was like trying to follow [Vince] Lombardi," Raftery said.

A few months later, in December 1967, Holzman and fellow scout Jerry Colangelo both attended a pre-Christmas tournament, the Marshall Invitational, in Huntington, West Virginia. At that point in the 1967–68 season, the Knicks were playing poorly and Ned Irish was antsy. After spending millions building a new Madison Square Garden, which was scheduled to open in February 1968, a losing team wasn't helping ticket sales.

When the tournament ended, Colangelo and Holzman were hustling to get home. They had arranged to meet up a few days after Christmas at the Far West tournament in Portland, Oregon. As they parted ways, Colangelo told Red that he wasn't going to make it to Portland; Colangelo insisted Holzman was going to be named the head coach of the Knicks. For a guy who had kept quiet and just listened the year before, it was heck of a prediction.

But Red was still once bitten, twice shy about coaching again.

He told Colangelo, "What are you talking about? No way."

CHAPTER EIGHT

"SEE THE BALL."

Jerry Colangelo was right. Holzman's scouting days were over.

Dick McGuire's job as coach of the Knicks had been in jeopardy since the second week of the 1967–68 season after the team had lost six straight.

McGuire's greatest challenge was a lack of team discipline; he was simply too nice a guy. Players were routinely late for practices, team buses and, on one occasion, a game. During McGuire's first season as Knicks coach, Barry Clemens, the player Holzman had scouted at Ohio Wesleyan, was playing bridge in the team's locker room with three veterans—Tom Gola, Emmette Bryant, and Len Chappell—when McGuire told them it was time to go out to the court for that night's game.

"Coach," Clemens said, "I have a good hand here. Can I play this one out?"

McGuire let them finish the hand.

He also allowed the players to eat at halftime. One player, Freddie Crawford, had the ball boys buy him two hot dogs and leave them in his locker. When McGuire would be in the middle of his halftime talk, Crawford would turn to listen with a mustard-covered mustache.

In Holzman's autobiography, he wrote that, in November 1965, when Harry Gallatin was fired as Knicks coach, general manager Eddie Donovan had approached him to take over coaching duties. But rather than accept the job, Red had suggested McGuire instead. That made sense. McGuire was a former franchise player with whom management had previously built a relationship. He also had four seasons of NBA coaching experience with the Detroit Pistons and was far from a novice, neither to New York (he grew up in Far Rockaway) or coaching.

But neither was Holzman. On some level, Red would have been satisfied with the security of spending the rest of his career as the team's chief scout. But he also had his pride. Holzman revealed in his book that, when he was a scout, he had received coaching offers from other NBA teams but turned them down out of loyalty to the Knicks. In 1965, when the coaching job was first offered to him, Red knew the team's personnel was improving but not ready to compete for a championship. In St. Louis, Holzman had been the coach that loosened the bottle cap long and hard over most of four seasons, only to be fired just before it opened and a championship flowed. He was too smart to do that again.

Holzman began his book describing the events of December 27, 1967—the day he took over for McGuire. The Knicks had just lost their fourth straight game at home and their record had fallen to 15–23. Ned Irish called Red into his office and told him that the Knicks wanted him to switch jobs with McGuire. The way Holzman later described it, if he didn't take over as coach, Irish would have let him go.

But Red insisted he would accept only as an interim appointment with the option to return to scouting at the end of the season. This took the pressure off and allowed him to run the team as he saw fit—especially with respect to instilling discipline. If the team didn't respond, he could return to his scouting job. But, if the Knicks improved significantly, Irish would be obligated to retain him as coach.

And Irish knew it. On the day Holzman was hired, Irish told the press, "We didn't think we could find anyone better qualified outside the organization. We don't look upon this as an interim job. If Red prefers to go back to scouting at the end of the season, we'll have to discuss that then."

Phil Jackson described this turn of events in *Maverick*, by referring to Red as "the sly old fox." Because he had scouted almost all the players on the Knicks and had seen McGuire's laid-back approach prove ineffective, Holzman knew better than anyone that the time was right for dramatic improvement. As he later wrote, "The talent that had taken so long to accumulate was ready to take off. All it needed was someone to point it in the direction of a championship." And he knew exactly how to blow reveille for this particular group of players.

Holzman had even started to wake the Knicks up before being named head coach. Once, Red happened to be in the Knicks locker room when Freddie Crawford was eating his halftime hot dogs. After Red teased Freddie about his yellow mustache, there was less eating and more listening during the intermission. In one game in the fall of 1967 before Holzman hit the road for his scouting duties, he was working as McGuire's assistant coach and noticed that Phil Jackson and backup center Nate Bowman were more focused on the young ladies in the stands than the action on the court. Even though there were only a few minutes left in the game and the Knicks were not so far ahead (or behind) to merit either one of the two benchwarmers seeing any action, Red jumped all over them. "How much time is there left on the clock?" he demanded. They said two minutes and 14 seconds. Holzman berated them, "The 24-second clock, not the game clock."

They said, "18 seconds."

"No, you fools. It's 17. If I ever catch you doing that again, I'll fine you. I want you to pay attention to the ball game instead of clowning around."

As Jackson wrote, "Then suddenly he [Holzman] was the coach, and 'Pay Attention' was all anybody ever heard."

The Holzman era began with a 10 a.m. team practice on Thursday, December 28, 1967. And when Red said 10 a.m., he meant according to his Bull's Eye pocket watch . . . which ran five minutes fast. Any player who reported to practice late was fined five or ten dollars, which was immediately payable to Knicks trainer Danny Whelan. First, Holzman fined Bradley, who was only a minute or two late, five dollars. At that moment, Walt Frazier was thinking, *If he's going to fine Bill Bradley, what the hell is he going to do with me?*

Then Dick Van Arsdale and Howard Komives waltzed in 10 minutes late. He fined them each ten dollars. The players moaned, but paid up. The fines weren't excessive, but Holzman was sending a clear message: there was a new sheriff in town. Eventually, his players not only showed up on time but started to point out to Red if a teammate was late. As he had intended,

Holzman-inspired discipline had become self-enforcing discipline.

And no one was beyond reproach. On one occasion, Red even fined trainer Danny Whelan for being late. Despite the fact that he had been an invaluable resource far beyond attending to the players' aches and pains during the team's glory years, it was clear that nobody was above the rules. Whelan, who had been the Pittsburgh Pirates' trainer when they won the 1960 World Series, not only became Holzman's companion and drinking buddy on the road but was a jovial "Friar Tuck" who kept players loose with his cutting humor and tall tales of old-time baseball trainers. Willis Reed referred to Whelan as "the big mom, keeping the troops happy."

Holzman set—and enforced—his rules from day one: no eating at halftime, no family or friends visiting during practices— which would be focused 100 percent on business. Practices lasted precisely 90 minutes. And, in the finest tradition of Nat Holman, not a minute was wasted. Red utilized numerous defensive drills which he would repeat over and over in order to form what Phil Jackson referred to as "habitual movements, routines, and patterns so they [the players] can do things instinctively."

Practices under Holzman always followed the same pattern.

"They started with defense," Willis Reed told me, "and ended with defense."

Red admitted his practices were "boring, repetitious grunt work." But he lived by a rule out of Vince Lombardi's playbook: "Practice doesn't make perfect. Perfect practice does."

A rookie on one of Holzman's later Knicks teams, John Rudd, described a practice session this way: "The practice was so well organized, and everything he did had a reason. If anything went wrong, he stopped the practice and made it clear to the guy what he was doing wrong. He also made it clear he did not want him repeating the mistake. I was very impressed."

There was one phrase that Red drilled into his players until they heard it in their sleep: "See the ball." The phrase reminded them to always know where both the opposition player they were guarding was, and where the ball was on the court. The goal was for them to instinctively be positioned between the ball and their man to take away the passing lane. Holzman instructed his players not only how to position themselves to accomplish this but also on the proper defensive stance, how to constantly communicate with their teammates when on defense, and how to make the transition from offense to defense in a quick and fluid manner.

* * *

In his first two seasons as coach, practices were held at Lost Battalion Hall, a dilapidated gym built during the Great Depression on Queens Boulevard in Rego Park, Queens. The contrast between their practice facility and the palace the Knicks would soon be playing in at the new Madison Square Garden was striking. Lost Battalion Hall, named after a group of American soldiers whose outlook appeared bleak after they were trapped behind German lines in World War I, was well named. The building was cold, the floors warped, the rims loose, and the showers short on hot water. But that didn't matter to Holzman. This was where he would put them through a grueling stretch of practices. According to Bill Bradley, during Red's first year as coach, in one twenty-five-day period, the Knicks played eight games and had twenty-one practices. Holzman would later refer to this period in biblical terms:

forty days and forty nights of practice. He joked that Whelan was exhausted just from watching. But that stretch proved Red was serious when he told his players, "If you win, your time is your own; but when you lose, you belong to me."

The practice venue may have been less than stellar, but the methodology became part of New York folklore: Knicks fans would soon be spontaneously chanting, "De-fense, De-fense," at crucial moments when the opposing team had the ball. Holzman had made his point about the importance of defense on the second day of practice. He took pages from the team's offensive playbook and held them up for every player to see. He then gestured as if using them to wipe his ass. He didn't win any style points, but the demonstration served as a visual preamble to Holzman's Law: if the Knicks were to become a winning team, a significant percentage of their offense would be a product of their defense. Or, more succinctly, as he insisted, "If you don't play defense, you sit."

In order to get his players to buy in, Holzman instituted a full-court pressing defense that began with the game's opening tip-off. This demanded much more effort from the players than could be sustained with a seven- or eight-man rotation. Since the Knicks had the benefit of a deep bench filled with players who wanted additional playing more, a pressing defense gave them such an opportunity. Holzman regularly utilized an eleven-man rotation: Willis Reed (PF), Walt Bellamy (C), Dick Barnett (SG), Dick Van Arsdale (SF), Cazzie Russell (SF), Walt Frazier (PG), Bill Bradley (SG), Howard Komives (PG), Freddie Crawford (SG), Emmette Bryant (PG), and Phil Jackson (PF).[1]

---

1   PG: Point Guard; SG: Shooting Guard; SF: Small Forward; PF: Power Forward; C: Center

According to Jackson, the Knicks were the first NBA team to use a pressing defense throughout an entire game—and opposing teams were taken by surprise. Before this, teams utilized a full-court press only if they were trailing late in a game and needed to force turnovers.

A pressing defense works only if all five players on the court move in a highly coordinated fashion. In the classic example, as an opposing player moved past midcourt, the player guarding him would force the opponent to dribble to one side of the court while the forward on that side ran over to double-team the man with the ball. This often resulted in either a steal or an ill-advised cross-court pass to a teammate whom the Knicks would strategically leave unguarded. The unguarded opponent was always the one farthest away from the player being double teamed. A forward or center on the other side of the court, away from the ball, would leave their man to intercept or deflect the pass and start a fast-break. The approach was risky, as it required perfect anticipation and timing. One mistake could easily result in the opponent having an uncontested shot. But that was what "perfect practice" sought to avoid.

When Holzman took over, the Knicks were far from popular. Prior to his first game as coach on December 29, 1967, hoping to boost the gate at the Garden, management scheduled an exhibition game between the Fabulous Magicians of Marques Haynes (the former Harlem Globetrotter star) and the East Coast Rens. That night, the Knicks already had many of the key pieces of their first championship team on the roster—just not in the right positions. The starting team in Red's first game had Reed and Russell at forward, Bellamy at center, and Barnett and Bradley in the backcourt, with Frazier coming off the bench.

But, in less than one year, when these pieces were realigned and a key addition made, the demand for a ticket to a Knicks game would rival the most popular shows on Broadway, and there was no longer a need for the Fabulous Magicians.

But it would take time for the Knicks to get used to Holzman's new system. Red lost his first two games as Knicks coach and on January 2, 1968, their record stood at 15–25. They headed to Philadelphia the next day to play the 76ers, the defending NBA champions.

Holzman knew that successful team play required more than the right offensive and defensive systems. It demanded players with confidence in their abilities. And this is where Red's empathy, as well as his thorough understanding of his player's abilities, made him the right man in the right place at the right time. As Ira Berkow wrote years later when contemplating the reasons for Holzman's success, "he gave people a boost, was sensitive and thoughtful of their feelings, left them with their dignity, and even when being critical did so with an underpinning of humor."

The Knicks benefited from Holzman's humanity before he even took over as coach. Never was this truer than after the team's first exhibition game of the 1967–68 season, which took place on the road against Philadelphia. Walt Frazier had to guard 10-time All-Star Hal Greer, then at the height of his abilities. Greer embarrassed the rookie Frazier, who fouled out trying to control the future Hall of Famer. In his book, *The Game Within the Game*, Frazier wrote, "Hal Greer humiliated me so badly that after that game, when the locker room cleared out, I sat down and cried. I thanked God that I had signed a three-year contract because I really didn't think I had what it took to make it in the NBA."

Luckily for Frazier, Holzman was traveling with the Knicks as McGuire's assistant coach. "Red Holzman changed my career around that night," Frazier told writer Mike Wise in 1998. "He said, 'I want you to sit by me on the bus back to New York.' I sat down and Red said: 'What the hell is wrong with you? I scouted you in college. You're a better player than that.' He kept talking. It became apparent that Red believed in me. It was the confidence I needed at that time in my career. Looking back, it seems he was always saying the right things at the right time."

At the root of Frazier's success was an ever-growing confidence and an unshakeable belief in his defensive abilities. So much so that just a couple of years later, when Frazier was introduced to LSU star Pete Maravich, one of the greatest scorers in NCAA history (who was in New York to play in the 1970 NIT at the Garden), Frazier told him, "I got something for you when you come to the pros next year . . . a little thing called 'D.'"

Beginning in early January 1968, the team's hard work began to pay off. Holzman's first win came on January 3 against Greer and Philadelphia. The Knicks pressing defense forced the 76ers into 36 turnovers, and the win started a six-game winning streak, the team's longest since 1958. And, in a sure sign of progress, five of their six wins were on the road. Over the last 44 games of the season, the Knicks finished 28–16: a better record over the same stretch than the Celtics—that seasons' NBA champions.

The Knicks finished in third place in the Eastern Division (they had been in fifth place when Red took over) and played the first-place 76ers in the opening round of the playoffs. After splitting the first two games, the Knicks lost the crucial third game in overtime, and later lost the series four games to two. It was no shame losing to the 76ers who were loaded with four future Hall of Fame players: Wilt Chamberlain, Billy Cunningham, Chet Walker, and Greer. Following the season, Irish didn't have to twist Holzman's arm to keep him on as head coach.

Despite their resistance, the Knicks' success put Red and Selma in the spotlight. Beginning that spring, Holzman was often asked to make public speaking appearances. In his standard talk, he joked that he had been invited only because Willis Reed was unavailable.

Ironically, there was some truth to that. In early May 1968, Red spoke at a University of Connecticut club dinner only because Reed was unable to attend. "We haven't changed our routine at all," Selma insisted that spring. "We're quiet people. I'd say we're uninteresting people. The only change is that now a few people out there know who Red is and the service is a little better. One thing Red values is his privacy. We like to take a place at a beach club in the summer and he stipulates that no one should be told who we are. He just likes to go about his business. It helps that Red is kind of small. He can pass in a crowd."

Going into the 1968–69 season, Holzman's greatest challenge was motivating Walt Bellamy into playing hard on a consistent basis. Bellamy had been the NBA Rookie of the Year, an All-Star in his first four seasons, and held his own against the league's two dominant centers, Wilt Chamberlain and Bill Russell. The problem was motivating him against everyone else. Dick McGuire's final two games as Knicks coach offered a perfect example. On December 27, 1967, Bellamy played Philadelphia's Wilt Chamberlain to a statistical dead heat. Both scored 27 points and Chamberlain had one more rebound than Bellamy

(21 to 20). But the night before, in a loss to Seattle, Bellamy was matched against rookie Bob Rule. Bellamy scored four points, while Rule had 24.

Red's approach to motivating his players was to treat them as professionals. He didn't give motivational speeches or set curfews.

> To this day, when Walt Frazier is asked to describe Holzman's approach he says, "We were on the first floor, Red was on the tenth." Frazier means that by booking his players on the lower floors of whatever hotel they were staying at and taking a room for himself on one of the higher floors, Holzman was sending an unspoken message to his players: If you guys want to keep late hours, that's your business—I'm not checking up on you. But at the next day's practice, I will immediately know who was out late partying just by watching your effort.

Besides limiting a player's minutes, Holzman believed there was little a coach could do to get a player to sacrifice his own game for the sake of the team. Either they did or they didn't, and Bellamy didn't. But as long as he was the team's biggest star, he was preventing Willis Reed from setting the right tone for the team. Red knew successful teams required an unselfish leader; and with Bellamy as their top player, the rest of the team could never be held accountable. For example, veteran guard Howard Komives didn't get along with Cazzie Russell. Things were so bad that they selfishly avoided passing each other the ball.

Because of the turnaround after McGuire was removed, expectations ran high for the 1968–69 season. But having lost some crucial players, the Knicks started the season poorly. In the NBA expansion draft following the previous season, they'd lost Dick Van Arsdale, a key player on the full-court press and the team's best all-around small forward, as well as Emmette Bryant, another vital component of the pressing defense. Bryant's role would be filled by Mike Riordan, Holzman's favorite New York City gym rat. Riordan had improved his game playing in the Eastern League the prior season.

But despite all the changes, Walt Bellamy remained. And to make matters worse, he refused to sign a new contract. In contrast, Reed had reported to training camp early and was working out with the rookies. Holzman, in typical fashion, took the high road. "I'm not worried in the least," he said that September, "Walt likes this sport way too much to stay away long. After all, he played in every one of our 88 games last year."

Bellamy eventually signed, but continued his inconsistent play. In an early November game against Seattle, when Red already knew the Knicks general manager Eddie Donovan was trying to trade Bellamy, he started Reed at center with the team's former star coming off the bench. The move was designed to send a message, but it was also an early test to see how Reed would play at his natural position. He had been the Knicks' center in his rookie season, but moved to forward in 1965 with the acquisition of Bellamy. To Reed's credit, whether he played center or forward, he had been named to the All-Star team every season of his career. Philadelphia 76ers guard Matt Guokas said of Reed, "He's a moose. He plays hurt. He beats you to death. He's got a great shot. No one in the league has more courage."

Unable to motivate Bellamy, Holzman realized that one player's actions meant the entire team suffered. After a one-sided loss to the Los Angeles Lakers in mid-November 1968, Red tried to shake things up, fining every player $100 for lack of hustle. But that didn't help. The solution, as Red knew, would have to come from his players. And it did.

The low point came on November 20 in Atlanta. That night, the Knicks record fell to 6–13 as they lost for the tenth time in twelve games. During that game, the Hawks and the Knicks engaged in several fights, with the main event being a fourth-quarter square-off between Lou Hudson and Willis Reed. In *Maverick*, Phil Jackson wrote there were some "bad feelings among the Knick players" because backup center Nate Bowman was the only other Knicks player who "had gone out there to support Willis." Bowman took on Bill Bridges, one of Atlanta's strongest players.

After that game, following a team meeting, the Knicks became focused—even Bellamy—as they won 12 of their next 16 games. After a win over Detroit on November 30 in which Bellamy scored 32 points, Thomas Rogers of the *New York Times* reported, "When Bellamy plays as he did last night, scoring, rebounding and running, it seems to be infectious."

On December 19, despite the improved record, Eddie Donovan traded Bellamy and Howard Komives to Detroit for All-Star power forward Dave DeBusschere. The son of a Detroit bar owner, DeBusschere was the kind of hardworking, smart, team-first player Red had coveted since seeing him play at the University of Detroit.

And it wasn't just the addition of DeBusschere that improved the Knicks. With Bellamy and Komives gone, Reed became the team's starting center and unquestioned leader. Walt Frazier moved into Komives's starting backcourt position alongside

Barnett. Cazzie Russell remained the fifth starter at small forward, with Bill Bradley backing him up off the bench.

Years later, Holzman told Ira Berkow that the DeBusschere trade made him so happy he got drunk for three straight days. Manny Azenberg told me that in all the years he knew Red, he never saw him drunk. But Holzman most likely exaggerated to make a point. He knew that with DeBusschere—a gifted shooter, defender, and rebounder who was effectively a coach on the court (he was a player-coach in Detroit at age twenty-four)—the Knicks would contend for a championship.

The change was instantaneous. In DeBusschere's first game with the Knicks, on December 20, 1968, they blew out his old team, the Detroit Pistons, 135–87.

Yet to the press, Holzman kept his cards to himself, made no predictions, and minimized his role. "Dave is going to help us tremendously," he said. "He's a solid pro who can do so many things, most of all play defense. Dave doesn't have to score to help us, he can do so many other things.

"I don't think I've been any kind of genius," Red went on to tell Sam Goldaper of the *New York Times*. "It's been hard work. Coaching has greater pressures than scouting and when a team puts it all together, you are a hero and if it doesn't, well you are a bum."

As usual, Red left it up to his players to express their views on his contribution. "Red brought an aggressive philosophy to the team," Willis Reed said that December. "He gave us positive thinking, always doing everything he could to build our confidence, even in defeat. Don't kid yourself, that's an important attribute, even in the pro ranks. He's a great exponent of defensive play and instead of the man-to-man defense Red instituted the press and instructed us to always try to keep pressure on the opposing backcourt men."

The trade for DeBusschere solidified a starting core . . . with the exception of the small forward position. Two college basketball player of the year award winners, Cazzie Russell and Bill Bradley, engaged in a fierce competition to prove who deserved to be the starter. Russell's strength was his ability to create his own shot. When his outside shot was working—in combination with his ability to drive to the basket—he was unstoppable. During the 1968–69 season he averaged over 18 points a game, the second highest on the team. Defensively, however, Russell didn't always *see* the ball. In contrast, Bradley was a tenacious defender. But, on offense, he was reliant on his teammates' passing to get his shot off. The flip side was that when Bradley didn't have the ball, he was constantly in motion pushing his teammates to keep moving until they found the open man with an uninhibited shot.

For two men used to being the star, a great deal of pride was wrapped up in who would be the starter. Russell's entire life had changed after he led Carver, his Chicago high school team, to the state championship game. After that, Russell told me, "Even the lunch room director knew who I was." In college, Bradley was enough of a national celebrity that John McPhee, one of the greatest nonfiction writers of the twentieth century, wrote a piece about him in the *New Yorker*. Red had to play the role of Solomon, deciding who started and who sat. In practice, Bradley and Russell went hard at each other, but Holzman was the real target of their frustration.

Russell told me of his interactions with Red. "We had a few disagreements. Nothing disrespectful. I wish I knew then what I know now. This [pro basketball] is a business. It's tough to talk about it now." Bradley's frustrations matched Russell's stride for stride. In his book, *Life on the Run*, Bradley admitted, "I had never felt about anyone in my life the way I did about Red." He even quoted from a journal he kept when his competition with Russell was at its peak, "If he [Holzman] wanted to keep me on the bench forever he could. It's always the tyranny of the unspoken. I feel helpless before his power over my life."

Since Holzman had become coach, Russell had usually been the starter and received the lion's share of playing time. But on January 21, 1969, in a game against Seattle, Russell broke the fibula bone in his right leg and would miss the rest of the regular season. Bradley grabbed the opportunity and ran with it. In the very next game, the Knicks lost to Philadelphia in double-overtime. Phil Jackson was also unavailable due to a severe back injury that would require spinal fusion surgery. As a result of such a thin bench, Reed, Frazier, Barnett, and Bradley each played at least 55 minutes (DeBusschere played 38) that night. Because of the injuries to Russell and Jackson, as well as the lack of other experienced bench players (Bill Hosket, Don May, and Mike Riordan were all rookies), those five got the majority of playing time for the rest of the season. As a result, they developed a familiarity with one another that was so strong they could communicate on the court without speaking. For example, Frazier and Bradley became so comfortable with each other that, if the situation presented itself, all they needed to do to run a backdoor play was to make eye contact. Even after a fully recovered Russell returned for the 1969–70 season, Bradley never relinquished the starting job. Holzman decided the team flow worked best with Bradley starting and Russell coming off the bench for a burst of offense.

It is ironic that a broken leg helped make the Knicks a cohesive team. In St. Louis, shortly after Red was fired, an analogous injury to Bob Pettit (a broken arm) forced Cliff Hagan into a starting role at forward. Like the 1968–69 Knicks, the 1956–57 Hawks developed into a tight-knit unit and won a championship the following season.

The 1968–69 season was not just a success on the court, where the Knicks set a team record with 54 wins to finish third in the Eastern Division, but a financial windfall for Madison Square Garden. They became the first team in the history of professional basketball to attract more than a million fans in a single season. Their success in the media capital of the world, where many Knicks fans were in the publishing and television industries, brought the NBA a level of popularity it had never experienced. As a direct result, the amount of money the networks were willing to pay to broadcast NBA games increased dramatically. With the subsequent advent of free agency, Holzman had helped usher in a financial era that left both management and players far richer.

* * *

In the opening round of the playoffs, the Knicks faced the first-place Baltimore Bullets. Earl Monroe and Wes Unseld, both future Hall of Fame players, were the team's two best players. Monroe proved to be as gifted a player in the professional ranks as he was in college.

With the addition of Unseld, a center, selected with the second pick of the 1968 draft, the Bullets had finished with the best record in the league, giving them home-court advantage.

However, the advantage did little to help the Bullets, as the Knicks took the opening game with a 113–101 victory and went on to sweep the series in four straight. After the series ended, Knicks general manager Eddie Donovan said of Holzman, "I've never seen anybody do a better job of coaching in all my association with basketball. He had complete control of every game. The confidence that the team has in Red never wavered. He was ahead of the action on every substitution and was able to deal with every situation that came up. It [Game One] gave us the momentum, and the Bullets never seemed to recover. When the Bullets opened with Wes Unseld bringing the ball up, it took Red only a few moments to adjust by putting DeBusschere on Unseld and letting Willis Reed drop back near the boards."

The Knicks sweep of the Bullets was their first winning play-off series since 1953.

After blitzing the Bullets, the Knicks advanced to the Eastern Division finals to face the Boston Celtics. Although the Knicks had defeated the Celtics in six of their seven regular-season games, Holzman preached caution. "Don't let the Celtics, or beating them in the season series ever fool you," he said. "They have so much playoff experience and so many great players. That Bill Russell during the playoffs just murders you."

Red was prescient. The Knicks lost to the Celtics, four games to two. The Celtics would go on to defeat the Lakers and win their eleventh championship in the thirteenth and final season of Bill Russell's playing career. But, with Russell's retirement, the Knicks looked forward to the 1969–70 season when they would be favored to win the Eastern Division title.

After the Celtics defeated the Knicks, Eddie Donovan was once again singing Holzman's praises, saying, "Red adds 6 to

8 points a game for us by the job he does on the bench." How Donovan came up with that figure is unknown, but under any analysis, Red had established himself as one of the best coaches in the NBA.

Prior to the 1969–70 season, Holzman's friend, Manny Azenberg, who had been hired to make the Garden a major entertainment destination, told his bosses that he wanted to produce a documentary film of what he sensed would be a historic season. Azenberg had arranged for the screenplay to be written by Academy Award winning screenwriter, William Goldman. Dustin Hoffman and Robert Redford would serve as narrators. All three were huge Knicks fans and would effectively work on the project without compensation. But Garden management turned Azenberg down. When they did, Azenberg decided he would have to work elsewhere. If they didn't support him for that project, they would never agree to anything worthwhile.

CHAPTER NINE
"HIT THE OPEN MAN."

The Knicks' preseason training camp for the upcoming 1969–70 season was held on Long Island at the SUNY Farmingdale campus (State University of New York). Based on team practices during the second half of the 1968–69 season, Dave DeBusschere sensed that Holzman would run a much more demanding training camp than he was used to in Detroit. Red didn't disappoint. He ran two practices a day, the first from 11–1, the second from 5–7. In his book *The Open Man*, about the 1969–70 season, DeBusschere described one torturous drill designed to increase a player's endurance. Holzman called it "pick-up."

Red stood on one end of the court with assistant coach Dick McGuire on the other. The sixteen players were divided into two groups with eight players standing on the end-line under each basket. One player began running down the court as Holzman would roll the ball ahead of him. The player had to catch up with the ball, bend down, pick it up in stride, and drive to the opposing basket for a layup. The player then had to retrieve the ball and hand it to McGuire, who would then roll the ball in the other direction for another player to repeat the process heading the other way. The drill was done with four basketballs so there was little time for a player to catch his breath before having to sprint back the other way. "Pick-up" went on for 10 to 15 minutes. Sometimes, if Red wanted to go easy on his players, he cut it down to five minutes. "I've never worked so hard in a training camp," DeBusschere later wrote.

Like his practices during the season, Holzman's training camp was regimented, repetitive, yet effective; each drill was designed to teach a specific offensive or defensive fundamental.

When the Knicks returned to Farmingdale from a road trip to Roanoke, Virginia, where they played the Bullets in their first exhibition game, DeBusschere, who had run his own practices when he was a player-coach in Detroit, told Holzman the team looked good and asked if they could have just one practice the next day.

Deadpan, Red replied, "It's still training camp."

Holzman wanted them to work hard, but he wasn't inhumane. He gave his players an occasional day off during the training period, usually on a Sunday. The players stayed at a nearby motel called Pickwick. As he did during the season, Holzman didn't set a curfew for his players; he let their own sense of professionalism be their guide. With this group of mature, responsible players who believed they had a good chance to win a championship, it worked like a charm.

To say the Knicks got off to a fast start to the regular season would be an understatement. They won 23 of their first 24 games, including a then NBA-record 18-game winning streak. The streak began in Detroit on October 24, and continued through November 28 with a win over the Cincinnati Royals. For the record-setting 18th win, the Knicks overcame a five-point deficit in the game's final 16 seconds. With 10 seconds remaining, after Reed's two free throws made it a three-point game, Cincinnati called time out. On the Knicks bench, Holzman tried to instill confidence in his players, telling them, "Let's do it. There's still time." Sure enough, two Cincinnati turnovers produced a 106–105 victory.

But no team can keep up that kind of pace indefinitely. The winning streak ended with a loss to Detroit on November 29. Rather than let the streak's end get to them, they went on to win four straight. They fell into a rut after that, losing three in a row. The third loss was a home defeat in overtime against the Hawks.

In his autobiography, Red wrote that he "was anxious not to let the losing streak go on too long." In their next game, facing the Bulls in Chicago, Holzman altered his usual substitution pattern, playing Reed and DeBusschere for more than 40 minutes. The Knicks won, 108–99. But, uncharacteristically, during that game, Bradley and Frazier both gave Red back talk after he seemingly called timeouts just to criticize their defensive play. DeBusschere wrote, Holzman "exploded twice . . . once at Frazier and once at Bradley." Holzman viewed it, as he later wrote, as "a flash rebellion" toward his authority.

* * *

Red knew it was the Knicks' year. His team had a real chance to win a championship, yet he feared that an extended losing streak could put that goal at risk. Normally, Walt Frazier told me, "No matter what happened on the court, even if we squandered a lead, you'd go back to the bench and he was always the same. And that calmed you down." To Frazier, Holzman was "a master psychiatrist." But that night he allowed Bradley's and Frazier's reactions to influence his behavior. So much so that he forgot the fine character of the two players he was dealing with. The results were memorable enough to merit subsequent written comments from Red and, in what at the time were the two most popular books written about that season: Phil Berger's agenda-ridden *Miracle on 33rd Street* and Dave DeBusschere's more subdued *The Open Man*.

Usually, Holzman closed the doors to the Knicks locker room for only a few minutes after a game so the beat writers could get some quotes and meet their deadlines. But the locker room was closed for a while after that game. According to Red, he told his players that, no matter what he said, he was right "whether they like it or not."

Berger didn't like Holzman and took a negative slant on both the coach and team management. He referred to Red's behavior that night as "an irreversible event," destroying the fragile "ego-librium" between the coach and his players. Berger was looking to sell books—and he did. But, in the process, the Knicks revoked his press credentials.

DeBusschere wrote that, "Red had to let out his feelings, had to let them [Bradley and Frazier] know once more who's the boss. I had to scream at teammates when I was a player-coach, and it was never pleasant, but it was necessary. It's the only way to get the player's respect. Somebody had to run the ship."

Whether it was Holzman's blast or his players' innate pride, it would be three months until the Knicks lost more than two games in a row. But at that point in the season, they had already clinched the Eastern Division championship.

Red's relationship with Bradley and Frazier seemed no worse following what Berger referred to as the "Chicago incident." But Bradley never felt completely secure until Cazzie Russell was traded following the 1970–71 season. With that transaction, Red sent Bradley the message he had been waiting to hear since Holzman took over as coach—you're my starting small forward for the foreseeable future. And, as team broadcaster Marv Albert told me, whenever Frazier got on the team bus, Holzman still took a key out of his pocket and told Frazier, "You're my key man." No matter how often Red did it, Frazier played along and laughed every time.

Years later, Frazier was quoted in the film *When the Garden Was Eden*, referring to Latrell Sprewell, who once physically attacked his coach, that "I wanted to do the Sprewell on him [Holzman] before there was a Sprewell." Frazier told me those were the times, "I'm trying to guard Earl [Monroe] or Oscar [Robertson]. And at halftime, Red would berate me, 'You're such a great defensive player, but look what they're doing to you.' There were times the whole team wanted to get him."

Marv Albert mentioned another routine Red had on the team bus that was more in line with the empathy he had shown Chuck Cooper in Shreveport. At the time, reporters from all the local newspapers would travel with the team. One of the beat writers was Sam Goldaper of the *New York Times*. According to Albert, Goldaper was meticulous about writing his stories. As a result, he invariably was the last writer to make it onto the team bus, and the other writers would tease him about his fastidiousness. Even though chided by his colleagues, Holzman always insisted that the bus wait for Goldaper. Albert told me that in all his years traveling with professional basketball teams, Red was the only coach he ever saw consistently hold up the team bus for a writer.

I sensed there was more to the story, and so asked former *New York Times* writers Ira Berkow and Gerald Eskenazi what they could share about Goldaper. I learned that he had polio when he was a child, walked with a limp, and periodically used a cane. (Goldaper's son, Robert, confirmed this, but told me his father didn't use a cane.) In return, he was respectful of Holzman in print. But it's an example of what Red's friend Manny Azenberg told me, "Red was a *mensch* (Yiddish for good person)."

On March 9, 1970, Eddie Donovan resigned as general manager of the Knicks and accepted the same position with the newly created Buffalo Braves (today's LA Clippers), who would be entering the NBA for the 1970–71 season. In addition to his duties as coach, Irish named Holzman to replace Donovan. As Red's approach was always straightforward, he didn't feel that having both jobs presented any type of conflict or problem. When he was coaching, that was his focus, and, when he was dealing with agents about player salaries, or with NBA executives about trades, being a general manager was his focus. But that approach would later prove to have limitations.

The Knicks finished the 1969–70 regular season with the best record in franchise history, 60–22. It was not until the 1992–93 season, the height of the defensively focused Pat Riley era, that another Knicks team would match that record. Holzman's players had seen the ball with remarkable clarity, allowing the fewest points per game in the league (105.9, with the league average at 116.7). The next closest were the Lakers, who allowed 111.8 per game. As a result of their defense, the Knicks had led the NBA with the highest average spread (points scored per game compared to points allowed) at 9.1. This despite the fact that eight out of the thirteen teams in the league scored more points per game than the Knicks that season.

In the opening round of the playoffs the Knicks faced the Baltimore Bullets, who they'd swept in the previous years' semis. These were two perfectly matched teams. Center Wes Unseld and power forward Gus Johnson were strong, physical players who could hold their own against Reed and DeBusschere. At small forward, Jack Marin was an outstanding shooter whose game was similar to Bill Bradley's. In the backcourt, Earl Monroe was a whirling dervish whose offensive moves left defenders befuddled; Frazier always used up a great deal of energy trying to guard Monroe. At the other backcourt spot, Baltimore started Kevin Loughery who was, like Dick Barnett, a determined professional. Loughery began the series wearing a brace that protected a month-old injury: four cracked ribs and a punctured lung.

With two evenly matched teams, coaching was crucial. The Bullets' Gene Shue had been named the NBA coach of the year the prior season, so Red had his hands full.

DeBusschere provides numerous examples of Holzman's coaching acumen and empathetic approach towards his players in his book. In the Knicks' practice session two days prior to the opening game of the playoffs, the team's timing was off and Red told them so. "What the hell do you guys think you're doing out there?" he yelled at his players. "Press your men, pick up all over!

Get back on defense! Once you make a mistake, run back. Don't stand there and brood about it." According to DeBusschere, Holzman was screaming louder than he had all season. Yet, once practice ended, he was jovial, saying, "That was a good practice today, wasn't it?"

In the locker room at Madison Square Garden prior to the series tip-off, Holzman called his players together and tried to loosen them up. "Clyde, how many times this year have you heard me say this is a big game?"

"Eighty-two, so far," he said.

"Well, forget whatever I said before. This is really a big game."

But it didn't start that way, as the Bullets jumped out to a 12–4 lead. Holzman called a timeout and tried to rally his troops. "We're forcing shots," he said. "We're calculating every move. You don't have to do that. Basketball's a game of instinct. Go out and play it that way!"

The game went into double overtime, but the Knicks prevailed, 120–117. DeBusschere called it "the most exciting, best-played basketball" game he had ever been a part of during his eight years in the NBA. During one of the overtime periods, Red got so caught up in the moment he looked down the bench at Bradley and yelled, "Come here, Riordan! Get in the game. Get in for Barnett." Bradley told Holzman that Riordan was already in the game.

"Holzman," Bradley told me, "was not a control freak but an enforcer of basic rules of how to play the game." According to Bradley, Red had only three rules: see the ball, hit the open man, and if you guys want a drink, go someplace else—the hotel bar is mine.

Unlike some who would micromanage, Red allowed his players to develop specific offensive plays on their own. The Knicks only had around fifteen plays that they used with regularity, but each had multiple variations depending on how the opposition defended them at that particular moment. Bradley's favorite play was BF, in which he ran his man off a pick and took his patented baseline jumper. But if the defense switched and Bradley was covered, he would pass the ball to a teammate who was open due to the switch. Frazier or DeBusschere called most of the plays, but every player on the court could call one if he sensed something might work. This was Holzman's way of empowering his players, an inherent part of his philosophy. Harvey Araton, a well-respected New York basketball writer who knew Red well, described his approach as "nurturing his players individuality. On the court or in the locker room, he wanted them to think for themselves."

Before the second game of the series, Holzman, concerned that Baltimore had figured out the Knicks play-calling system, asked for input from his players as to how to rename some of their most frequently used plays. Whatever they came up with worked. The Knicks won, 106–99, to take a 2–0 lead. After the game, Holzman locked the reporters out of the locker room so he could school his team in his credo—never say anything negative about anyone. "Let's not knock Baltimore," he said, "Say nice things about them. Watch yourselves. I don't want anybody saying anything that will get them up for the next game."

For Game Three, it didn't matter what the Knicks did or didn't say to the press. Reed had an off game; Unseld outrebounded the entire Knicks team, and Baltimore won easily, 127–113. Now, Red's postgame tune changed. "Maybe that game will do us some good," he told the team. "It shows what happens when you don't play together. Now let's get some rest and forget this one."

After the fourth game, a 10-point loss in Baltimore, the seven-game series was tied at two. During the regular season, the Knicks had dominated Baltimore, winning five of six games played, outscoring them by an average of almost 20 points a game. Yet, in this series, the Knicks were in the fight of their lives. But, publicly, as Pete Axthelm noted in his classic book, *The City Game*, Holzman remained his old laconic self.

"Well, it all comes down to two-out-of-three series now," a reporter said to Holzman after the loss. "I guess so," Red replied, deadpan. "I thought it was three of five, but somebody straightened me out."

"What will you do with the team now?" another writer asked, deluding himself into thinking Holzman would give away his plans for Game Five back in New York. "I guess our first worry is to make sure we catch the plane in the morning."

But Red did have a plan. He told Frazier to forget about scoring and focus on defending Monroe. He also suggested Frazier and Barnett move the ball into the forecourt quicker so the team had more time to move and hit the open man. The Knicks won handily, 101–80. Frazier held Monroe to 18 points, his lowest total in the series. But the key was Reed, who once again saved the Knicks with 36 points and 36 rebounds.

Baltimore went on to win Game Six, forcing a decisive seventh game at Madison Square Garden. A few hours before tip-off, Holzman was asked if he worried.

"I'm always worried," he replied.

"More than usual tonight?"

"I try to keep my worrying on an even keel."

To DeBusschere, the players and their coach seemed nervous before game time. Red's pregame talk was even briefer than usual, "There's nothing I can say, fellas. Just run your plays and move and hit the boards and play as a unit. Play tough defense. That's it."

For Game Seven, Holzman told Barnett to bring the ball upcourt so Frazier would have more energy to guard Monroe. In an unintended benefit, Barnett decided that, since he had the ball, he might as well shoot it. He and DeBusschere led the Knicks in scoring with 28 points each. With their best team effort of the series, they won the seventh game, 127–114, and advanced to the Eastern Division finals against the Milwaukee Bucks.

Milwaukee had finished in second place in the Eastern Division. Their star was 7-foot-2 Kareem Abdul Jabbar, then in his first year in the league and still using the name Lew Alcindor. In college, he had led UCLA to three consecutive national championships. His go-to shot, a "sky hook," which he released with his right arm fully extended above his head, was virtually unstoppable when he got position close to the basket. By the time his career ended, he had scored more points than any other player in NBA history.

In practice before the series began, Holzman mapped out a strategy for how the Knicks should defend Alcindor. Reed would try to muscle him away from the basket as much as possible; the guards would drop off their men to help out, looking to steal the ball from him if he brought it too low; and the forward on the weak side would block the middle to challenge Alcindor as he moved across the lane to take his sky hook. Red was gambling that making Kareem work harder for his shot was worth the trade-off of allowing the Milwaukee guards, Flynn Robinson and John McGlocklin, open looks at the basket. The Knicks had defeated Milwaukee the first four times they had played during the regular season, but Alcindor had improved as he gained experience over the course of the season. In fact, the last two times the teams had played, Milwaukee had won handily.

Coaching would again make a significant difference. After defeating Baltimore, Red gave his players two days off and then ran them through a light workout on their first day back. Milwaukee had defeated their first-round opponent, Philadelphia, in five games and ended up with a week off. During that break Bucks head coach Larry Costello had been running practices, according to one of their veteran players, Len Chappell, "like training camp." As a result, Milwaukee was "dull at the start."

The Knicks took the opening game of the series with ease, 110–102. Flynn Robinson, who was the Bucks second-leading scorer, averaging 21.8 points a game, was particularly dull, making only 4 of 16 shots. Frazier's defense added to his dullness. In Game Two, the Knicks prevailed again, 112–111, with Reed scoring 36 points and pulling down 19 rebounds.

On April 16, the Knicks was set to travel to Milwaukee for the next two games in the series. Unfortunately, they would be short one key player: Dave DeBusschere. Early that morning, DeBusschere's wife had a miscarriage. He called Holzman to tell him he wouldn't be able to fly out with the team. Red said, "Your family comes first."

The next day, DeBusschere brought his wife home from the hospital and then flew out to Milwaukee in time for the third game. Playing their worst game of the series, the Knicks somehow managed to lose by only five points, 101–96. Before the next game, Holzman asked his players if anyone had suggestions. DeBusschere said that, early in the game, Reed should get the ball often. Barnett agreed, saying that would put pressure on Alcindor from the word go. Barnett suggested Reed act as a pivot man, with the others cutting off him; if they were open, Reed would pass the ball; if not, he would drive to the basket. It was the kind of discussion that would have made Nat Holman and his five moving pivots proud. Red obviously had the last word, but having everyone on the same page was key. He looked at Reed and said, "Willy, you've got to move for the ball better than you did last game." Reed agreed.

The Knicks started fast in Game Four and led by 20 points at the half. Unable to come out of the locker room with the same intensity, Milwaukee scored 16 straight points to put the Knicks on the ropes. A Milwaukee win would tie the series at two games, but Cazzie Russell came off the bench to score three quick baskets early in the final quarter to turn the momentum back in the Knicks' favor. They would not give up the lead and cruised to a 117–105 victory.

Back in New York, before Game Five, Holzman was more nervous than usual. He once told Marv Albert that if he could arrange it, in order to avoid waiting around all day as his anxieties mounted, the Knicks would play all their games at 10 in the morning. That night, Frazier, seeing his coach more wound up than usual, told him, "Hey, Red, don't sweat it. We're gonna handle this game for you." The Knicks won the game in a rout, 132–96, taking the series from the Bucks in five.

Near the end of the game, knowing victory was confirmed, Holzman cleared the bench. Everyone played except Bill Hosket, who had twisted an ankle in practice. The Garden crowd was chanting, "We want Hosket." Red finally told the Garden PA announcer, John Condon, to announce that Hosket was injured and couldn't play. The crowd cheered upon hearing the news. Later, after a timeout, Hosket trotted back to the bench. "Limp a little, will you?" Holzman said.

In the championship round, the Knicks faced the Los Angeles Lakers. They had taken four of six from the Lakers during the regular season, but Wilt Chamberlain had missed most of the year due to a knee injury and played in only the first of those games (which the Knicks had won by just three points). With Chamberlain out of action, the Lakers often ran isolation plays for their best shooter, Jerry West. Holzman responded by often double-teaming West. For the championship series, the Lakers would have all three of their stars—Chamberlain, West, and Elgin Baylor. This presented a defensive challenge for the Knicks. Chamberlain was an offensive powerhouse who demanded the same level of attention as Alcindor.

At practice the day before the championship series began, Holzman asked his players what they thought the best way would be to defend against the Lakers. Frazier made it clear he had to guard West closely and could not help out on Chamberlain. DeBusschere, would be guarding Baylor, who was averaging 24 points per game that season. "I can't leave Baylor for a second," DeBusschere said. Reed would have to do his individual best to cover Chamberlain with nominal help from only Barnett and Bradley. On offense, Holzman instructed Reed to shoot from the outside to pull Chamberlain away from the basket. Red also asked that whichever Knicks player Baylor was covering to keep moving on offense to tire the thirty-five-year old out so he had less energy when the Lakers had the ball.

Things started well. In the series opener, Reed was hitting from outside and the Knicks led at halftime, 65–54. But the Lakers came back in the third to go ahead by three. Settling down in the fourth, the Knicks outscored the Lakers by 15 points to take Game One, 124–112. Afterward, Holzman closed the doors to the locker room and told his players not to share any trade secrets with the press. "Don't tell them we're using Willis as an outside pick all the time or that we're trying to run Baylor."

After giving his players a day off following Game One, team practice focused on defensive techniques for end-of-game situations—those when the Lakers would most likely go to Jerry West for the game's final shot. Red must have seen how tired his players were. After only an hour, he said, "I think you guys have had enough. What do you think?" DeBusschere agreed, and practice promptly ended.

Before Game Two, Holzman implored his players to make the Lakers, especially Baylor and Chamberlain, run throughout the game . . . but they didn't, and their coach was not pleased. At halftime he screamed at his players, "When we move, we win! When we don't, we lose!" The Knicks went on to lose, 105–103. After the game, Red was singing a different tune and looking ahead to Game Three, rather than looking back at a loss he could no longer do anything about. "The way we played," he said, "they could've beaten us a lot worse. Don't worry about this one. Shake it off."

In Game Three, Los Angeles was ahead by 14 points at halftime, but the Knicks staged a second-half comeback. With only seconds left and the game tied, 100–100, Holzman called timeout. He didn't tell his players what play they should run, but instead asked for their thoughts. It was decided that 3-2F, where

DeBusschere set a screen for Bradley to take his jump shot, would work. But Bradley was covered and so Barnett had to pass the ball to DeBusschere—the second option on 3-2F. DeBusschere hit the shot to give the Knicks the lead with only three seconds left. Chamberlain inbounded to West, who dribbled a few steps and released a desperation shot from beyond halfcourt.

Incredibly, it went in to tie the game.

Normally in total control of himself, Frazier was so drained after seeing West make the shot that Red had to call him twice to get him to come to the huddle before the beginning of the overtime period. The Knicks' captain and inspirational leader, Willis Reed, told his teammates to forget the shot and focus, "It's incredible, but we got an overtime to win now." The Knicks won the game, 111–108.

Holzman held a practice the following day, in preparation for Game Four. DeBusschere told his coach that he didn't feel like running. "Then don't even dress," Red replied. He also gave Reed the day off. Of all the Knicks players, Reed and DeBusschere, the two leading rebounders and interior defenders, had taken the greatest physical pounding. Similarly, Auerbach would let Bill Russell skip team practices knowing how much he needed the rest.

Jerry West scored 37 points two nights later, proving Holzman correct when he said, "When the going gets shaky they feed the ball to West." With nine seconds left in the fourth quarter and the game tied, the Knicks had a chance to win it. Holzman told his players to set up the same 3-2F play that had worked at the end of regulation in Game Three. But Red had gone to the well once too often. The Lakers had Frazier well-guarded and he was unable to pass the ball. All he could do was force his own shot, which missed. The Lakers won in overtime, 121–115.

The teams returned to New York, tied at two games apiece. At practice prior to the pivotal fifth game, Holzman again gave Reed the day off and allowed DeBusschere to just walk through the plays. Red tried to pump up his players with a short talk after practice. "There's no need to tell you how important this week is. These are the most important games any of us have ever been in. And I know how tired you all are. But you're just going to have to ask your bodies for something extra. Maybe it's there. Maybe it's not. But you're going to have to push yourselves harder than you're ever pushed in your lives."

In Game Five, Willis Reed pushed too hard. In the first quarter, with the Knicks already trailing by 10 points, Reed fell down in terrible pain as he tried to drive past Chamberlain, injuring the tensor muscle in his right leg. This muscle is crucial for walking, running, and jumping. Reed would be unable to play for the rest of the game and would be ruled out for Game Six.

After Reed's injury, Holzman was just trying to avoid a blowout before halftime. To replace Reed, he first tried Nate Bowman. At 6-foot-10, Bowman was the team's tallest player—but was not strong enough to guard Chamberlain. He then tried 6-foot-8 Bill Hosket, hoping he could hit a few shots to draw Chamberlain away from the basket. But Hosket missed his first couple of shots and, with about four minutes left in the half, Holzman tried DeBusschere on Chamberlain. The half ended with the Knicks down by 13, 53–40.

In the locker room, Knicks players saw Reed lying on the trainer's table and knew he wasn't coming back for the second half. Holzman then gave his version of a win-one-for-the-Gipper speech. "Willy's won a lot of games for us this season," Holzman said. "Let's win one for him."

But the crucial words spoken at halftime came from Bill Bradley. He suggested the Knicks try a 1-3-1 zone offense to combat the quasi-zone the Lakers were playing, with Chamberlain defending the basket and not any specific player. Red unhesitatingly gave his blessing to the idea, hoping it would take the Lakers by surprise. Frazier played the point, Bradley was in the middle at the top of the key with Barnett and Russell on the wings, and with either DeBusschere or Stallworth running the baseline to try and pull Chamberlain from under the basket. The plan was a gamble, but it worked. On offense, the Knicks were in constant motion. Bradley and Russell began hitting their outside shots. On the defensive end, the Knicks applied constant pressure, switching and swarming and helping each other out. Los Angeles was totally befuddled. The Lakers had 19 turnovers in the second half, Chamberlain took only three shots, and West was held to four points. At the end of the third quarter, the Knicks trailed by seven points.

With about nine minutes left in the fourth and trailing by four, Holzman replaced DeBusschere, who had five fouls (one short of fouling out), with Stallworth. After hitting three outside shots, Stallworth had forced Chamberlain to defend him away from the basket. At the crucial moment of the game, with the Knicks ahead and the Lakers desperate for a defensive stop, Stallworth saw an opportunity. He drove past Chamberlain for a twisting reverse layup, using the rim to prevent Chamberlain from blocking his shot. That basket broke the Lakers. After that, the Knicks extended their lead and never looked back.

The Knicks won, 107–100, outscoring the Lakers in the

second half by 20 points. After their remarkable come-from-behind win, Red uncharacteristically let his feelings rise to the surface. "These guys can do anything," he kept telling reporters. "There's nothing they can't do."

After the game, Lakers coach Joe Mullaney said, "They gambled in the second half and it paid off. They made us resort to something different, and we couldn't do it."

Heading back to Los Angeles for Game Six, Holzman chose not to use either the 1-3-1 offense nor the pressing defense that had taken the Lakers by surprise in Game Five. "On another night," he said after the game, "playing that gambling defense, we might have been killed."

Red was never one to concede anything, but logic dictated the Lakers would be well prepared and highly motivated to avenge their failure in Game Five when, as Jerry West said, "We couldn't do anything right in the second half. We couldn't even call a time out right." Despite having some of his player's lobbying for a return to the 1-3-1 offense that was so successful in Game Five, Holzman, believed his team's best chance to win the series would be in Game Seven on their home court when Reed might be able to play. To the press, Holzman revealed nothing. He just started Bowman who gave his all, scoring 18 points. But even with Bowman's solid performance, Chamberlain was unstoppable scoring 45 points and pulling down 27 rebounds. West, who had been held to 20 points in Game Five, had 33 points and 13 assists. The Lakers led by 20 points after the first quarter and won handily, 135–113.

An entire season now came down to one final game. But the Knicks' greatest vulnerability—what to do if Reed was injured—had come home to roost. The Knicks players knew their championship hopes depended on whether or not Reed could play in the deciding game. Without him, they knew they had little chance of winning. What they had accomplished in a rush of emotion in the second half of Game Five would be impossible to sustain for an entire game. Several players came back to the training room to see if Reed would make it onto the court. Finally, Holzman had had enough. He berated his players, telling them that whether or not Reed played didn't matter, as *they* had a game to play.

In Danny Whelan's training room shortly before game time, Reed saw the team doctor pick up the biggest needle he had ever seen and get ready to stick it into his leg to numb the pain so he could play. Although on injured reserve, Phil Jackson was in the training room taking photos for a book he would do with Knicks' photographer George Kalinsky. No other photographer was allowed that kind of access. Jackson took a photo of Reed immediately before the shot was administered when his face showed, what Jackson called, "the anticipation of pain." Holzman saw Jackson take the photo and made him promise he would never use it, saying it would be unfair to both Reed and the other photographers.

"That," Jackson told me, "was Red in his most ethical moment."

Spike Lee later offered Jackson a significant sum for the photo; but out of respect for Reed and Holzman, Jackson didn't sell it.

Following a now legendary walk onto the court in which he intentionally bumped into Sam Goldaper for good luck, Reed started the game by hitting his first two shots. No one knew it at that moment, but thanks to Reed's remarkable act of courage to play, the game was effectively over. The Knicks broke out to a

15–6 lead in the first five minutes and were up by 27 at halftime. Reed toughed it out for 20 minutes in the first half, and Red limited him to seven minutes in the third quarter and then took him out for good. The Knicks led, 94–69, at the end of the third, and won, 113–99. Because of Reed's heroics, it's often forgotten that Walt Frazier not only had one of best games of his career, but one of the greatest closing games in NBA history. Frazier's line for the game: 36 points, 19 assists, seven rebounds, and five steals.

After the game, Holzman told Leonard Koppett, "He [Reed] gave us a tremendous lift just going out there. He couldn't play his normal game, but he did a lot of things out there and he means a lot to the spirit of the other players."

For the first time in their history, the Knicks were champions. They won because they had great players; four of the five starters would be elected to the Basketball Hall of Fame. But there was more to it. Bill Hosket told me that from the beginning of training camp, every player on that Knicks team—even the benchwarmers—had just one overriding thought: "What do we have to do to win a championship?"

The only starter on that team who is not in the Basketball Hall of Fame, Dick Barnett, told me almost half a century later, "You got to have the guys playing together. Minimize your own abilities in order to fit into the greater good of the team."

In this regard, Holzman's role was not just critical, but influential. On offense, he had drilled into his players the importance of hitting the open man. On defense, it was his never-ending focus on the importance of playing team defense that had his players feeling like the words, *see the ball*, were tattooed across their foreheads. Nothing Red demanded of his players was new. As Mike Riordan pointed out to me, Holzman didn't revolutionize the game; he was merely part of its evolution. For example, other coaches made offensive-defensive substitutions late in games to maximize a player's strengths. But Holzman turned it into an art form. If the Knicks were leading by two and their opponent was throwing the ball into play to set up a final shot to tie the game, Phil Jackson and his unusually long arms would be leaping and whirling like a windmill to prevent the inbounds pass. And if the opponent did manage to score, Jackson would suddenly be on the bench and Cazzie Russell would be in for his instant offense.

Throughout everything, Holzman made sure the spotlight was solely on his players. Through his scouting and coaching, Red had helped form a team in his own image: hardworking, selfless, and color-blind. As Walt Frazier said, "When I make a pass, I don't see the face, only the uniform."

Oscar Robertson, one of the greatest players in NBA history, had competed against Holzman's Knicks many times. In his auto-biography, Robertson wrote, "Those Knicks were probably the best purely defensive team of that era. Red Holzman had them hustling all over the floor. In a half-court situation, they weren't flashy or tricky, but simply settled in. They made you take tough shots, and then they got the rebound when you missed."

Following the 1969–70 season, Red Holzman, the "ordinary man" who never wanted to coach again, was named NBA Coach of the Year.

CHAPTER TEN

"DID I SCINTILLATE YOU WITH MY RETORTS?"

Red Holzman didn't have time to rest on his laurels. The Knicks defeated the Lakers in Game Seven to win the NBA championship on Friday, May 8, and the expansion draft was held on Monday, May 11. That year, three teams joined the league: the Buffalo Braves, Cleveland Cavaliers, and Portland Trail Blazers. Red had to decide which seven players on his roster he wanted to protect from being selected in the draft. With a roster as deep as the Knicks, he had some tough choices to make.

Willis Reed, Dave DeBusschere, Bill Bradley, Walt Frazier, Cazzie Russell, and Dick Barnett, who turned thirty-four prior to the beginning of the 1970–71 season, were all almost surely protected. Other general managers might have left Barnett unprotected since expansion teams building for the long-term would typically pass on an older player, but Barnett was one of

Holzman's favorites; an integral part of the team both on the court and in the locker room.

With Phil Jackson not on the Knicks' roster due to a back injury, Holzman had to decide between Mike Riordan and Dave Stallworth as the final player to protect. Both had the talent to be starters on an expansion team.

The way the expansion draft worked was that once a player was selected off a team's unprotected list, one of the remaining listed players could be pulled. Former Knicks general manager Eddie Donovan ran the draft for Buffalo, and selected two Knicks players: Don May and Bill Hosket. Once May was selected, Red must have pulled either Riordan or Stallworth, whichever one he left exposed, off the list. The Knicks also lost a third player, John Warren, to Cleveland. A month later, Holzman and Eddie Donovan engaged in a trade, with the Knicks sending Nate Bowman and Mike Silliman, a star at West Point whom the Knicks had drafted in 1966 and who had just completed his military service, to Buffalo for cash. There was speculation that this trade indicated that Holzman and Donovan had made a prior agreement whereby Buffalo would select May—not Riordan or Stallworth. When asked about this, Holzman said, "I've heard all the talk, too. But we've done nothing wrong or illegal."

However Red maneuvered it, by retaining both Riordan and Stallworth, the Knicks could later make a crucial trade that would produce a second championship.

In his own way, Holzman had forewarned May and Hosket they were vulnerable. During the 1969–70 season, after the team had held a team practice in San Francisco, May and Hosket were playing HORSE, a game where a player wins by sinking shots from locations his opponent is unable to match. The Cow

Palace, where practice had been held, appeared empty. May and Hosket thought everyone else had left, so they were fooling around taking shots from distances and angles they would have never attempted during an actual game. They even took shots from beyond the out-of-bounds lines. Suddenly, Holzman, who must have been silently watching their shot selections, appeared.

"Do you two guys ever stop screwing around?" he said.

Holzman never liked to see practice time wasted—not even during a game of HORSE. If you're going to be taking shots, he felt, take those you would actually use during a game. On his way out, Holzman said, "You both are going to play in this league. But there's a good chance it won't be for me."

In 2017, when Hosket told me the HORSE story, I said, "Red was pragmatic."

"That's putting it mildly," Hosket replied.

Holzman was tough when he needed to be, but his toughness was diffused with humor. Gwynne Bloomfield, Holzman's secretary with the Knicks, told me, "Red was gruff, but a sweetheart." He came into work each morning at around 10 singing showtunes, and often joked with her, saying, "I wouldn't trade you for a barrel of pickled herring." Yet, Holzman was firm in insisting that none of the women working for the Knicks date any of the players, or players from any other NBA team.

Red's personnel planning had assured Knicks fans that the team's best nine players would all be back to try and win another championship. May, Hosket, Warren, and Nate Bowman were replaced by rookies who would, like their predecessors, see little playing time. As was his usual preference, Red would usually use an eight- or nine-man rotation. But as Dick Barnett told me, even if you maintain player continuity, repeating as a championship team is harder than winning the first time around because now everyone is gunning for you.

The Knicks finished the 1970–71 season in first place in the Atlantic Division with a 52–30 record. They once again had the best defense in the NBA, but there were no 18-game winning streaks. In fact, they proved to be beatable, losing six games in a row during the month of February. The Milwaukee Bucks, who had improved with the addition of Oscar Robertson, had finished the regular season with the best record in the league (66–16) and were favored to win the championship.

But the playoffs were a new season for a veteran team like the Knicks, and they easily defeated the Atlanta Hawks in the first round of the playoffs, four games to one. The Knicks then faced the Baltimore Bullets for the third consecutive season—this year in the Eastern Conference finals. After losing the previous two seasons to the Knicks, Baltimore badly wanted to avenge those defeats. With the series tied at three games each, a decisive Game Seven was played at Madison Square Garden. The Knicks led by four at halftime, but a strong third quarter by the Bullets gave them the lead. With three seconds left and Baltimore up by two, Bill Bradley's shot was partially deflected by Wes Unseld. Gus Johnson grabbed the rebound and the Knicks were eliminated from the playoffs.

After losing the series, Holzman, never one to cry over spilled milk, said, "The game's over, the season's over, and it's like death—you can't change it. You can't go out and add up the score again."

But Red knew he had to make changes to his roster to keep the team strong. After years of playing through injuries and pain while battling much taller centers, Willis Reed had a chronic knee condition. In the series-ending game against Baltimore, Reed was able to run and jump better than he had in weeks, but only after taking the painkiller xylocaine for his bad knee—once before the game, and again at halftime. Holzman decided to acquire a player who could fill in for Reed for extended periods of time without a significant drop-off in quality. With that in mind, he traded for a player he'd scouted and admired years before, Jerry Lucas. A high school basketball star in his native Ohio, an All-American at Ohio State, and a 1960 Olympic champion, Jerry Lucas was, in his day—long before LeBron James—the most successful player ever to come out of Ohio. The Knicks had been unable to acquire Lucas because Cincinnati made him their territorial pick in 1962. At 6-foot-8, Lucas had justified the pick by becoming an All-Star in his first six seasons. Playing the power forward position, he was a gifted scorer, rebounder, defender, and passer, averaging 19.7 points, 19.2 rebounds, and three assists in his six year with Cincinnati. But despite the combination of Lucas and Oscar Robertson, Cincinnati had never won a championship, and had shipped Lucas to San Francisco.

Off the court, Lucas had his idiosyncrasies. When he was barnstorming in Ohio with four of his fellow Ohio State teammates—one of whom was the future Hall of Famer John Havlicek—Lucas made it clear that since he was the one drawing in the fans, he should get half of all gate receipts. He also had a photographic memory. Once, at a party, he totally flummoxed chess champion Bobby Fischer with his ability to memorize the phone book. Yet, after missing a team practice with the Knicks, Lucas told Holzman it was because he had forgotten. Holzman fined Lucas, telling him he could understand that happening to any other player—but not him. Before the trade, Holzman didn't know how Lucas would fit in with his teammates off the court, but believed he would be invaluable on the court.

In order to acquire Lucas, Holzman decided that with Bill Bradley approaching the apex of his career, Cazzie Russell was expendable. So, on May 7, 1971, Holzman traded Russell to San Francisco for Lucas. Russell felt he should be starting ahead of Bradley and was never shy about making his feelings clear to Holzman. Yet there was never any ill will between the two.

About two weeks after Russell was traded to San Francisco, Red and Selma were involved in a car crash. They both sustained serious injuries and ended up in St. Joseph's Hospital in Far Rockaway. Selma had a broken right hip and would end up using a cane the rest of her life, while Red suffered injuries to his head, ribs, and arm. Selma remained in the hospital after Red was discharged. During her stay in the hospital, numerous Knicks players visited to see how she was recovering, including one former team member with a lot of class, Cazzie Russell, who brought Selma an azalea plant. When she was discharged, Selma planted it in the Holzmans' backyard. Years later, Russell told me Selma had "a nice smile and spirit about her." The trade for Lucas proved well-timed. Reed's injuries again caught up with him and he would miss the final 67 games of the season. Thankfully, Lucas was able to successfully fill in for Reed for the remainder of the season. As Holzman later said of Lucas, "he just fit in perfectly with us because he was so intelligent and a fine passer."

But even with the addition of Lucas, in early November 1971, the Knicks were in last place in the Atlantic Division. A shake up was needed. On November 10, Holzman traded Mike Riordan and Dave Stallworth, as well as a significant sum of cash, for Baltimore's Earl Monroe. Holzman needed a long-term replacement for Dick Barnett, and Baltimore was unwilling to offer Monroe a contract he found acceptable. Monroe was an electrifying one-on-one player, and many wondered how he would fit into the Knicks' team-oriented style. The prevailing thought was that the team would need two basketballs: one for Monroe, one for Frazier.

But Holzman knew better. He had scouted Monroe in college and considered him a flamboyant but multifaceted player with amazing court vison. In a 1978 interview, Red waxed poetic about Monroe, saying he was "a master player, a great player who can do everything. I don't think he's been given credit for being able to do a lot of things that he can do because he's such a master at doing the magic."

At the press conference introducing Monroe, Holzman said, "We made the trade because Monroe is a great basketball player. I'm sure he can adjust to our system."

Monroe agreed. "There shouldn't be any big problems. As a professional, I can be compatible with anyone. I can adapt, but there may be some little problems at first. Learning the plays will probably be my biggest."

Red then joked, "No Earl. Everybody on the Bullets knows our plays."

All joking aside, the reality of the situation was more serious. According to Monroe's autobiography, *Earl the Pearl*, immediately before the press conference, Monroe told Holzman that he had been playing in considerable pain and needed to have bone-spur surgery on his left foot. That's probably not what Red wanted to hear, considering that Monroe had just signed a two-year contract with the Knicks.

Holzman told Monroe, "We've just made this trade for you

because we need you and want you with us. Willis is out and we need to have you on the floor. Plus, we don't want any letdown at the guard position. That's why we brought you in. So, you might have to just play through the pain this season."

Monroe said, "Well, Coach, I'm cool with that. Let me go slowly at first."

Monroe wrote that, in response, Red "looked at me and nodded his head. I could see he had respect for my saying that."

Holzman didn't demand much from Monroe that season. Dick Barnett remained the starter, and Monroe played about twenty minutes a game. In addition, rookie Dean Meminger, who grew up in New York City and had played in college at Marquette for Al McGuire (the brother of Knicks chief scout Dick McGuire), proved to be an excellent defensive player. Red utilized Meminger when the Knicks needed to shut down an opposing backcourt player with a hot hand.

Monroe, as a veteran coming from a team where he was the star, offered some interesting insights into Holzman's system. Unlike Baltimore, the Knicks had game statistics available to them at halftime. And Red, thanks to his statisticians, was always aware of a players' shots, rebounds, assists, and turnovers. But the biggest adjustment for Monroe, who had always been his team's top scorer in college or the pros, was that on this team he was valued even if he only scored 10 points in a game by following Holzman's rule that great players don't have to score as long as they are lifting up their teammates' performance.

The Knicks finished the 1971–72 season with a 48–34 record for a second-place finish in the Atlantic Division behind Boston. The Knicks had slipped defensively without Reed, but were still good enough to advance past the Bullets and Celtics in the first two rounds of the playoffs. In the championship round, they once again faced Los Angeles.

But this was a better Lakers team than the one the Knicks had defeated to win their first championship. With Elgin Baylor's retirement, the team still had Wilt Chamberlain and Jerry West, but the aging Baylor's replacement at small forward, Jim McMillian, in only his second year in the NBA, proved to be the right man to make them the best team in the league. A graduate of Columbia, McMillian was to the Lakers what Bradley was to the Knicks: an intelligent, unselfish player who was constantly in motion creating opportunities for his teammates. In the other guard spot opposite Jerry West, was Gail Goodrich, a future Hall of Famer who was an outstanding scorer. That season, the Lakers had the best record in the league, 69–13, and a 33-game winning streak, still the longest in NBA history.

But in Game One, the Knicks easily defeated the Lakers in Los Angeles, 114–92. Holzman, taking advantage of Chamberlain's reluctance to come out and defend the oppositions' center, created a pick-and-roll play for Jerry Lucas and Bill Bradley. The two veterans, both deadly outside shooters, ran it to perfection. If Chamberlain switched to cover Bradley, he'd pass the ball to Lucas. If Chamberlain stayed with Lucas, Chamberlain wouldn't usually chase him 25 feet away from the basket—which was well within his shooting range. Bradley scored 29 points; Lucas, 26. The Knicks had taken away the Lakers' home-court advantage and appeared to have a chance of winning the series. But, in Game Two, DeBusschere was injured in the first half and didn't return. With that, the Knicks lost the game and their momentum. In New York for the third game of the series, DeBusschere played for only 20 minutes and the Knicks lost again. In Game Four, which turned out to be the pivotal game of the series, DeBusschere toughed it out and started the game, but the Knicks lost in overtime, 116–111. The Lakers won easily back in Los Angeles, 114–100, to take the series and win the championship.

That offseason, Holzman made no major moves anticipating that with a healthy Reed, DeBusschere, and Monroe, the Knicks could win another championship.

* * *

For generations, politicians have associated themselves with winning sports teams. In the fall of 1972, George McGovern headed the Democratic ticket against the incumbent, Republican President Richard Nixon. That year, Knicks assistant general manager and director of public relations Frank Blauschild gave permission for the Democratic vice-presidential candidate, Sargent Shriver, to visit the team's locker room before a game. Blauschild made the mistake of not first asking Holzman for his approval. Red insisted that for approximately 30 minutes before game time, his players not be disturbed by anyone: not family, friends, the press, or politicians. He knew how important that time was for some of his players, especially Bradley and DeBusschere, as they psyched themselves up for the game. But Blauschild either momentarily forgot Holzman's preference or figured Red, who was a Democrat, wouldn't mind.

From his office adjacent to the locker room, Holzman heard the commotion as Sargent Shriver made his rounds among the Knicks players. Red asked Blauschild, "Frankie, what going on?"

New York Knicks head coach Red Holzman on Knicks Media Day at
Madison Square Garden, 1968. *(George Kalinsky)*

Holzman, Willis Reed (left) and Walt Frazier at Knicks training camp in Farmingdale, New York, 1969. *(George Kalinsky)*

Willis Reed, captain of the Knicks, holds the World Championship trophy with Holzman at a presentation ceremony at Madison Square Garden on October 13, 1970, prior to a game with the Boston Celtics. *(AP Images)*

The often even-keeled Holzman shouts disapproval of referee's decision as the Knicks lose Game Four of the Eastern Division finals against the Boston Celtics on April 13, 1969, putting them down three games to one. *(AP Images)*

Holding the role of both coach and general manager of the Knicks, Red speaks on a conference call with NBA Commissioner Walter Kennedy during the 1970 NBA Draft. Team president Ned Irish (left) and chief scout Dick McGuire flank Holzman. *(AP Images)*

Never sticking with an unsuccessful game plan, Red was known for making in-game adjustments, here doing so during a time out. *(George Kalinsky)*

Always the teacher, Red takes the time to "educate" a referee during the Eastern Conference finals against the Boston Celtics in April, 1973. *(George Kalinsky)*

New York Knicks team portrait,1972–1973 season. Bottom row (left to right): Henry Bibby, Walt Frazier, Ned Irish (president), Irving Mitchell Felt (chairman), Red Holzman, Earl Monroe, Dick Barnett, and Harthorne Wingo.

Top row (left to right): Bill Bradley, Phil Jackson, John Gianelli, Dave DeBusschere, Willis Reed, Jerry Lucas, Tom Riker, Dean Meminger, and Danny Whalen (trainer). *(AP Images)*

With Jerry Lucas at the projector, Red and the Knicks study film before Game Five of the 1973 NBA Finals against the Los Angeles Lakers. *(George Kalinsky)*

New York City Mayor John Lindsay (right) congratulates Holzman after presenting the city's diamond jubilee medals to the coach and other members of the Knicks team and organization on the steps of City Hall, May 15, 1973. Also in the photo are MSG board chairman Irving Felt (third from left) and team captain Willis Reed (standing next to Lindsay). *(AP Images)*

Bill Bradley (right) and Red Holzman thank the MSG crowd honoring them prior to a game against the Boston Celtics on April 5, 1977. *(AP Images)*

Earl Monroe (center) holding his retired jersey No. 15 with former teammates (left to right) Dave DeBusschere, Walt Frazier, Bill Bradley, and coach Red Holzman, on March 1, 1986. "The Pearl" would be the fifth of sixth Knicks coached by Holzman to have his jersey retired. *(AP Images)*

Two of the winningest coaches in NBA history, Red Auerbach (center) and Holzman, pose with commissioner David Stern at the NBA's 50th anniversary celebration at the Boston Garden, 1997. *(George Kalinsky)*

Always his rock, Red's wife Selma poses with him at an MSG Collection signing and reunion of the Knicks 1973 Championship team at Caesar's Palace in Atlantic City, New Jersey, 1998. *(George Kalinsky)*

With three decades in the sport, as a player, coach, and executive, Red Holzman left his mark on the game of basketball. His 613 hangs high in the MSG rafters, reminding all Knicks fans of the glory he brought to the franchise. *(George Kalinsky)*

"That's Sargent Shriver, he's running for Vice President on the Democratic ticket."

"I don't give a fuck if he's General Shriver," Holzman yelled, "get him out."

Blauschild would have been better off arranging for Shriver to give a motivational speech. In *The Open Man*, DeBusschere wrote, "If Red has a weakness, it's his pre-game talks." Holzman repertoire ran the gamut from, "Well, this is another big game," to "Well, this is a really big game." According to DeBusschere, Bradley (and from his tone, DeBusschere himself) tuned Red out before games so as to work themselves up to the right state of mind for the opening tap.

Blauschild wasn't the only one to make the mistake of violating Holzman's 30-minute rule. In the early 1970s, Ira Berkow was writing a book with Walt Frazier called *Rockin' Steady*. One night, Berkow asked Knicks business manager and director of publicity Jimmy Wergeles for permission to be in the locker room right until game time to observe Frazier's routine. After spotting Berkow in the locker room, Holzman approached him, asking for an explanation. Berkow said he had gotten the okay from Wergeles, to which Red, certain that Wergeles wouldn't break the 30-minute rule, replied, "Don't bull-shit a bull-shitter." By chance, Wergeles walked into the locker room at that moment and backed up Berkow's story. It's doubtful Wergeles made that mistake again.

Because of his flashy clothing, Rolls Royce, and famed nickname, Walt "Clyde'" Frazier was the best known Knicks player. Yet, Holzman had no problem holding him accountable. Once, after the Knicks had clinched a playoff spot, Frazier asked Red if he could sit out a regular season game against a second-tier opponent struggling to make the playoffs. In the same way Holzman never publicly embarrassed his players, he never wanted to shame the opposing teams' players. He told Frazier that if he kept him out of the game, it would be insulting to their opponent. How would you feel, Red asked Frazier, if an opponent thought so little of the Knicks they didn't feel the need to play their star player? As a compromise, Holzman suggested Frazier suit up for the game, promising to substitute for him after he played only a few minutes to open the game and the second half. Red then looked down at the floor and ceased making eye contact with Frazier. At that moment, his suggestion became a mandate.

* * *

The Knicks began the 1972–73 season winning 17 of their first 20 games. Holzman's rotation began with his four veterans from the 1970 championship team: Reed, DeBusschere, Bradley, and Frazier, with Monroe as the fifth starter. Jerry Lucas was the primary reserve at power forward or center. Phil Jackson continued to wreak havoc on the defensive end, as did Dean Meminger, the first guard off the bench. Two rookies provided more depth: John Gianelli, a rangy 6-foot-10 center, and Henry Bibby, a 6-foot-1 guard from UCLA who had learned from the master, John Wooden. Thanks to his UCLA coach, Bibby was one of most fundamentally sound first-year players Red ever coached. Barnett remained on the roster for spot duty, as well as providing an indispensable hand on the pulse of what was transpiring in the locker room. The Knicks finished with a 57–25 record, their highest win total since their championship season. Although they seldom pressed the opposition full-court, they again led the NBA in defense, allowing only 98.2 points per game.

The high point of the regular season was a remarkable come-from-behind win on November 18, 1972, against the Milwaukee Bucks at Madison Square Garden. Holzman would later write how that game symbolized his coaching philosophy: "We played as a team, and we won as a team."

With less than six minutes left in the game, the Knicks trailed by 18 points, 86–68. Long before the three-point line was established, that was usually an insurmountable lead. But Holzman wasn't ready to concede. "I always felt," Holzman said, "you got no place to go, anyway. You can't go to the movies until the game is over. You can't go out to dinner until after the game is over. So you might as well give it your best shot until it's over."

The Knicks ran off 19 consecutive points while holding the Bucks scoreless to win the game, 87–86. This was no mean feat playing against a team with Kareem Abdul-Jabbar and Oscar Robertson. The final Knicks basket of the night could serve as the high point of Holzman's credo to hit the open man. With less than a minute left in regulation, Reed grabbed a rebound off a missed Bucks free throw and passed the ball to Frazier, who moved into the forecourt and got enough separation from his man to take a jump shot. But at that moment, Monroe had a better shot. Frazier passed to Monroe, who sank the shot that would ultimately give the Knicks the win. After that game, the Knicks felt they could accomplish anything.

A few months later, Holzman sensed that Monroe needed one of those "boosts" that he had given Frazier after Hal Greer had embarrassed him. According to Monroe's autobiography, Holzman told Monroe that he "seemed to have lost his ego."

When asked by Monroe to explain, Holzman said, "if you want greatness you got to have an ego. And you don't seem to have the same ego you had before. So I think you have to go back to playing with more ego."

Monroe wrote, "it was only then that I realized that Red actually liked me . . . for him to come up and talk to me this way kind of freed me up to be me . . . 'Earl the Pearl' again. That was much appreciated on my part." After the talk, Monroe felt comfortable enough to be more aggressive offensively, and his scoring improved.

Later that month, Monroe's mother, who was in a hospital in Germantown, Pennsylvania, after suffering an aneurysm, took a turn for the worse. Holzman told Monroe he could take off as much time as he needed. And after Monroe's mother passed away a short time later, Monroe remained in Germantown for about a week. "No one from the Knicks," Monroe wrote, "bugged me with telephone calls asking when I was coming back."

Holzman showed his empathetic nature with Walt Frazier in a different context. Seeing the expensive lifestyle Frazier revealed with his cars and wardrobe, Red must have thought back to his own career where he went from being one of the highest paid players in the NBA to being unemployed a decade later after being fired by Kerner. He didn't tell Frazier what to do. He simply asked, "Clyde, you saving any money for a rainy day?"

* * *

In the opening round of the playoffs, the Knicks defeated the Baltimore Bullets in five games to advance to the Eastern

Conference finals. They would be facing the Celtics, who had taken the Hawks in six games.

During the 1972–73 season, the Boston Celtics were the Knicks primary competition in the Atlantic Division. For the first time since the retirement of Bill Russell, the Celtics had a legitimate shot at a championship. Auerbach had rebuilt the team around three future Hall of Famers: Dave Cowens at center, John Havlicek at forward, and Jo Jo White in the backcourt. But, hoping to be able to get past the Knicks in the playoffs, Auerbach had improved his team's defense and rebounding by trading for All-Star forward Paul Silas. The Celtics finished the regular season in first place in the Atlantic Division with the best record in the NBA at 68–14. The Knicks had finished 11 games behind the Celtics, but were confident that they could hold their own against Boston in the playoffs. During the regular season, the two teams had evenly split the eight games they played, with each team managing one win on the road.

In Game One at the Boston Garden, the Celtics won easily, 134–108. After that game, an unknowing reporter asked Holzman for reasons behind the one-sided score. In response, Holzman waxed poetic, "We played badly, and they played well."

The Knicks returned the favor in New York, blowing out the Celtics, 129–96. After the game, another reporter was silly enough to ask Holzman if it mattered to him if the Knicks were blown out of Game One or Game Two. Holzman, who always focused his attention to the next game, not the previous ones, said, "If you knew ahead of time there had to be two games like that, you'd be glad to have the second one go your way. But if you don't know, you'd rather have the first."

Back in Boston, the Knicks won Game Three, 98–91; they

never trailed after the first eight minutes of the game. Behind by 12 at the half, the Celtics got within two points early in the fourth quarter. But, with Havlicek missing most of the fourth due to an injured shoulder, the Celtics' rally fell short. Neither Monroe, whose bone spurs were acting up, nor Havlicek, played in Game Four back in New York—yet the game was a classic. The Knicks would come out victorious in double overtime, 117–110, to take a three-games-to-one lead in the series. But the Knicks didn't give their usual all-out effort knowing they could close out the series back in New York, and lost Game Five in Boston, 98–97. Then, in Game Six, the Celtics broke open a tie game entering the fourth quarter and won, 110–100, forcing a seventh and deciding game in Boston. That didn't bode well for the Knicks. In their entire history, the Celtics had never lost a Game Seven on their home court. Ned Irish came to practice the next day and berated the Knicks for failing to win the series in New York.

In those years, when the Knicks played at the Boston Garden, Red Auerbach, now the team's president and general manager, would try to frustrate them by frequently changing which locker room they'd be using. And, whichever one they were assigned, it was invariably overheated or too small. Holzman's response was to tell his players to take their frustrations out on the court.

Before Game Seven, Holzman, who felt there had been some bad calls by the referees in the series, told off John Nucatola, the league's supervisor of referees. Whether that helped or not is questionable; Nucatola wore hearing aids and may have turned them off while Red was berating him. During the seventh game, Holzman uncharacteristically berated the officials. Normally he just reprimanded them when he thought a poor call had been made. In contrast, Red Auerbach typically voiced his displeasure to the referees on each and every call made against his Celtics. Auerbach figured this relieved his players of the responsibility.[5]

Auerbach and Holzman also differed in terms of their pre-game approach. Holzman, who could be wound up immediately prior to games, usually stayed in the team locker room until almost game time. Figuring he had a leader like Willis Reed out on the court during warm-ups should any issues arise, there was no reason for him to be a distraction. Auerbach, on the other hand, was out on the court during warm-ups watching the opposing team, looking for anything that might give his Celtics an advantage—such as a player favoring one leg indicative of an injury.

Another major difference in coaching style was their respective approaches to picks or screens. Auerbach's Celtics were schooled in using a switching defense, while Holzman advised his players to not switch on defense. Instead, Holzman demanded that his players fight through screens and continue to defend their man. The contrast between the two approaches would play a big part in the seventh and deciding game.

Against a smart team who moved the ball as well as the Knicks, the Celtics' switching defense created moments of vulnerability. When center Dave Cowens was forced into pick situations, he ended up chasing one of the Knicks' guards. That was when they would pass the ball to the player Cowens had been guarding before the switch. Invariably, it was a player (either Reed, Lucas, or DeBusschere) who was momentarily being covered by a much shorter opponent, providing a situational advantage. If Cowens

---

5   Tom Heinsohn was the Celtics coach for this series, as Auerbach had moved from the bench to the role of general manager.

moved back to help out, the guard he had been covering was now the open man.

Though only 6-foot-1, Dean Meminger was a tough defender due to his exceedingly long arms. In a film session after the game six loss, Meminger complained his teammates weren't warning him about screens. Holzman told Meminger, "Don't bitch about the screen—just get through it."

Despite being in considerable pain due to his bone spurs, Earl Monroe started Game Seven, but was ineffective in guarding Jo Jo White. At the beginning of the second quarter, with the Knicks trailing by three, Red replaced Monroe with Meminger, and the game turned in New York's favor. Just as the fourth quarter of Game Five of the 1970 championship series belonged to Dave Stallworth, the final three quarters belonged to Dean "The Dream" Meminger. He forced his way through screens and made Jo Jo White work for every shot. On offense, he scored 13 points and was so active that White fouled out trying to guard him.

Monroe, one of the NBA's greatest stars, never complained that Holzman didn't put him back into the game. All that mattered was moving on to the championship round against the Lakers . . . and the Knicks did. They were ahead by five at halftime, 15 after three quarters, and won the game, 94–78. It was the team's finest defensive performance of the season, holding the Celtics to their lowest point total of the season—34 points below their season average.

The injury to Havlicek factored greatly into Boston's poor offensive production. With Havlicek playing hurt, Jo Jo White and Dave Cowens—the Celtics' other two leading scorers— needed to have dominant offensive games to win. Meminger did the job on White, but Holzman made another move that helped the Knicks shut down Boston: He started DeBusschere against the highly mobile Cowens. Reed, who was still battling knee pain, covered power forward Paul Silas, who was not just slower than Cowens but also much less of an offensive threat. In Game Seven, Cowens scored 24 points, but that was his lowest-scoring game of the series since Game Two.

Stu Inman, who at one time or another served as a scout, coach, or general manager for the Portland Trail Blazers, was speaking with Red Auerbach at the height of the Knicks' successful run in the early 1970s. As quoted by David Halberstam in his book, *The Breaks of the Game*, Inman said to Auerbach, "that's nice about all the media attention Holzman is getting. He's such a terrific coach."

"Yeah," answered Auerbach, "but he ain't got no charisma like me."

Holzman's conscious decision to avoid speaking negatively about anyone—or, if possible, never really say anything—guaranteed he would never be a celebrity. But as Bill Bradley pointed out in his book, Red had no interest in fame and "only wants to be Knick coach." In contrast, Auerbach never hesitated to draw attention to himself by saying or doing anything—negative or otherwise—he felt would give the Celtics an edge.

But, following their victory over the Celtics, Holzman uncharacteristically let himself go. His postgame statements revealed the multiple layers of his true feelings.

First, you had the top soil. To the press, he gave only what he wanted to share publicly, ever mindful to avoid saying anything negative about his rival, Red Auerbach. "I say this was the most satisfying victory I've ever been connected with." Holzman told the *New York Times*. "Right now, in view of all the things that have been said about us in this series, this has been the most satisfying victory I can remember."

To his players, how much the onion skin came off depended on the player.

Holzman always respected Bill Bradley for his intelligence and selflessness, as well as his unique basketball skills. But in the first few years of Bradley's professional career, when he and Cazzie Russell engaged in a struggle to be the starting small forward, Holzman was the ultimate arbiter. And, as a result, Holzman knew he bore the brunt of Bradley's competitive anger and made sure to follow Nat Holman's approach and never get "too chummy" with either player. But, by 1973, he was comfortable enough with Bradley to open up after their win over the Celtics. As Bradley documented in his book, Red told him, "It's days like this that do it. You get hooked—this job, this profession, you live for days like this. It's so great to get them. Everyone was great. We really responded. But you know, it's not real, all this ecstasy, this isn't what life's about. But you get hooked. I always have. Seems like I've played thirty thousand years but today was the greatest thrill. We beat Boston in *their* year. Hell of a satisfaction. Tomorrow I'll call you dumb cocksuckers again, but today, well, today even the scotch will taste better."

To Phil Jackson, a player Holzman felt simpatico with because he saw not only the ball but the entire court, Red revealed a brief, but intense, glimpse of the lifelong rivalry he had with Red Auerbach. As documented in Jackson's book, *Eleven Rings*, Holzman said, "You know, Phil, sometimes life is a mystery and you can't tell the difference between good and evil that clearly. But this is one of those times when good definitely triumphed over evil."

Whatever his exact words were, the Game Seven win over the Celtics in the Boston Garden was the high point of Holzman's coaching career. None of his players ever saw him happier. His team had beaten the Auerbach's Celtics in "their year." After a lifetime of playing second fiddle to Auerbach, Holzman had finally come out on top.

Both Red and his players felt that, after defeating the Celtics—whom they saw as the biggest threat to their winning a championship—the Western Conference champion Lakers would not be as great a challenge.

They weren't.

The first two games were played in Los Angeles, with the Lakers winning Game One, 115–112. But none of the Knicks lost confidence, and they defeated the Lakers in Game Two, 99–95. Back in New York, the Knicks won Games Three and Four (87–83 and 103–98, respectively).

With a three-to-one lead in the series, Holzman decided that the team should fly to Los Angeles immediately following Game Four. That night, as Earl Monroe was walking down Seventh Avenue, three drunk white men in Knicks caps and shirts who had just come from the game were walking in the opposite direction. One of them pushed Monroe, punched him in the jaw, and called him the N-word. An angry, upset Monroe was late to the airport, but Red had waited for him. Monroe told his coach what had happened. In his autobiography, Monroe wrote that a "shocked Holzman shook his head and put his arm around me and told me that, as much as it hurts, I had to forget about it." Red must have told the other players about what Monroe had gone through, and they all left him alone on the flight.

In Game Five, Monroe focused all his anger through his performance. He was the team's top scorer with 23 points—eight of which came in the fourth quarter. The Knicks won their second championship with a 102–93 victory.

The next day, Leonard Koppett, who had covered the NBA since the 1950s and knew Red as well as any writer could, wrote, "Red Holzman, coach and general manager, is the most private of all the Knicks. As strong willed as he is, untalkative, Holzman has succeeded brilliantly in both jobs by imposing his philosophy of team unity on the players to the point where it has become part of them. He also makes all the proper moves during a game, and made the proper personnel changes as needs arose.

But his victory celebration consisted of a few uninhibited smiles, a good night's sleep and calm acceptance of the fact that he could not get bagels and lox for breakfast in a Los Angeles hotel coffee shop."

* * *

In the spring of 1974, the Knicks finished the 1973–74 season with the second-best record in the Atlantic Division (49–33), seven games behind the Celtics. They defeated the Bullets in the opening round of the playoffs and once again advanced to the Eastern Conference finals against Boston. But with Willis Reed and Dave DeBusschere both hurting and on their last legs, there would be no more heroics.

After losing the second game at Madison Square Garden, 111–99, falling behind two games to none in the best-of-seven series, Holzman demonstrated his usual obfuscation in his repartee with the press. The dialogue, as reported by Dave Anderson in the *New York Times*, makes it clear that Red's ability to separate from it all was crucial to his long-term survival under the unrelenting pressures of coaching in New York.

Holzman was asked, "Do you think you can win four out of five?"

"Maybe we can beat 'em four out of five. The best thing to do is start with the next game."

Red was sitting in front of his wooden desk in his cement block office next to the players' locker room. He wore a dark blue suit, a light blue shirt, and a dark blue tie with small white polka dots. "Tomorrow is a good day to take a day off," he said.

"I thought," somebody mentioned, "that you were going to say tomorrow is a good day to die."

"This is important," Red said, "but not that important."

After folding the statistics sheet from the game in his pocket, Red continued, "I'll take tomorrow off. I'll stay home. Maybe go to the race track. We'll practice Thursday, then go to Boston and when we get there, I'll look at the films myself, then I'll show it to the players, Friday morning."

"What will you look for?"

"Just things we might not have been doing that we should have done and things they're doing. They're not doing things different, but sometimes you become aware of certain things just by seeing them."

"Did they run because Reed can't run?"

"They ran so much because they got the ball off the boards. That is usually why you run. You get the ball off the boards. In the second half they just started doing their things better and we started doing our things worse. We didn't have to change our game. We just have to do it better. Our defense is very important to us. Our defense creates our offense. We didn't have it the last two games."

"How come Frazier hardly played in the last quarter?"

"The coach thought he should sit down," Red replied.

"DeBusschere looked like he was limping."

"I can see him limping, too. He's got that stomach muscle. He'll probably take both days off. If we play a good game Friday, that'll get a lot of guys well. If you win, the players tend to overlook a lot of minor things."

"Your team really looks tired."

"I think every team in basketball is tired at this point. Losing makes you tired. If we got a couple of wins, we wouldn't be so tired."

"Do you have any strategic plans?"

"I have a lot of strategic plans," he said, smiling. "Even if I didn't have any, I'd say I did . . . a man who gets paid as much as me, even if [he] doesn't have a plan in the world, I'd say I had a plan."

"Can you control Dave Cowens?"

"He's tough. He's a big, strong guy. He rebounds well, he gets his points."

"Are this year's Knicks as good as last year's?"

"That's hard to say. We had a good team last year. But nobody came around asking me that question after we won the seventh game from the Bullets last week."

"But what's happened in this series?"

"They got off to a good start, they won the first two games."

Finally, Holzman smiled, then asked, "Did I scintillate you with my retorts?"

The Knicks lost the series to the Celtics, four games to one. Nineteen seventy-four would be Boston's year. The Celtics defeated the Milwaukee Bucks in the NBA Finals, winning Auerbach yet another championship.

After the season, Reed, DeBusschere, and Lucas all retired. Holzman faced the impossible task of replacing three Hall of Fame players in one fell swoop. Since taking over the coaching duties from Dick McGuire, Red enjoyed a run of seven consecutive winning seasons. But after seven years of feasting, it was time for seven years of famine.

CHAPTER ELEVEN

"NEVER LET A BALD BARBER CUT YOUR HAIR."

Entering the 1974–75 season, with the retirement of Willis Reed, Dave DeBusschere, and Jerry Lucas, Red Holzman was forced to start John Gianelli at center and Phil Jackson at forward. In comparison to the players they were replacing, Gianelli and Jackson were limited offensively and better suited coming off the bench. With the loss of three future Hall of Famers, the Knicks finished the season in third place in the Atlantic Division with a record of 40–42. Defensively, they missed Reed, DeBusschere, and Dean Meminger, who had been selected by the New Orleans Jazz in the expansion draft. Even with Walt Frazier and Earl Monroe scoring over 20 points a game (21.5 and 20.9, respectively), the Knicks hit the open man enough to have all five starters averaging at least 10 points a game. Despite their losing record, they were able to qualify for the playoffs. But the Houston Rockets, coached by former Knick Johnny Egan, beat them in the first round, two games to one. The decisive third game was a blowout, 118–86.

Holzman had to rely on Gianelli and Jackson because most of the Knicks' top draft picks during his tenure as general manager had not worked out. Because they had been one of the most successful teams in the NBA from 1970 to 1974, their draft selections came late in the first round, reducing their chances of selecting an All-Star–caliber player. But, looking back on their selections with the benefit of hindsight, Holzman passed on some great players.

In the 1970 draft, which took place after Holzman had taken over for Eddie Donovan mid-season, they selected Illinois guard Mike Price with the last pick of the first round when two future Hall of Fame backcourt players, Calvin Murphy and Nate "Tiny" Archibald, were both available. Price played only one full season in the NBA.

In 1971, the Knicks did well picking Meminger. But, out of loyalty to a legendary player, Red chose to protect Reed in the 1974 expansion draft—not Meminger. The Knicks ended up losing both players since Reed, who had been playing with painful leg and knee injuries, retired prior to the 1974–75 season.

In 1972, with the eighth pick in the first round, the Knicks chose 6-foot-10 Tom Riker with the hope that he'd be Reed's eventual replacement. According to Dick Barnett, Holzman said that Riker looks like "the second coming" in practice, but during games, "He disappears." Even in the 1974–75 season, when the Knicks desperately needed solid front court play, Riker averaged less than 10 minutes per game. Red waived Riker after that season, and he never played in the NBA again. To draft Riker, the Knicks passed on a player from Long Island who was a local legend before he even went to college—Dr. J, Julius Erving.

In 1973, the Knicks could have selected another future Hall of Fame player, George McGinnis. Instead they picked Mel Davis, a star forward at St. John's who could never recapture his college success in the NBA.

Although Holzman was the general manager during that period, the blame for making some questionable decisions does not rest solely on his shoulders. As Red often said, whether he was a scout, coach, or general manager, all personnel decisions were the product of a process involving numerous individuals. However, as a scout, Holzman actually saw all the players he recommended compete during their college careers—many on numerous occasions. But, as a general manager, he depended on chief scout Dick McGuire. It's also possible that executives in the Garden hierarchy had input. In any case, Holzman the coach wished Holzman the general manager had made wiser choices.

During the course of the 1974–75 season Red traded Henry Bibby to New Orleans for center Neal Walk and guard Jim Barnett. The move ended up being a huge failure. Barnett, who had broken into the NBA with the Celtics, preferred to play on a running team and was a terrible fit in New York, since both Frazier and Monroe preferred a slower-paced half-court game. Holzman hoped Walk, who had been an outstanding player earlier in his career with Phoenix, would contribute significant minutes in relief of Gianelli. But he was no longer the same player. Physically, he had lost too much weight after becoming a vegetarian; and mentally, his will to win had vanished. Bibby remained productive long after Barnett and Walk retired.

Barnett and Walk were also characters. After one game, Holzman saw Walk getting dressed and noticed that when he put on his jeans, he wasn't wearing any underwear. "No underwear, huh?," asked Red.

"Nonfunctional, Red. Nonfunctional," Walk replied.

When Jim Barnett was playing for the Knicks, *New York Times* reporter Jane Gross became one of the first woman to be allowed into the locker room of an NBA team. Other teams decided the issue of whether or not to allow female reporters access based upon a vote by their players. But Holzman, who was in favor of allowing them access, made the decision unilaterally on behalf of his players. Barnett didn't like the idea and, to show his unhappiness, he surprised Gross by suddenly giving her a kiss on the back of the neck. Red wasn't happy with such behavior. But in his own style, instead of yelling, Holzman got his message across in his own way, asking Barnett, "Would you have done that to a guy?"

Decades later, when I discussed this incident with him, Barnett recalled kissing Gross on the cheek, not the back of the neck. Jane Gross has no recollection of the incident. Nearly half-a-century before the #MeToo movement, she emailed me that, "the players were sweet and affectionate in a nice way."

Back then, when many players and coaches were having issues with female journalists, Red was a trendsetter. One of the first times a female journalist entered the Knicks' locker room, someone on staff came running into his office shouting, "Red, there's a woman in the locker room."

Holzman asked, "Does she have proper credentials?"

"Uh, yeah."

"So?"

* * *

Things didn't get better the following season. Despite the addition of All-Star power forward Spencer Haywood, the 1975–76 season was a particularly frustrating one. The Knicks failed to qualify for the playoffs for the first time in nine years, and their 38–44 record was the team's worst since Holzman had become head coach.

Early that season, the Knicks played a game against the New Orleans Jazz in the newly completed Superdome. The Jazz were the first team to have courtside VIP tickets sandwiched in between the scorer's table and the team benches. Holzman, who was known for his all-consuming focus during games, was about to discover that the NBA had entered a new era of commercialism. As documented by Wayne Federman and Marshall Terrill in *Pete Maravich*, when Red realized that a fan would be literally sitting in the seat right next to him during the game, he unleashed a torrent of curses at Jazz management, everyone seated at the scorer's table, and even at the poor referees. For Holzman, it was an uncharacteristic display of unfocused frustration—and it did little good. The fan seated next to him remained, and the Knicks lost in double overtime.

Normally, Holzman was much more targeted when it came to blasting the refs. He picked his spots to maximize their impact.

And he was even specific as to which referee to blast. At that time, two referees were assigned to call each game. Typically, a veteran referee would be paired with a novice. Former NBA referee Joey Crawford told me that, "The veteran guys [referees] got us through. Red didn't bother with the younger guys and it was refreshing. He knew we didn't know what we were doing. He left me alone. I'm not even sure he even knew who I was." Another NBA referee, Ed Rush, confirmed that Holzman, unlike many NBA coaches, would not go after the least experienced member of the two-man crew. "Holzman was quietly effective, very professional, and at the same time very aggressive when needed," said Rush.

During Rush's early years in the league, he was often paired with veteran referee Mendy Rudolph. In those days, when Red was upset, "He went to Mendy. There were times when he went after Mendy really hard."

Crawford became an NBA referee in 1977 and doesn't recall working many Knicks games before Holzman's coaching career ended following the 1981–82 season. Yet, even from a relatively small sampling, Crawford told me, "I was impressed with Red. Coaches like Dick Motta and Hubie Brown ate you up as soon as you walked on the court. Not Red."

This is not to say that Red didn't get his share of technical fouls. The list of referees that ejected Holzman includes some of the best in NBA history: Mendy Rudolph, Richie Powers, and his old teammate at CCNY, Norm Drucker.

Ed Rush had a long history of working games Holzman was coaching. The youngest referee in NBA history, Rush began in 1966 at age twenty-four and was still working games long after Holzman retired. Rush referred to Holzman as "a great coach" and "a very good person." To Rush, what made Red a great coach was his ability to get his players to share the ball offensively and to understand their well-defined roles. "He got people to think as one," Rush said. He admired Red because "He was honest in his communications. He was not calculated. If Holzman said it, it wasn't just posturing looking for the next call. He was just coaching his team. If he had something to say, it was valid. A lot of coaches have a paranoia. If the opposing coach gets a technical, they feel they have to get one too—but not Red. He didn't feel he had to get one to make up for it. He wasn't going to take a chance in a tight game to get a technical. He knew every point counts."

But Red was easily heard when he felt it was justified. "Giving Red a technical was easy," Rush said. "When he took it to another level, he would explode. It came out of his personality." This was his way of saying that when Holzman exploded, the flavorful street language of his Brooklyn youth came out—but always for a good reason.

For example, in the first half of a game against the Warriors in Oakland on March 17, 1973, the Knicks were trailing when Holzman had one of his justifiable explosions. In the space of nine seconds, Richie Powers hit Red with two technical fouls, ejecting him from the game. Prior to his explosion, seven fouls had been called on his players, and only one on the Warriors. In the 79 seconds following Holzman's blast, the Warriors were called for four fouls, and the game's momentum quickly changed. Having trailed by 17 points, the Knicks pulled to within eight at halftime. In the second half, with Dick Barnett coaching in Holzman's absence, the Knicks won, 117–108.

Not all NBA players followed Holzman's approach of only

complaining to the referees when circumstances warranted it. When a player was protesting too often for his taste, Red encouraged the refs to show they were running the game from a position of strength. When he saw a referee taking a lot of unjustified abuse from an opposing player, "He didn't like it," said Rush. "His demeanor was such that if a guy on the other team was off the reservation, he would ask the referee who was the target of the abuse, 'How much more of this are you going to take?'"

The Knicks players, on the other hand, "were not constant complainers. Frazier never said anything."

The natural tendency for referees is to get caught up in the moment resulting in too many calls in the home team's favor. For referees first coming into the league, Holzman had a phrase for determining if they were strong enough to not favor the home team. "I want to see him on the road [not at the Garden]," Holzman would say. Back in those days, the league was much smaller, and word got around fast whether a new referee would stand up for himself. Early in his career, Rush was calling a game in Cincinnati. Royals future Hall of Famer Oscar Robertson, was, according to Rush, "nasty to young referees." That night, Rush hit Robertson with a technical and soon hit him with a second for an automatic ejection. "Word went around the league fast," Rush said. "In my next game, which was in Chicago, the players were pointing at me and asking, 'Is that him?'"

When Spencer Haywood arrived in New York in the fall of 1975, the press touted him as a savior. Haywood put more pressure on himself, saying, "Then I'll save." An established star used to leading his team in scoring, Haywood didn't fit into Holzman's team-first offensive philosophy, nor did he mesh well with the team's long-established star, Walt Frazier. In one game, Haywood picked up a loose ball near halfcourt with a defender on him while Frazier stood alone under the Knicks basket. But instead of passing the ball to the open Frazier, Haywood drove to the basket and dunked. The basket didn't count, as he had traveled. At that moment, Ira Berkow wrote, "Frazier's shoulders slumped, his eyes twirling in his head."

Years later, in his autobiography, Haywood enumerated the reasons for the Knicks' terrible play in the 1975–76 season. The first reason he gave was that Holzman "had us running the same offensive patterns his team had been running for fifty years and opposing teams were no longer caught by surprise." Bill Bradley told me that the team's problem was not the predictability of their plays but a failure by the players to execute them properly.

In either case, Holzman wasn't in love with Haywood either. In his autobiography, in one of his few negative comments about a player, Red wrote that Haywood "couldn't or wouldn't give up the ball" and "had defensive lapses."

In difficult times, Holzman could be surprisingly inventive when it came to keeping his players loose. Holzman once bet Frazier, one of the best defenders of that era, that he could get a two-handed set shot off against him. "Yeah," Frazier told me confirming that the story was true; and adding, after a brief pause, "and Red lost." Frazier blocked every shot. "All I had to do," Frazier said, "was watch his feet. A two-hand set shot is like a golf swing. There is no improvisation. I didn't even look at his body. I just waited for him to set his feet."

* * *

Within only a few seasons of Red taking on the general manager job in addition to coaching, Ned Irish disliked the idea. "I don't feel the jobs can be combined because a coach can't and shouldn't negotiate contracts with his players," Irish said. "He can't talk to them like a general manager." Irish believed Red wasn't tough enough in his negotiations regarding salaries. According to Phil Jackson, Holzman was exceedingly fair regarding his compensation. Bill Bradley, on the other hand, whose compensation was significantly higher than Jackson's, never negotiated his contract with Red but dealt directly with Irish. The two would meet at a French restaurant once a year, and, by the time dessert arrived, they had an agreement. Walt Frazier's first contract negotiation with Holzman proved Irish was right. As a coach he was, more often than not, telling Frazier how good he was; but with his GM cap on, Red was not so generous in his praise. "You can't be fair," Frazier told me, "because you're an organizational man." After negotiating that first contract—which marked the only time Frazier and Red had a serious difference of opinion—Frazier only worked with Irish directly or other members of the team's upper management.

With Irish handling the salary negotiations for his most highly compensated players, Red's dual role did not create financial challenges for management nor issues of fairness in his player interactions. But what Irish missed is that a coach has a focus on winning in the short term so he can keep his job, but a general manager must always be looking to keep his team competitive in the long term. As long as Red the coach still had the five starting players he inherited from Donovan, Holzman the general manager didn't have to worry about the long-term until injuries or age demanded adjustments. But, when the time came, his inclination was to bring in veterans via trades so the winning continued—as opposed to experiencing some lean years while restocking through the draft. This approach prolonged the period in which the Knicks were viable championship contenders, but also set a pattern for the team solving its problems by bringing in high-scoring players, like Haywood, who would fail to mesh on a team-focused squad.

Following the 1975–76 season, Holzman's contract to be both coach and general manager had ended. He was removed from his GM duties, as the Knicks brought Eddie Donovan back to take the role he once held. It was hoped that with Holzman focused only on coaching and Donovan handling player transactions, the team would return to the playoffs. The process started off well. In the 1976 draft, the Knicks selected Lonnie Shelton, a 6-foot-8, 245-pound power forward out of Oregon State. Shelton's physical build was comparable to Willis Reed's. And that fall, with Bradley retiring at the end of the season, the Knicks acquired small forward Jim McMillan, who had helped bring a championship to Los Angeles in 1972. In December, the Knicks added Bob McAdoo, a 6-foot-10 scoring machine. The hope was that with a lineup consisting of four future Hall of Fame players—Frazier, Monroe, Haywood, and McAdoo—the Knicks would be unstoppable. But, despite all that talent, they didn't play as a team. In his autobiography, Haywood quotes McAdoo, who told him upon being traded to the Knicks, "You sacrificed your game last year, and what did it get you? I'm not sacrificing anything."

On January 21, 1977, the Knicks were, in the words of Leonard Koppett, "taken apart by the Los Angeles Lakers, 108–94." After the game, a frustrated Holzman told the press,

"Everyone comes in and asks me about our superstars and how good we look on paper. But I have to look at what we do on the floor, not on paper. On a good team there are no superstars. There are great players, who show they are great players by being able to play with others, as a team. They have the ability to be superstars, but if they fit into a good team, they make sacrifices, they do the things necessary to help the team win. What the numbers are in salaries or statistics don't matter; how they play together does. We haven't been playing that way, the right way. In this game, things can turn around pretty quick, and I certainly hope they will. But until we show we can do it the right way out on the floor, in games, the reputations don't mean a thing, mine or theirs."

That season, Haywood was injured and played in only 31 games. Lonnie Shelton showed potential, but was prone to getting into foul trouble. McAdoo finished fifth in the league in scoring, but failed to lift his teammates' performance. One writer later described McAdoo's time with the Knicks as "firing away as if in a gym alone."

Holzman had several humorous sayings he utilized when appropriate. One of his favorites was, "Never let a bald barber cut your hair." The implication being, how could someone without hair have any appreciation for yours? With Haywood and McAdoo, Holzman was dependent on two highly gifted—but effectively bald—players who had no appreciation for hitting the open man.

In the spring of 1968, when the Knicks first started to show marked improvement under Holzman, he had joked, "I suppose I tried to make the team fit my philosophy. But if it hadn't worked, I would have thrown my philosophy out the window and used someone else's." But almost a decade later, saddled with two stars who didn't fit his philosophy, Red himself—and not his approach to how the game should be played—would soon be out the window.

By the end of the 1976–77 season, the pieces still hadn't jelled and the Knicks were once again a losing team. In that era, no coach, not even one who had guided his team to their only two championships, was going to hold on to his job in New York after three consecutive losing seasons. After months of speculation, in March 1977, management officially announced that Willis Reed would replace Holzman at the end of the season. The Knicks' public relations staff said Red was retiring, but everyone knew he had been fired.

Holzman, always the company man, still had a year left on his contract but stepped aside gracefully. The handwriting had been on the wall for some time. After the Knicks ended November with four straight losses to fall to 9–11, it was clear that Reed would replace Red. The only question was when. During that season, Holzman had suggested Reed become his assistant coach, which would have allowed for a transitional period. But, according to Holzman, "He [Reed] didn't want to do it." Instead, emulating Holzman's role prior to coaching the Knicks, Reed did some college scouting.

The Knicks' season mercifully ended on April 10, 1977, with a win in Detroit. They had missed making the playoffs for the second season in a row. After the Detroit game, Red broke his long-standing rule that the hotel bar was off-limits to the players. That night, he had a drink with Phil Jackson and Bill Bradley. Holzman spoke about what a great run it had been and how much he appreciated his coaching tenure with the

Knicks. He also noted the fact that current NBA players were entitled to a pension when they retired, but players from his era received no such benefit. They also toasted Bradley, who had just played the final game of his Hall of Fame career. Bradley's NBA career began the same season that Holzman replaced McGuire as coach. Ten years later, as a perfect bookend, Red's coaching career appeared to be ending on the same day Bradley hit his final shot. That summer, Bradley officially began his political career and was elected to the US Senate the following year.

One of Holzman's brethren in the NBA coaching fraternity, Jack Ramsay, was upset by Red's firing. That season, Ramsay's Portland Trail Blazers won an NBA championship playing a team-oriented hit-the-open-man brand of basketball that was the best the league had seen since the Knicks won their two championships. Ramsay was blessed with a future Hall of Fame center in Bill Walton, who could handle the ball and pass so well that Holzman once said if the 6-foot-11 Walton was shorter he could play guard in the NBA. Ramsay was so troubled by Red's firing that at a Fourth of July celebration that summer, when some other guests—who didn't make their livelihood in basketball—spoke about how vulnerable their careers were, Ramsay became angry. To him, no profession was as competitive and in the spotlight as an NBA coach. "Look at Red Holzman," Ramsay said. "One of the best coaches in the league. When New York was winning all those years, everyone applauded. Two or three years later, they stocked up on the wrong kind of players, no one blamed management. They blamed the coach. It was Holzman that got canned. The players can always hide their inadequacies by blaming the coach."

Holzman thought he was finished coaching basketball. He had no interest in college coaching since his style worked best with mature professional players. In his 1978 interview, which took place during the spring of the first year of Reed's tenure as Knicks coach, Red was asked, "Is there anything that could get you to coach again?"

He laughed and said, "I guess everybody has some kind of price. I would doubt it, but, you know. I shouldn't say that positively. I mean I think I could coach again if I had to and maybe by the end of this year I'll feel like I want to, but it would take a pretty good deal because I've got five years left on my contract here. Not my old coaching salary, but a pretty good salary, and for me to come out and start getting into that hassle again, it would take something really good or something that would be pleasant for me."

It turned out, the Knicks weren't finished with him. But it's debatable whether his return to coaching was "pleasant."

At a minimum, he got his fill of Sugar.

CHAPTER TWELVE

"I DON'T CARE IF THEY'RE RED, BLACK, OR GREEN."

Following one of Willis Reed's first press conferences as Knicks head coach, he asked *New York Times* basketball reporter Sam Goldaper, "Well, Sam, how did I do? How was the press conference?"

"You sounded just like Holzman. He never said anything either," Goldaper answered.

"I had a good teacher, huh," Reed replied.

With Reed as their coach, the Knicks were a team in transition. In a move that shocked hometown fans, Walt Frazier was sent to the Cleveland Cavaliers as compensation for the team signing free agent guard Jim Cleamons. Holzman later wrote that, had he still been in a decision-making position, he would have insisted that Frazier—like Reed—be allowed to end his playing career as a Knick. In 1974, Holzman had demanded that Reed, after all he had sacrificed for the franchise, not be placed on the expansion draft list, which would have potentially reduced salary costs.

Red had a special affinity for Frazier and had selected him to be the team captain after Reed's retirement. Like Reed, he would use Frazier as the player he would criticize in front of teammates in order to motivate the group. Reed had told Holzman that it was okay to criticize him in front of the other players—he just shouldn't overdo it. But, for Frazier, the role of team captain did not come as naturally as it did for Reed. During Frazier's final season with the Knicks, he was quoted as saying, "if we win, it will ease the pressure on everybody. But if we don't win, it's a panic situation." Holzman disagreed with Frazier's choice of words. "No time," Red said upon hearing Frazier's comment, "is the time to panic."

This is a good example of why Frazier would later say of Holzman, "When we were at our worst, he was at his best."

With Frazier gone, Jim Cleamons and Butch Beard, another veteran who had been acquired during Holzman's tenure, shared backcourt duties with Earl Monroe. The Knicks finished the 1977–78 season in second place in the Atlantic Division with a record of 43–39. The team improved offensively under Reed, but their defense regressed. In fact, they were the worst defensive team in the NBA based upon average number of points allowed.

In the opening round of the playoffs, they defeated the Cleveland Cavaliers, 2–0. But in the second round, their defensive limitations cost them, and were swept in four games by Philadelphia. The 76ers featured two players the Knicks could have drafted, but didn't: Julius Erving and George McGinnis; and another they sent off in an ill-advised trade: Henry Bibby.

As a player, based upon his physical strength and force of will, Reed exerted great control over the Knicks' destiny. As a coach, he expected a similar level of control. After his first season at the helm, Reed believed the team needed a legitimate center to improve their defense and advance further into the playoffs. As a result, just prior to the 1978–79 season, the Knicks signed 7-foot-1 center Marvin Webster to a five-year contract as a free agent. Webster, known as "The Human Eraser" because of his shot-blocking abilities, was coming off the best season of his career. He had averaged a double-double (double digit totals in points, as well as rebounds, per game) and helped Seattle reach the NBA Finals. But, as compensation for the signing, the Knicks had to give up Lonnie Shelton, a player Holzman had had high hopes for. Plagued by hepatitis, as well as tendinitis in his knees, Webster never fulfilled expectations and became a career backup. In Seattle, Shelton matured and became an integral part of a championship team.

But the most significant move the Knicks made prior to the season was drafting Micheal Ray Richardson out of the University of Montana with the fourth pick in the 1978 draft. Richardson's game was so sweet, they called him Sugar. At 6-foot-5, he could play either guard or forward and was fearless driving to the basket. On the defensive end, Richardson's hands were quick and powerful; if he got just one finger on the ball, he would invariably gain control of it. The hope was that Richardson, along with Ray Williams, the team's first-round pick in the previous years' draft, would form the Knicks' starting backcourt for the longterm. Comparisons were made to Frazier and Monroe, putting undue pressure on a pair of young men and ultimately leading to a heartbreaking tale of what might have been.

As a player, in order to educate the Knicks' rookies in the ways of the NBA, Reed always had one as his road roommate. As a coach, he was just as attentive. Holzman ran the Knicks' rookie camp for just three days immediately prior to the regular training camp. But Reed set up his rookie camp two months before regular camp began and ran it for a full week. Because of this, and because Reed had personally spent time out west with Richardson, he became a father figure to Sugar, whose own father was out of his life by the time he was six.

The Knicks started the 1978–79 record with a 6–8 record. As a result, the latest management group running Madison Square Garden were unhappy. With Ned Irish retired, the new man in charge was Sonny Werblin, a former entertainment industry executive who knew little about the game. His only sports management experience was with the New York Jets football team.

With the poor start to the season, Reed made the mistake of forgetting what Holzman had taught him. Speaking through the press, Reed sought assurance that Werblin still had confidence in him. Not surprisingly, Reed's comments were misinterpreted and translated into sensationalist headlines on the sports pages of the *New York Post*. Werblin, already displeased with the Webster signing, wrongly concluded that Reed—despite sacrificing his long-term health to lead the Knicks to two championships—was not loyal enough. Werblin fired a heartbroken Reed and offered the job to Holzman. Red suggested other coaches for the job, but Werblin insisted and Holzman signed a two-year contract to return as Knicks coach.

Werblin hadn't hired Reed and didn't give him a fair chance to turn the season around. In hindsight, Reed might have benefitted from serving as Holzman's assistant before assuming the head coaching position. Even after Reed took over as coach, Red was still on the payroll as a consultant; but he was rarely consulted. Sportswriters referred to Holzman's office deep in the bowels of Madison Square Garden as Elba, the island where Napoleon was sent in exile.

During the transition from Reed to Holzman, veteran Jim Cleamons was still with the team. As a rookie, he had played on the Los Angeles Lakers' 1971–72 championship team. That experience gave him a firsthand education in winning basketball. As Cleamons told me, "Basketball is a simple game. You move your bodies. You move the ball. You find the open man. You win."

But Cleamons played on Knicks teams that, despite having "some very good basketball players," were "not disciplined" and lacked a "charitable team spirit." He added, "Someone has to sacrifice. You play the game to win, not to score points." The Knicks were then a "young team looking for an identity, learning how to become a team."

Much of the blame lay with upper management; consistency was not their strong suit. During the 1976–77 season, Holzman was deemed too old; but by the fall of 1978, he was regarded as a timeless classic. "Management didn't know what they wanted," Cleamons said. "They were trying to determine what assets they had and what to do with them. They were flying by the seat of their pants, happy to put out a competitive team, and things were not very well thought out. There were no real goals or expectations. Holzman was brought in to bring security and experience to a team that was looking for an identity."

"The better teams," Cleamons added, "keep it simple." This, Holzman did. But his methodology was also based upon treating his players as men—professionals who, according to Cleamons, knew "what to do." That worked when Reed was team captain and set an example based upon personal sacrifice. It was another case entirely when the team leader was Micheal Ray Richardson, a player, as Cleamons politely put it, with "personal issues that became a hindrance to his professional longevity and impacted his career negatively."

When Red was rehired as Knicks coach on November 10, 1978, his first task was to find an assistant coach. Dick Barnett, Holzman's previous assistant, had moved on to life outside of basketball. Decades later, when I asked Barnett if he ever wanted to be an NBA head coach, his hearty laugh told me his answer before he said, "No."

Holzman's first choice was Phil Jackson. But Reed had traded Jackson to the New Jersey Nets where, in addition to playing almost 20 minutes a game, he served as an assistant to head coach Kevin Loughery. Red called Jackson and offered him the job. Had Jackson not suffered from the typical professional athlete's disease of wanting to continue playing beyond his period of natural obsolescence, his career trajectory might have been very different. But Jackson told Holzman, "I have an opportunity to play here and I have a contract and feel responsible, so I'll stick it out here."

Red then called Butch Beard.

When the Knicks had picked up Beard off waivers in December 1975, Holzman was impressed with how quickly he had learned the team's playbook. Dick Barnett, then Red's assistant coach, said that Beard knew the plays better than he did. Beard joked that when you played for as many teams as he had, you have no choice but to learn quickly. Given that self-effacing response, as well as an innate love for the game, Holzman had found a kindred spirit. Beard told me that he was the son Red never had.

Butch Beard was born in Hardinsburg, Kentucky. He attended Breckinridge County High School, where he was such a good player that he won the prestigious title of Kentucky's Mr. Basketball. Although he became a star at the University of Louisville, his NBA career was more of a travel log as he bounced around from Atlanta to Cleveland to Seattle to Golden State and back to Cleveland. Yet, he was selected as an All-Star in 1972 and was the point guard on Golden State's 1975 championship team, where he showed sufficient interpersonal skills to befriend the team's notoriously prickly superstar, Rick Barry. Beard then played for the Knicks for three seasons—one for Reed and two under Holzman.

Only a few weeks before Red's call, the Knicks had waived Beard and he had returned to his Louisville home. "Hey ass-hole," Holzman lovingly said over the phone to Beard, "come back and be my assistant."

Beard told me he had never given any thought to becoming a coach before that call. But, a few days later, despite wanting to continue his playing career, Beard accepted Holzman's offer. "I came back for one reason only, Red Holzman," Beard said at the time. "I hope to coach someday, either at a major university or in the pro ranks. With the Knicks I will be serving an apprenticeship under the best—Holzman. Basketball is my life. I know how to play it. I think I can coach it, and this is the best place to learn."

"Butch was the guy I wanted," Holzman said. "He's intelligent, he knows the game, and he has good rapport with the players."

In addition to hiring Beard, Red made two other moves that showed loyalty was a two-way street for him. First, he hired his old friend Fuzzy Levane as a scout. He then insisted the Knicks re-sign Earl Monroe to a new contract. Although Monroe was no longer the player he had been in his prime, Holzman knew that without Monroe's selflessness the Knicks never would have won their second championship.

Red's first game back was at home against the Celtics on November 11, 1978. As he stepped onto the court, the largest home crowd so far that season gave him the biggest ovation of his career. Red liked to joke that the biggest ovation he ever received was prior to the seventh game of the 1970 championship against the Lakers. But he would add, after a brief, well-timed pause, that Willis Reed—making the most dramatic player appearance in NBA playoff history—just so happened to be walking onto the court in front of him. But, Holzman's favorite entrance story was the time a Garden security person didn't recognize him and refused to let him on the court until he got confirmation that Holzman was really the Knicks' coach.

Things started off well as the Knicks defeated the Celtics, 111–98, which would be the first of five consecutive victories. Holzman did a lot of screaming that first night, but the Knicks "saw the ball," holding Boston under 100 points for the first time that season.

On December 2, Jack Ramsay's Trail Blazers visited the Garden. It was Portland's first game against the Knicks since Holzman's return. As Red made his usual appearance only minutes before the game began, Ramsay, elated that his comrade-in-arms was once again coaching, rushed out to the court and hugged him. It's rare to see one NBA coach embrace another prior to a game, but it's doubtful Ramsay was in a hugging mood after the game—the Knicks won easily, 111–77. That night, the Knicks not only saw the ball but hit the open man. All five starters— Earl Monroe, Ray Williams, Micheal Ray Richardson, Toby Knight, and Spencer Haywood—scored in double figures (with a high of 19 points and a low of 12).

When asked about the team's initial success when he took over as coach, Holzman said, "We've been very fortunate." Being a veteran coach, Red knew the positive start was illusory. The Knicks had lost the three games immediately preceding their win over Portland, as well as their next four games. At midseason, management decided to rebuild with younger players.

On January 5, 1979, Spencer Haywood was traded for Joe C. Meriweather, a player more in synch with Holzman's team-oriented style. In February, Bob McAdoo was traded to Boston for three picks in the 1979 draft. Those selections produced two starting players: Bill Cartwright, an offensively skilled 7-foot-1 center; and Sly Williams, a talented yet troubled forward. The Knicks finished Holzman's comeback season in fourth place in the Atlantic Division with a 31–51 record, but a plan was in place to build the team around Cartwright, Ray Williams, and Sugar Ray Richardson.

* * *

During the 1978–79 season, like most rookies, Richardson had a hard time adjusting to the speed and physicality of NBA play—and the coaching change from Reed to Holzman didn't help. The move shocked Richardson, who told me he had no inkling the Knicks were going to fire his mentor. In his biography, *Sugar: Micheal Ray Richardson, Eighties Excess, and the NBA*, Richardson is quoted as saying of Holzman, "he was an older man and very set in his ways. Besides Holzman didn't like rookies. Didn't like them and wouldn't play them. . . . Needless to say, Holzman and I did not get along very well."

Red's preference was to play his veterans and bring his younger players along slowly. But, if a rookie showed he could play under control and help the team, he was utilized. In Bill Cartwright's rookie season, for instance, he averaged 38 minutes per game.

The problem was that Richardson's greatest strength—his hyperactive energy—was also his greatest vulnerability. Richardson was impetuous. He wanted it all and had no time to wait. He drove his Mercedes through the streets of New York so intensely he made cabbies move out of his way. On the court, he was no different. He would go right at his opponents—even future Hall of Famers such as Magic Johnson and Isiah Thomas—as if they were cabbies he could intimidate right off the road. But Richardson had no neutral gear. For him, going from being *the star* at the University of Montana to the fourth guard on the Knicks behind Cleamons, Williams, and Monroe was a blow to his ego.

In his autobiography, Red wrote, "Richardson and Williams were not thoughtful players, but they had so much talent they were able to excel at times, to get by on raw ability." For Holzman, who was resolute in not saying anything negative about anyone, the fact that he wrote that two of his players were "not thoughtful" indicates much deeper problems. He even lamented how, in the

1978 draft, the Knicks passed on Larry Bird to pick Richardson. Although he notes that the Knicks needed immediate help—and that Bird, who through a quirk was eligible to be selected after his junior year, would not be available until the following season—he must have hated how Bird ended up being selected by Auerbach's Celtics. Bird embodied Holzman's definition of a great player: one who "lifts his teammates' performance."

Instead, Red had Richardson, an incredibly talented yet inconsistent player. Once, when Richardson was pulled out of a game, he screamed at his coach, not only demanding to know why he was being yanked but saying, in front of his teammates, that he was a better player than they were. Holzman later made Richardson apologize to his teammates for the outburst, but not before telling him what he wanted: "I want some discipline. I want you into the flow. I want you thinking."

With all the other players from the championship years gone, it fell to Monroe to provide leadership to keep his young teammates focused on playing with a modicum of pride. After the Knicks lost several games in a row at home, Monroe finally had enough. As documented in Dennis D'Agostino's *Garden Glory: An Oral History of the New York Knicks*, Monroe entered the locker room and started yelling at his teammates, "You guys think it's funny?! These teams are coming into the Garden and kicking our butts and you think it's funny?! I don't think it's funny."

Red was looking on the entire time, "nodding his head and thinking, 'Yeah,' and amening to everything he [Monroe] was saying."

Frustrated about his limited playing time, Richardson once felt so out of sorts he complained to reporter Harvey Araton. "This old man, he don't want me," Richardson said. "I'm calling my agent to get me out of here. Write that." Holzman overheard what Richardson had said. As Araton walked past Red to file his story, Holzman said, "That poor schmuck thinks you're going to help him."

Red wasn't doing himself any favors by referring to Richardson as "*Meshuggah*," which means crazy in Yiddish, instead of Sugar. When Richardson learned what *meshuggah* meant, he called Holzman on it. After that, Holzman referred to Richardson only as Sugar Ray.

In the fall of 1979, near the end of the preseason, Holzman asked Beard to give him a list of the twelve best players on the team; a decision had to be made as to who would make the Knicks' 1979–80 regular-season roster. Red had his own list, but in the same way he encouraged his players to think for themselves by calling their own plays, he was training Beard to make his own choices in preparation for the day when he would be an NBA head coach. Beard's list included only black players, as did Holzman's and Knicks general manger Eddie Donovan's. Although it seems inconceivable today, at the time no NBA team had ever had a roster comprised of only black players. The previous season the Knicks had only two white players on the team. One was John Rudd, whose playing time was negligible. But the other, Glen Gondrezick—or Gondo as he was called—averaged 20 minutes a game and was extremely popular with fans. Gondo was the final player Red waived, which left the Knicks with the NBA's first all-black roster. Beard told me, "Back then, that was a very big statement."

Every other NBA team took notice. It became fodder for an infamous story in the *New York Post* with the line, "It's not like anybody is going to call them the New York N-bockers." Some fans wrote angry letters. Others called up the Knicks office to complain to Donovan. But Holzman understood that if he had kept Gondo as a token, the other players would know it and he would lose their respect. Red told Beard, "I don't care if they're red, black, or green. They're the best we have."

In his Dorot interviews, whose transcripts Holzman had reviewed and signed off on only a few months before releasing Gondo, he was asked several questions that may have convinced him it was time for an NBA team to finally pick its roster strictly upon ability—not color. Red was asked, with reference to his playing days in the early 1950s, "Was there a sense of unease among the white players to see the influx of black players?"

Holzman responded, "I don't think that was ever a problem because the guys who were coming in were all good ball-players and should have been there a lot sooner."

"When blacks began to come into the league was there a quota?"

"No," Holzman replied, "there was never a quota that I knew of."

The interviewer, knowing full well there had been quotas, asked a follow-up question.

"Did you hear them complaining about it though, especially if they got cut?"

"Well, I'm sure they complained, but there'd be no reason to complain to me about it. I know a lot of white guys complained too [laugh] because they got cut."

In his 1987 autobiography, when discussing his decision to establish the NBA's first all African American roster, Holzman made no reference to the unwritten quotas that—despite his denials—he knew existed in the NBA right up until the day he cut Gondo. Instead, Red took the high road, pointing out how much things had changed since he and Fuzzy Levane ate their meals in hotel rooms with Dolly King after he was turned away from segregated restaurants.

* * *

In his second season, Richardson's play improved dramatically and Holzman made him the Knicks' starting point guard. Richardson led the NBA in both assists and steals, but turnovers as well. He had started thinking, which was a positive. Unfortunately, at times his thinking was only about his own statistics. In D'Agostino's oral history, his teammate Mike Glenn— whom the players called "Stinger" because of his accurate outside shooting—recalled that when Richardson passed him the ball he would say, "'Stinger, when you get the ball, don't dribble it. Just shoot it.'" According to Glenn, Richardson did this "because he knew he'd lose his assist if I put the ball on the floor."

Yet with Richardson playing better and Cartwright developing into one of the league's best rookies, the Knicks' record improved to 39–43.

The following season, 1980–81, they began to play team basketball with Campy Russell and Sly Williams at forward; backcourt holdovers Richardson, Williams, and Glenn; and a combination of Cartwright and Webster at center. The youngsters started to buy into Red's system. Their offense was firing on all cylinders, with all five starters averaging in double figures. On defense, the Knicks improved dramatically, going from 20th to 9th in points allowed per game. They finished 50–32, their best record since their championship-winning season of 1973.

But in the opening round of the playoffs, the Chicago Bulls, led by one of the most physically imposing centers in the league, 7-foot-2 Artis Gilmore, swept the Knicks in two straight games. The young team was unfamiliar with the increased pressures of playoff basketball, and reverted to one-on-one play. "You really can't know it [playoff pressure]," Holzman once said, "until you've been through it."

Mike Glenn's lasting memory of that series was of Richardson getting several shots blocked as he challenged Gilmore head-on. Gilmore was no New York City cabbie. That series was the high-water mark of Red's second stint as Knicks coach. The following season, things didn't just go backwards . . . they sank.

After their quick playoff elimination, Sonny Werblin didn't have the patience to maintain a consistent roster that had played well during the regular season and would improve if given time to mature together. Instead, Richardson's backcourt partners and close friends, Ray Williams and Mike Glenn, signed as free agents with other teams. This proved detrimental for Richardson not just on the court, but off. As compensation for Ray Williams, the Knicks received All-Star forward Maurice Lucas, whose offensive game did not jell with Cartwright's, leaving the Knicks with an updated version of Bellamy/Reed circa 1965. Another young backcourt player, Mike Woodson, fit in well with Holzman's approach. Woodson would go on to have a successful career as a player—and decades later, as that rare twenty-first century breed, a Knicks coach with a winning record. But Woodson was traded for Mike Newlin, a veteran whose best days were behind him.

The net effect was that the 1980–81 Knicks team, which had a nucleus of seven or eight players who understood their roles, metamorphosed into a roster of too many ill-fitting pieces complaining of not enough playing time. To make matters worse, Richardson, missing his two friends, fell in with the wrong crowd and began freebasing cocaine. Sly Williams, who had been a starter the previous season, succumbed to the same temptations and saw his skills and playing time reduced. Williams began to miss practices, even games. Eventually, Holzman suspended him. But Red had to live with Richardson, who was still the team's best player and leading scorer. This, although, as Richardson would state in his 2018 biography, as a result of his drug use, "basketball didn't seem as important as getting off."

Holzman's coaching approach relied on his players acting professionally. As Butch Beard would later say, "Red was so good at what he did, he truly believed the only way to win was to have the players learn to motivate themselves." That worked when Willis Reed set the tone, but failed miserably when leadership was in the hands of a player who was as irresponsible as Richardson was during the 1981–82 season. The twenty-six-year-old Richardson never intended to hurt anyone. As Beard told me, "The city had adopted Sugar and he could do no wrong. But, if you're not mature enough, the city will gobble you up."

Richardson was New York City's main course. A counselor up in Harlem who knew Beard let him know that Richardson and Williams were out in the streets buying drugs at 3 a.m. Beard brought it up to them, saying the drug use was altering their personalities.

"You're like *One Flew Over the Cuckoo's Nest*," he told Richardson.

"Regardless of what Richardson may say or think," Beard told me, "Red wanted to help. But Sugar did a good job of covering up from all of us."

The low point came when a reporter asked Richardson what was happening to the Knicks.

"The ship be sinking," he said.

When Nat Gottlieb of the *Newark Star-Ledger* followed up and asked how low it could go, Richardson famously replied, "The sky's the limit."

That spring, Red knew his time with the Knicks was running out. But he never publicly blamed his players. Instead, he reverted back to his well-worn line of, "Win or lose, I'm going home to have my scotch and steak with Selma."

The Knicks finished the season in last place in the Atlantic Division with a record of 33–49. To add insult to injury, in their final game of the season, they lost to Boston by 20 points (119–99). Red Auerbach, still the Celtics' president and general manager, sat opposite the Knick's bench smoking his victory cigar watching what would be Holzman's final game. That season, the Celtics finished first in the Atlantic Division with the best record in the NBA, 63–19.

After the game, Holzman said goodbye to his players, telling them he might not be back. He put on a brave public face telling the press, "We have a good team, but we have not had a good season. Some key players have been hurt, but that goes along with the job. I can't really pinpoint the players."

After the game, Celtics coach Bill Fitch said, "Red Holzman is a great coach. If he was sitting on my bench with my type of players and I was sitting on his bench with his kind of players, he would have had a record that matched ours."

In the 1980s, Larry Bird led the Celtics to three championships.

In the 1980s, Richardson violated the NBA's substance abuse policy three times.

RED HOLZMAN

After his final game as Knicks coach, Holzman was asked to comment about his player's effort. "Not now, it's too close," he said. "Maybe I'll say something soon."

Red looked away, then back, flashed his wise guy smile, and added, "Probably not."

CHAPTER THIRTEEN

"YOU NEVER THINK IT WILL HAPPEN, AND THEN IT DOES."

After being fired by the Knicks for the second time, Holzman knew he would never coach again. Although he still enjoyed the chess matches with opposing coaches, the back and forth with the referees, eating at his favorite restaurants on the road, he was done. The burdens of coaching finally outweighed the benefits. According to Michael Whelan, the son of the Knicks longtime trainer Danny Whelan, Holzman told his father, "The worst mistake I ever made was coming back the second time. It wasn't as pleasurable."

But that doesn't mean Red didn't wish things had worked out differently. In his autobiography, published five years after his coaching career ended, Holzman wrote that if the Knicks had drafted Larry Bird instead of Sugar Ray Richardson, "I could have coached Bird and might still be coaching the Knicks today."

But he never said that publicly when he was "officially" retired in May 1982. Instead, Holzman, who was then sixty-one, spun the end of his coaching career by way of a recurring dream. "I dreamed I was playing in a league and not doing well," Red said, "My passes were bad, my shooting was off, and the man I was guarding was scoring. But the teams I played for, Rochester and Milwaukee, still wanted me. And I thought, well, I guess it's not so bad, how many people at fifty-seven-years-old are still playing in this league?" Holzman smiled. "When I turned sixty, the dream mysteriously ended. In my dreams I finally retired."

Yet, Red remained a loyal company man. In his second stint as Knicks coach, he told his players that, as a matter of professional pride, wearing the Knicks uniform meant something special. And, after being employed by the Knicks in one capacity or another for almost a quarter of a century, he wasn't going anywhere else. One of Holzman's closest friends within the NBA coaching ranks, Cotton Fitzsimmons, had a similar bond with the Phoenix Suns when they were run by Jerry Colangelo—Red's former scouting travel companion, who, as Holzman had predicted, did "pretty well." Colangelo not only ended up owning the Suns, but baseball's Arizona Diamondbacks. "Red Holzman was always a company man, always a Knick," Fitzsimmons once said. "If they wanted him to coach, he coached. If they wanted him to be a consultant, he was a consultant. If they wanted him to scout, he was a scout. So, I'm a company man for Jerry Colangelo. That simple."

In May 1982, at a CCNY Alumni Association Hall of Fame dinner attended by both Red Holzman and Nat Holman, Holman spoke about his most famous disciple. "I taught constant movement with or without the ball. At no time would any player not be in a position to receive the pass. When Red coached those great Knick teams, he had them doing that. But I would think that the last couple of years were painful ones for him when he saw his teams playing one-on-one. That was not his kind of basketball. You don't win games that way."

Shortly after Holzman's coaching career ended with 696 wins, Thomas Rogers, who covered the Knicks for the *New York Times*, asked Holzman if he was frustrated that he didn't reach 700 wins. "The 696 is just a number," Holzman replied. "It's not much different than 700. Sure, I can think of lots of games that we should have won, but I can also think of some games that maybe we should have lost and didn't. Right now, I'm concerned about my tennis game. I keep getting beaten by eighty-year-old ladies. I may have to try serving overhand."

* * *

Holzman's NBA coaching career had lasted for all, or part, of 18 seasons. His 696 career wins were then second only to Red Auerbach's 938.

During his coaching career, Red was fond of saying that the best feeling in the world was "waking up early when you don't have to go anywhere." After his coaching career ended, he enjoyed his free time. Holzman once described his retirement routine this way:

Well, summer season was the same as always, except I took up tennis; I had some free time. I played some tennis, went to the beach, had some lunch, came home. Winter season I did some chores for my wife. Then I played my tennis later in the day, came home, had some cocktails, some dinner, watched TV—you know me, any movie with a horse in it. Went to bed. Got up and did it again the next day. Some guys retire, their friends tell 'em, "You won't like it." I loved it. I've always been a great relaxer.

Red and Selma also enjoyed attending boxing matches at the Garden, as well as Broadway shows. Manny Azenberg recalled that one of Holzman's favorite shows was a Yiddish musical called *Those Were the Days*. He loved that show so much he saw it twice and was literally dancing in the aisles. And not all the ladies Red played tennis against were old. He once played against Martina Navratilova. But, because Selma didn't like to fly, and he never would have dreamed of traveling internationally without her, Holzman never got a chance, as he would have liked, to visit Italy and Israel.

In the years after being fired as Knicks coach, he often spoke to Phil Jackson, who had been an assistant coach with the Nets, a position he would hold until 1981. Then he became the head coach of the Albany Patroons. In 1984, he coached the Patroons to the championship of the Continental Basketball Association (CBA). Following Red's advice, in order to gain further head-coaching experience, Jackson coached in the Puerto Rican summer league. Yet, despite his success in Albany, he was unable to get another assistant coaching position in the NBA. His reputation as someone who marched to the beat of his own drum, as he had documented—despite Holzman's advice—in *Maverick* preceded him. Red had told Jackson that books, unlike newspapers, have legs, and don't end up at the bottom of a bird cage the following day like a newspaper. No matter, Holzman very much hoped to see his protégé coaching in the NBA.

In his 1987 autobiography, Holzman wrote, "Phil has his sights set on an NBA coaching job." Jerry Krause, who had known Red since the 1960s when Holzman told him to "cut the bullshit," was then the general manager of the Chicago Bulls. In 1987, Krause offered Jackson a position as the Bulls' assistant coach. Jackson accepted and, a few years later, was promoted to the head coaching job. Before Jackson's coaching career was over, he won 11 championships—more than any other coach in NBA history. And Jackson took particular pleasure that the coach whose record he had broken was Holzman's nemesis, Red Auerbach. I asked Jackson if Red ever spoke to Krause on his behalf. Jackson replied, "I have no knowledge of Red ever speaking to Jerry K. about me. When we would talk about the future of a coaching position Red would always say, 'I don't have a cabal like some of these coaches: Hubie Brown, Five-Star, or the Boston clique.' So I doubt it. They would sit together during scouting assignments, and both saw my last college tournament game."

The reality was that before Krause hired Jackson, he was also considering Butch Beard for the assistant coaching position, and had even called Holzman asking for his thoughts. But Red would have never recommended one of his two most beloved protégés over the other. Instead, much as he did with his players or assistant coaches, Holzman passed the ball back to Krause telling him he would figure it out on his own. Krause did, and Jackson coached the Bulls to six championships.

Following his firing, Holzman was again under contract as a consultant. But once again he was rarely, if ever, consulted. Sonny Werblin referred to Red as "a luxury," saying he was available for advice if needed. But three subsequent Knicks general managers, from Dave DeBusschere who, according to Ed Rush, "loved Red," to Scotty Stirling to Al Bianchi, all came and went without benefitting from Holzman's experience.

No matter, Red and Selma continued to attend all the Knicks home games sitting seven rows behind the home bench. Selma still kept score. On December 25, 1982, they were at the Garden for a game against the New Jersey Nets. That night, Holzman viewed the game as a basketball fan but also as a former coach.

As a coach, he was often looking at what was happening away from the ball in the unoccupied sections of the court in anticipation of a play that would soon fill those open spaces. But now, as a mere fan, he had the luxury of keeping his eye on the man with the ball. As a result, he could enjoy the remarkable abilities of players such as Knicks star Bernard King. But his thoughts were still those of a coach looking for an edge to win the game. That night, he noticed the Knicks' poor free-throw shooting. During the game he asked Selma what King was shooting from the line. "Two-for-four," Selma replied after searching her scorecard. "And Marvin [Webster], what's he doing?" After checking her scorecard again for the Knicks' center, she said, "One-for-three." Holzman then said, "They've got to do better. We have a chance to win this thing."

Fans paraded past where Red and Selma were seated just to get a close glimpse of him. Some stopped to wish him well. One even pleaded with him for the Knicks to put Scott Hastings, an unheralded rookie, into the game. The legendary coach could only smile and shrug. "What can I do?" Holzman asked. "I'm only watching the game."

The game was close. The Knicks led, 100–99, with 14 seconds left. Craig Wolff of the *New York Times* asked Red his take on what the two coaches were going through. That night, Hubie Brown coached the Knicks; Larry Brown the Nets. It was one year ago to the day that Holzman was coaching the Knicks to a one-point loss to the Nets. "I'll tell you," he said as he looked down at the Knicks who were huddled in a timeout, "you enjoy the ordeal of coaching only if you win. But right now, for these guys, at a moment like this, it is nothing but sheer work. There are no magic words."

As Holzman had anticipated, the Knicks failed to improve their free throw shooting and it cost them the game as they lost in overtime by two points. King finished by making only 4 of 8 free throws; Webster 1 of 5.

The game's result may have been the same as the previous year, when Holzman's team had lost to the Nets on Christmas Day, but the contrast in coaching styles between Red and the current Knicks coach was apparent to anyone who understood the game. Hubie Brown called every single offensive play that night. Fans heard him shout a steady stream of numbers from the bench, "32, 42, 54." On offense, even during his second stint as coach, when his key players lacked experience, Holzman left some decisions up to them. His aim was, as always, to teach them to think for themselves. Both John Warren, who played for Holzman in the 1969–70 season, and Mike Glenn, who played for him from 1978 to 1981, told me they only came to fully appreciate Holzman after they played for other coaches. As Mike Glenn told D'Agostino: "Red wanted you to be a student of the game. More than any coach I ever played for, he wanted guys to talk about the game. Red allowed his players to mature and utilize their intelligence and knowledge more than most coaches. He had no inferiority complex whatsoever. He'd say, 'How you guys gonna handle that pick-and-roll?' Or, 'I don't wanna call a play. Any play you call will work. You just have to execute.' I appreciated Red so much for that. Afterwards, it was so hard for me with coaches who would try to be domineering."

Butch Beard was fired as the Knicks' assistant coach when Holzman was dismissed. Beard later become a head coach, first at Howard University, and later with the New Jersey Nets. It's worth noting that it was Willis Reed, then the Nets' general manager, who hired Beard to coach the team. Reed knew better than anyone that Beard had learned from the best.

Beard had not only spent countless hours talking basketball with Holzman, but had also been taught about the importance of being up-front with his players. "Never lie," Holzman told Beard. "If you're not honest with your players, they will know it." Beard took that advice with him for the rest of his coaching career, long after he left the NBA and was coaching the women's team at Simmons College in Louisville. "Some people might not like my honesty," Beard told me, "but that is what works best for me."

* * *

On May 6, 1986, Red Holzman was inducted into the Naismith Memorial Basketball Hall of Fame. With his professional basketball roots extending back to 1945, Red had a connection to all the other inductees that year: Billy Cunningham, Tom Heinsohn, Fred Taylor, Stan Watts, and Red Mihalik. He coached against Philadelphia 76ers teams that Cunningham played for, and later coached. Holzman could say the same about Heinsohn during his long association with the Boston Celtics. In fact, Red's most satisfying coaching victory, the seventh game of the 1973 Eastern Conference finals, came against a Celtics team coached by Heinsohn. Holzman scouted Jerry Lucas when Taylor was his coach at Ohio State. Although the Knicks never drafted any of his players, he scouted BYU games when Watts was their coach. And in the 1950s, Mihalik refereed NBA games Holzman had coached.

At the induction ceremony, Holzman selected Rochester Royals owner Les Harrison to escort him to the podium. Red selected Harrison for this honor since his years in Rochester were the happiest of his playing career. Not surprisingly, since public speaking was never his thing, he gave a very brief acceptance speech. After the inductees were instructed to keep their remarks to no more than two minutes, Holzman must have been relieved. But, for a coach who prided himself on making sure his teams were always well-prepared, the fact that Red spoke without the benefit of prepared written remarks was unusual. Billy Cunningham, another product of the Brooklyn schoolyards, not only utilized index cards and spoke for twice as long as Holzman, but appeared much more at ease. In his autobiography, Red concedes as much, noting that some of the other speeches were much longer and that he should have spoken "a little more." Someone—my guess is Selma—pointed out that he never once mentioned the Knicks or any of the great players on the two championship teams he coached. That was quite an omission. Without those players, Red never would have been inducted.

Why the omission? Perhaps it was just done in haste. If he had prepared for his speech, he would have used index cards like Cunningham. In fact, when Red ran team practices, Butch Beard once asked him how he kept track of what offensive and defensive techniques he wanted to cover that day. In response, Holzman pulled out a stack of index cards with specific plays written on each. After a play was covered in practice, Holzman noted it on the card and moved it to the bottom of his stack. But it could also be that, had he mentioned the Knicks, in order to be evenhanded, he would have felt the need to mention the Hawks, the other NBA team he coached, and where the memories were far from pleasant.

Holzman did condition his remarks, saying he was sure he was going to leave someone out. He did make sure to thank his coaches, Les Harrison and Nat Holman, and spoke of how "lucky" he was as a player to be associated with a great Rochester Royals team. He named several of his Rochester teammates who were at the ceremony: Al Cervi, Bob Davies, Bobby Wanzer, and Fuzzy Levane. Holzman didn't forget Selma or his daughter Gail, who were both in attendance. He asked that they stand up to be recognized, even using Selma as a foil for an attempt at levity saying, "My wife is a great coach. Unfortunately, she coached some of the bad years."

In an interview with the *Springfield Morning Union* that took place when Holzman was in Massachusetts for the induction ceremony, he spoke more straightforwardly. On his getting fired by Ben Kerner in St. Louis, he said, "It wasn't exactly the kind of situation you expected to retire from. I knew that was coming. Besides, at that time coaching was a learning experience. I like to think I was better at it the second time around."

Holzman knew his time coaching the Hawks—however painful—was part of a learning process which helped make him the right man to bring a championship to New York; a championship which raised the NBA to a new level of popularity. "It was a great thing for New York, and it came at a time when the league needed it," he added. "Boston had been winning everything. The league needed to be strong in New York. We helped with that, and with some television things that were being worked out at the time. It was all good for the future of the NBA."

And, as to his great Knicks teams, perhaps making up for their omission in his speech, Red said, "We just had the right blend of intelligent players who knew how to be unselfish, and knew how to play defense. They were willing to play the game I wanted to play—it was the ideal marriage. They should all be in the Hall of Fame." At the time, Willis Reed, Bill Bradley, Dave DeBusschere, and Jerry Lucas had already been elected. Holzman said he would like to see Walt Frazier, Earl Monroe, and Dick Barnett elected. Frazier and Monroe would later be.

Regarding his induction, although he was then one of only ten men in NBA history who had won championships as both player and coach, Holzman tried to disappear into, as a writer once put it, a cloud of humility. "The funny thing about getting into the Hall of Fame," Holzman said, "is you never think it will happen, and then it does."

In March 1990, at halftime of a game with the New Jersey Nets at Madison Square Garden, the Knicks honored both Holzman and Dick Barnett. That night they retired Barnett's number 12 jersey, and raised it to the rafters of the Garden to join those of his former teammates: Willis Reed, Dave DeBusschere, Bill Bradley, Walt Frazier, and Earl Monroe. A banner was also raised for Holzman with the number 613, as those were all the wins while at the helm of the Knicks. Until it was pointed out to him, Red was unaware of the fact that the number 613 represents the number of mitzvot, or commandments, in the Torah. In subsequent years, he would take great pride in that fact. But, on the night the banner was raised, he was happily making self-deprecating jokes about being honored.

"I thought it was going to be my button-down shirt, but it's going to be a banner. I was afraid I was going to be in that shirt they put up there."

Barnett also had a sense of humor; but his was cool and cutting—never corny. When Red reprimanded a Knicks player for letting an opponent get off too many shots—even though those shots were missing—Barnett disagreed. "Let that Ray Charles shoot," Barnett said. Another time, when a referee was missing flagrant fouls by the opposing team, Barnett stared at him and said, "That a dog whistle in your hand? Nobody can hear that whistle but a dog?" When Bill Bradley first joined the Knicks, he took little interest in his clothing choices. As a result, Bradley looked shabby when compared to some of his better-dressed teammates. At the time, Barnett told Bradley that he would never have to worry about getting mugged—he dressed as if he already had been. And once, when Barnett's backcourt mate Mike Riordan was having trouble covering his former Providence teammate Jimmy Walker in a game the Knicks were playing against Detroit, Barnett told Riordan, "I can tell you know Walker's best move. You stood there all night watching it."

At halftime on the evening Barnett and Holzman were honored, Barnett took the microphone and reminisced about a night when the Knicks were on the road. "Some of the players felt it would improve our eyesight if we went to the burlesque show at the hotel even though we might miss curfew. When we mentioned it to Red, he told us not to go because we might see something there we shouldn't see. But we went anyway. And we did see something there we shouldn't have seen. We saw Red."

On the evening Barnett and Holzman were honored, he was once again forced to dust off his remarkable ability to obfuscate. When asked by a journalist to evaluate the current Knicks squad, Holzman said, "I think they're a good team. They have some dead spots, but they have a lot of high spots."

When asked to describe the team's two championship teams, he said, "I'm always accused of double-talk, but with those players it was a case of being selfish by being unselfish."

That phrase, "being selfish by being unselfish," was one that Red used often when talking about the importance of team chemistry. He did so in his 1978 interview in describing the great Boston Celtics teams that won eleven championships in thirteen seasons, with Bill Russell setting the example for the team. "If you get the first guy doing it right," Holzman said, "like a Bill Russell, if he's doing everything right, nobody else dared to do it any other way. And the thing is, it was beneficial to him for the team to be team-oriented and to play that way. So, in a sense, even though it was beneficial, he was being selfish too because that was the best way for him to play and the best way for him to be part of the team. So, when you get that type of person, like a [Bill] Walton , it's beneficial to him to have the team play team basketball. If they don't play team basketball, he'll do all right, but he won't do as well. So, you know, it's a funny kind of selfishness, but it's a good type, but that's the way it is."

In a best-selling 2017 book, *The Leadership Class: A New Theory of Leadership*, author Sam Walker wrote about dominant teams with elite captains in multiple sports who inspired their teams to extraordinary success. Walker used Bill Russell as his lead example. Though far less articulate than Walker, decades before, Red had understood the importance of leadership.

In this regard, Holzman knew his success was because on his championship teams, he not only had a leader in Willis Reed but also an extraordinary group of men. As Holzman told Craig Wolff of the *New York Times* on Christmas Day in 1983, after being asked how he twice molded a group of unique personalities into a championship team: "By taking advantage of the more subtle talents that each player brought to the team. They could all pass. They could all move well without the ball. They all had a special instinct on defense. With those guys, a coach could do no wrong."

It was therefore not surprising that when I interviewed Dick Barnett and asked him what was Holzman's greatest strength as a coach, Barnett replied, "He didn't get in our way."

Somehow, over three decades before I spoke with Barnett, Red knew how his former player would respond. In 1987, for the epigraph to his autobiography, Holzman selected a poem on leadership written by Chinese philosopher Lao Tzu. The poem, quoted below in full, sums up Holzman's approach to coaching—to attribute his team's success to his players, to set firm rules but not attempt to control his players' every action, to treat his players respectfully, and to do more observing and listening than talking.

A leader is best when people barely know he exists.
Not so good when people obey and acclaim him.
Worse when they despise him.
Fail to honor people. They fail to honor you.

"YOU NEVER THINK IT WILL HAPPEN, AND THEN IT DOES."

But of a good leader
    who talks little
    when his work is done
    his aim fulfilled
    they will say:
    "We did it ourselves."

CHAPTER FOURTEEN
"YOU DON'T CALL ANYMORE."

Dave Checketts grew up a Knicks fan, which was unusual for a teenager coming of age just outside Salt Lake City in the early 1970s. At the time, there was no NBA franchise in Utah, as the New Orleans Jazz wouldn't move to Salt Lake City until 1979. Checketts's friends all rooted for the Los Angeles Lakers. But, as he told me, "The Knicks were my team. They were the Golden State Warriors of their day."

After his parents went to sleep, Checketts would quietly go downstairs, carefully close the living room door, turn on the television, and watch Knicks-Lakers games which ran at 11:10 p.m. after the evening news. That was when Checketts first took notice of Holzman. "I saw Red in action, and I admired him so much. He was competitive, intense, and always put his players ahead of himself."

It was therefore no surprise that on March 1, 1991, when Checketts was appointed as president of the Knicks, the first thing he did was call Holzman and arrange to come out to Cedarhurst to meet with him. Checketts had spent most of his life in Utah, where he graduated from the University of Utah and received his MBA from Brigham Young University. At twenty-eight, when he was named president of the Utah Jazz, he became the youngest chief executive in the NBA. The Jazz were floundering, and there was a high likelihood the team would be sold and moved out of Utah. But Checketts was instrumental in convincing successful Utah businessman Larry H. Miller not only commit to keeping the team in Salt Lake City, but invest in them. In a few years, with the drafting of future Hall of Fame players John Stockton and Karl Malone, the Jazz became one of the NBA's most consistently successful franchises.

In the nine seasons since Holzman had been let go, the Knicks initially started winning with a team built around Bernard King. "He's the greatest scoring machine I've ever seen," said Holzman of King. But, after King suffered a severe injury, general manager Dave DeBusschere made Patrick Ewing their first-round pick in the 1985 draft (first overall) and built the team around the future Hall of Fame center. After four losing seasons, that approach appeared to be working when the Knicks finished the 1988–89 season in first place in the Atlantic Division. But three coaching changes within a three-year period, from Rick Pitino to Stu Jackson to John MacLeod, had them going backwards. The Knicks ended the 1990–91 season at 39–43.

Checketts was hired to bring stability, and that's why he contacted Red. He believed that, as a New Yorker and the most successful coach in team history, Holzman understood better than anyone "what made the Knicks go, what made them relevant to the city."

"Well, you know, I'm here if you need me," Holzman said over the phone.

"No, no, no. I want you to be here. Because I need you," Checketts replied.

That conversation was the beginning of an unlikely friendship between a seventy-year-old Jewish New Yorker and a thirty-five-year-old Mormon who had moved to New York only six months before.

When Checketts's limo pulled up in front of 408 Ocean Point Avenue in Cedarhurst, he told the driver he must be mistaken. Although he didn't parrot the kid who had bicycled past the same house twenty years before, convinced the coach of the Knicks would never live in such a dump, Checketts had imagined Holzman living in far more opulent surroundings. But the driver assured him, "This is it. This is the address you gave me."

Their initial meeting lasted four hours. They sat in Red's living room where, as Checketts told me, "There was hardly enough room for both of us."

In 1991, when people first met Checketts, they typically asked him, "How does a thirty-five-year-old end up president of the Knicks?" But not Holzman. He was gracious and engaged. "I saw the job you did in Utah. Congratulations," he said. "We're lucky to have you."

Checketts had spent the past six months working as VP for International Development for the NBA. His boss, Commissioner David Stern, wanted Checketts to continue working for him. But once the offer had been made to come work for his "dream team," he "couldn't wait to go."

Checketts viewed Holzman as "the guy that holds the keys to the franchise. The person every team with a history has who understands the market, the press, the veterans who played there, who is part of the spirit of the place." He wanted Red to be his confidant. "He was my complete safety valve," Checketts said. "I could say anything to him."

Before Holzman agreed to work for Checketts, he had one requirement. "Dave," Red said. "If I'm going to be around, promise me you won't react." Holzman's philosophy, firmly rooted in his belief that the glass is always half-full, was to never be overly reactive—especially when it came to the press. The key was to stay focused on the long-term stability of the organization.

Checketts agreed. And in early June 1991, Holzman was hired as a consultant; once again a valued part of the Knicks organization. His consulting agreement with the organization was fortified by the amount of time he worked, as well as his compensation. But Red didn't want an office in Madison Square Garden; he didn't want to feel obligated to come into Manhattan every day. His preference was to come in when he was needed. He would attend the pre-draft camp, preseason training camp, and playoff road games.

Checketts got Holzman involved immediately. His first job was to attend the NBA pre-draft camp in Chicago. Red also sat in on coaching job interviews which were held with Doug Collins and Paul Silas. Checketts soon decided that Pat Riley was the man he wanted to coach the Knicks. But this presented him with a chicken or the egg scenario, as Patrick Ewing's contract was expiring. Although negotiations to re-sign him had started, Riley resisted signing on as coach before knowing he would have Ewing on his team. Much as he did with his players, Holzman set out some basic rules for Checketts to follow, but never told him what to do. "Just keep your head—stay calm," Holzman said. "At the same time, you must protect the franchise. It's bigger than any one individual. We want to keep Patrick. We want to get Riley. But you need to put your feet down firmly."

What Red meant by "feet down firmly" was for Checketts to let everyone know he was now the man in charge. As a result, he took an aggressive approach—which worked out, as they hired Riley and retained Ewing. With those two in place, a solid foundation was set.

The Knicks began a run of ten consecutive winning seasons—433 consecutive sellouts. The high-water mark came when the team won two Atlantic Division championships (1993 and 1994) and emerged as the Eastern Conference champions in 1994—unfortunately losing to the Houston Rockets in seven games in the NBA Finals. A ticket to a Knicks game at the Garden once again became as hot as it had been in the championship era of the early 1970s—especially if Phil Jackson, Michael Jordan, and the Chicago Bulls were in town.

Holzman was impressed with Pat Riley's coaching ability. He watched many practices and took particular notice of the intensity Riley brought to every aspect of coaching, from video analysis to defensive planning. The coach's preference in those years was to have his first assistant be an older, veteran coach, and his second assistant be a younger coach he could develop. Riley offered Red the role of being his first assistant for all Knicks home games, but Holzman turned him down, as he preferred to sit in the stands with Selma.

The same year Holzman returned to the Knicks fold, Fuzzy Levane nearly died after suffering a ruptured aortic aneurysm. Levane was in a coma for three days. During that time, *New York Times* writer Harvey Araton called Holzman for a quote about his former teammate. Red replied, "You never heard anyone say, 'Here comes that asshole Fuzzy.'"

Every day for two weeks, until Levane was out of danger, Holzman made the drive from Cedarhurst on the South Shore of Long Island to St. Francis Hospital on the North Shore, to visit his old friend. Levane would make a full recovery.

Throughout the 1990s, because Red was not involved with the team on a day-to-day basis and didn't necessarily know every detail of what was going on, he was able to stay out of the limelight. He rarely if ever made an appearance in the Knicks locker room. On occasion, Checketts would "drag" Red into the locker room after a game, and it was easy to tell which of the players valued his presence. All the players would be sitting there icing their knees and the last thing they wanted to do was stand up. But, as Checketts recalled, two players, Anthony Mason and Charles Oakley, were very respectful. They would get up and greet Red, always referring to him, as "coach."

But more than the locker room visits, Holzman greatly enjoyed being part of the conversation again, especially during preseason training camp down in Charleston, South Carolina, at diners with Riley, his assistant coach Jeff Van Gundy, and general manager Ernie Grunfeld.

At the pre-draft camp in Chicago, while all the other scouts and general managers were sitting, folders open, scoring guys, Holzman didn't bother with documentation. He paid much more attention to how hard a player went at it. According to Checketts, Red still had a razor-sharp memory and could tell you what he liked, or didn't like, about each player he had seen without having taken notes.

During the Checketts era, as Red was serving as a consultant,

New York's rivalry with the Chicago Bulls reached a crescendo. With Phil Jackson coaching the Bulls, Red was conflicted. He remained loyal to his team, but was also pleased to see one of his favorite former players enjoying a level of success beyond anything he or Selma could have envisioned for the gawky kid from North Dakota who needed to take the hanger out.

"Red," Jackson told me, "was always there to congratulate me and tell me what a good job I was doing."

That was not so easy for Holzman to do publicly when Jackson's Bulls came to play in the Garden. In those years, as Holzman and Selma would sit in their usual seats, Jackson always waved hello to them right before the national anthem was played.

Once, when Selma couldn't make it to a game against the Bulls, Dolly Berkow, the wife of the Pulitzer Prize–winning writer Ira Berkow was sitting in Selma's seat. After Holzman had retired, Berkow had befriended him and the two had grown close. That night, right before the national anthem, Dolly noticed something strange, as Red had excused himself and disappeared. He didn't return until the jump ball to start the game. She asked Holzman about his behavior. Red was superstitious and apparently had reason to believe Jackson might be as well. He indicated that, because the Bulls had defeated the Knicks in their last visit to the Garden, if he wasn't around when Jackson waved, the Knicks would have good karma and win the game.

Holzman instructed Dolly, "Don't tell Ira until I'm dead."

Dolly respected Red's wishes. Only after his death did she tell her husband the story. Berkow later asked Jackson about it. According to Berkow, Jackson replied, "I was wondering when Red would catch on."

Seeking confirmation for the story, I asked Jackson who said that superstition had nothing to do with his waving to Red and Selma. He added that he had no recollection of Holzman ever disappearing from his seat in anticipation of a Jackson wave. Berkow believes Jackson is "suffering from a severe lapse of memory." But no matter what the reality, Holzman figured out a way to pay his regards to Jackson privately. At some point, whenever the Bulls came to the Garden, Holzman began asking former Knicks player and broadcaster Cal Ramsey to stop by the visiting locker room before the game and give Jackson his best regards.

Ramsey wasn't the greatest player, but was good enough to spend time on the rosters of the St. Louis Hawks and Knicks from 1959 to 1961. Perhaps, due to the fact that Ramsey was black, he was cut from both teams despite being a better player than a number of his white teammates. At the time, with the exception of the Celtics, NBA teams only had two or three black players on their rosters. Holzman had previously scouted Ramsey at NYU; and after Red took over as general manager, he hired Cal as his statistician. That job eventually led to Ramsey becoming a Knicks broadcaster.

Jackson wasn't the only one who would wave hello to Red when the Bulls were in town. On a night when Selma wasn't able to attend the game, Holzman invited Josh Azenberg, the eight-year-old son of his friend Manny Azenberg, to sit next to him. When Michael Jordan waved hello, Red didn't disabuse young Josh of his misperception that out of 19,500 people in the Garden, Jordan had waved hello just to him.

Holzman was a great admirer not just of Jordan, but also of his teammate Scottie Pippen. "He thought they were both sensational," Manny Azenberg told me.

During Checketts's tenure with the Knicks, ownership changed from Paramount to Viacom and then to Cablevision. Despite these changes, Checketts—as Holzman had suggested—prided himself on consistency. Ernie Grunfeld was the team's general manager throughout most of Checketts's time at the Garden. Not counting a brief stint by Don Nelson, the Knicks had only two head coaches during that same period: Pat Riley and Jeff Van Gundy—who had first been Riley's assistant. Interestingly, Holzman had told Dave he didn't think Nelson should have been let go just because his players didn't like him. Red believed that a coach's lack of popularity with his players should never be a reason for terminating him, especially one who, like Nelson, had a winning record.

One other area where Holzman had definite opinions was in dealing, or more specifically not dealing, with league officials regarding how games were called at Madison Square Garden. Checketts was convinced that the referees never gave the Knicks a fair shake because the whole NBA staff—which is based in New York City—was at the Garden for home games. As a result, the referees went overboard so as not to favor the home team. Red said to leave it alone. If Dave brought the issue up to league officials, Holzman said, "You will create more problems than you will solve."

* * *

During the years Holzman held the keys for Checketts, he would sometime be asked to write a letter of recommendation to nominate one of his contemporaries to the Basketball Hall of Fame. When the request was made, Red would call Dennis

D'Agostino for assistance. He was a senior member of the Knicks public relations staff and the editor-in-chief for all team publications. Red referred to D'Agostino as "Boswell." Originating as a specific reference to the eighteenth-century Scottish writer James Boswell, who was best known for his biography of Samuel Johnson, the term refers to anyone who details the life of a famous contemporary.

Holzman would call D'Agostino and say, "Boswell, are you ready to do me a service?" A recommendation from him carried considerable weight— a responsibility that Red took very seriously. Thanks to him, players like Dick McGuire, as well as coaches such as John Kundla and Alex Hannum, were elected to the Hall of Fame.

Sometimes the request was for someone who was "a lot short of Hall of Fame caliber"; but Red never refused. On more than one occasion, D'Agostino suggested to Red that a particular individual was not deserving. Holzman always replied: "Look, what right do I have to judge who belongs in the Hall of Fame and who doesn't? Who am I to say, 'This guy is a Hall of Famer and this guy isn't? Hell, I don't even know if I belong in the Hall of Fame. So, we're gonna write the damn letter."

Another Garden employee Holzman befriended was Francis Murphy, a senior vice president at MSG Sports. Although Murphy and Red had a nominal work relationship—Murphy worked on matters such as the salary cap—the two men grew close. Like Holzman, Murphy was the son of immigrants. For Murphy, whose Irish father and brother were both deceased, Red filled a void. "I loved him," Murphy told me in 2018. The two men shared many meals together at Suite 200, the restaurant in the Garden for executive management. Murphy can't recall a single time that they talked basketball, but Holzman still favored steak and scotch—preferably Dewar's White Label. Red was fond of Murphy's children and always inquired about them. "Red would have been successful in whatever he did. He was the sort of person you put on a pedestal—and he knew it. He was the best." One year, after the Knicks' MetLife cap night, Holzman asked Murphy if they had any leftover caps. They did. Red asked for a dozen. He took them to the Children's Hospital for Cancer and give them to patients there.

In December 1996, Holzman, Reed, DeBusschere, Bradley, Meminger, and Monroe attended a book signing for a new tome about the Knicks. The line of fans was long, and they all agreed to only sign their names—and not add any personal messages—to keep the line moving. But one player broke the pact, jamming things up. As *New York Times* reporter George Vecsey noted, "Suddenly, the old coach turned his head, and with the caustic tone from a long-ago practice, Red Holzman snapped, 'Monroe, you still won't pass.'" With that, they all broke out in laughter.

In early January 1998, Murphy received a phone call from Red. "I won't be at the game tonight," he said. "I've got leukemia."

Although word soon spread to the press, initially, Holzman shared the news with only three people in the organization: Checketts, Grunfeld, and Murphy.

Holzman was admitted to Long Island Jewish Hospital in New Hyde Park, New York. Privacy still mattered to Red. "At the request of the Holzman family," reported the *New York Times*, "a hospital spokesman said there would be no details released on his condition."

Jackson and the Bulls happened to then be in New York around that time, and Jackson made a phone call to the hospital to speak with his old coach. Not long after, Jackson referred to Holzman as "the ultimate Zen Buddhist seeking the middle." Holzman could not be reached for his response to Jackson's comment, but Harvey Araton wrote, "I can assure you Holzman's response to that would not be printable."

Red soon was well enough to return home, and Frank Murphy called him every day to see how he was feeling. On one occasion, Holzman, sounding a bit exasperated, replied, "Geez, Murphy. Why the hell do you have to call and bother me every day?"

When Murphy finally missed a day, Red called him up early the next morning. "What's the matter, Murphy?" he asked. "You don't call anymore?"

That year, Holzman needed to do whatever he could to retain his sense of humor. At the end of July, Selma passed away of congestive heart failure at age seventy-five. For over twenty years, ever since their car accident, Red would cradle Selma's cane on his arm during games so she could keep score. And he had protected her for far longer than that. Back in Rochester, after a particularly good game, a fan had asked Selma for her autograph. She was nervous and signed using her maiden name, 'Selma Puretz.' The confused fan asked if Selma was Holzman's wife. Before Selma could answer, Holzman responded, "That's OK, buddy, that's her pen name."

"He loved her," Manny Azenberg told me. "And when she died, it disrupted his existence."

During Holzman's years coaching the Knicks, Bill Raftery's Irish immigrant mother often wrote letters to Red, wishing his team good luck. He always wrote back, thanking her and wishing her well. Holzman saved those letters. In 1998, knowing he didn't have much time left, Red bound up all the correspondence from Raftery's mother and sent it to him.

Jon Segal, a writer who had wanted to do an in-depth piece about Holzman in the early 1970s for the *New York Times Magazine*—which Holzman refused to do—later befriended the former coach. They shared a love of basketball and a wicked sense of humor. On occasion, Segal sat with Red at Knicks home games. He taught Segal that he shouldn't watch the ball—as most fans do—but instead turn his attention to the open spaces on the floor to see how plays develop. Segal brought his brother Jim to one game, joining Red. When he went to the bathroom, Holzman conversed with Jim for the first time. When Segal returned, Holzman, his half-glasses resting near the end of his nose, was staring down at the stat sheet from the first half. "You know, Segal," Red said without lifting his eyes, "your brother is a hell of a lot smarter than you are."

By 1998, the two men had grown close. Holzman felt comfortable enough to ask Segal to speak with his doctor on his behalf.

In the later years of Holzman's life, whenever he interacted with Walt Frazier, then a beloved Knicks analyst for the MSG Network, he would end their conversations with the words, "I'm still here, Clyde." During that same time period, Holzman was once honored at the Garden. That night, Frazier ended his remarks regarding Holzman saying, "You're still here, Red. You're still here."

In the fall of 1998, as part of that year's celebration for the new inductees to the Naismith Memorial Basketball Hall of

Fame, a fleet of vintage cars was hired to parade the current Hall of Famers around Springfield. Holzman arrived early and stepped into what he believed was his car. He made small talk with the driver, who was also the car's owner. Always inquisitive, Holzman asked a lot of questions about vintage cars. A few minutes later, Red Auerbach arrived. By then, there were no more cars available. The organizers determined that there had been a mix up—Holzman was in Auerbach's car. After some back and forth as to what should be done, Holzman rolled down the car window, pointed at Auerbach and said, "That's Red Holzman. I'm Red Auerbach. I'm in the right car."

In October 1998, when Bill Bradley was promoting his new book, *Values of the Game,* at Michael Jordan's Steakhouse on the balcony at Grand Central Station, an unusual mix of athletes and politicians—from Willis Reed to Geraldine Ferraro, the former candidate for vice president—were in attendance. Although his leukemia had worsened, Red was there as well, lending support to one of his most famous players.

Later that same month, he was invited to attend the wedding of longtime Garden photographer George Kalinsky. Red very much wanted to be there, but, until the evening before the wedding, wasn't sure if he would be feeling well enough to make it. Cancer patients have good days—and bad ones. But October 25 turned out to be a good day. Kalinsky sent a car to pick Holzman up and take him to the wedding. Reed and DeBusschere also attended. Red had such a good time that he was one of the last people to leave.

"For our wedding present," Kalinsky later said, "Holzman sent a check with a note. The note read, 'Dear June and George—This is the best I can do. I don't know about these things. If Selma were alive, she would have known what to do.'"

A week later, Butch Beard drove to Cedarhurst and spent the weekend with Red. They took a walk and talked about basketball. But Beard's lasting memory of that weekend was Red admitting how much he missed Selma. As he drove home to Maryland on Sunday, he came to grips with the fact that he would never see his coaching mentor again.

Red Holzman died on Friday, November 13, 1998, at Long Island Jewish Hospital.

Holzman's daughter, Gail, asked Checketts to give the eulogy. In his speech, which Francis Murphy helped him write, he spoke about Red not just as a basketball professional, calling him "the patriarch of the Knicks," but as a person. No written copy of the eulogy still exists, but Checketts later said, "Red was the finest human being I've ever known. I can say that without hesitation."

When I met with Checketts in 2017, he could still recall one story he told as part of his eulogy. Once, when he was at dinner with Holzman and Ernie Grunfeld, Checketts said he was unhappy with Knicks backup point guard Greg Anthony. Checketts viewed Anthony as a wise guy and told Grunfeld to trade that "little a-hole." Red replied, "He is a little a-hole. But, Dave, he's *our* a-hole." Holzman was sending a message: however challenging Anthony might be—and Red had dealt with his share of personalities—it was in the best interests of the team to "make him more valuable, not less." In the eulogy, Checketts said "*putz* (fool)," one of Holzman's favorite Yiddish words, instead of "a-hole."

A teary-eyed Fuzzy Levane was in attendance for the funeral. The connection between the two was so long-standing that many in the crowd didn't even know who Levane was or that he had been the one to bring Holzman into the Knicks' fold. Levane couldn't understand how he had come so close to death, yet outlived his old busboy. Because Red appreciated all that Levane had done to keep him in basketball—and that Levane never achieved his level of financial success—Holzman made a specific bequest to Levane in his will.

When Holzman died, the NBA was in the midst of a players' strike and the opening of the 1998–99 season was delayed until February. When the truncated season began, the Knicks players wore a black patch on their uniforms in his memory. With the acquisition of Marcus Camby and Latrell Sprewell prior to the beginning of the season, the Knicks had been expected to be a playoff team. But, after losing four straight games in mid-April, their record was 21–21 and it seemed unlikely that they would qualify for the postseason. With eight games left in the season, for the first and only time in his basketball management career, Checketts felt the need to address his players directly. In the locker room on the campus of Purchase College where the team practiced, using "a few colorful words," he invoked Holzman's name hoping to motivate his players. Checketts told them the black patch on their uniforms was in memory of the greatest coach in Knicks history, and he would be ashamed about their recent lack of effort. They were a playoff team and they should show it.

Like Red, Checketts was no Knute Rockne. But, after his speech, the Knicks won six of their last eight games and qualified for the playoffs as the eighth seed, where they defeated a heavily favored Miami team (who was the top seed in the East) in the first round, then swept Atlanta in four straight, and defeated

Indiana in the Eastern Conference finals. In the championship round, with Patrick Ewing injured and unable to play, the Knicks lost to a heavily favored San Antonio team.

Fuzzy Levane later surmised that if Holzman had lived only a few more months, seeing the Knicks back in the NBA Finals might have given him a reason to carry on. That was wishful thinking. Even if the team had won a championship, it wouldn't have brought Selma back. But one thing can be said for certain regarding that playoff run. Well into the new millennium, that spring remains the last time a Knicks team reached the NBA Finals. And they did it wearing a black patch in memory of the only coach ever to lead them to a championship, William "Red" Holzman.

ONE NIGHT IN STAMFORD

Red Holzman was once asked how he wanted to be remembered.

"The same way Arthur Treacher, the old-time movie star, did when someone asked him the very same question," he said. "I came, I said the words, I took the money, I went home."

Although it's interesting that Holzman responded by citing Treacher, an actor best known for playing servants, Red never thought much about his legacy. That fell into the category of things he deemed beyond his control and not worth worrying about. Red loved basketball and considered himself fortunate to have spent most of his working career involved in the game. For him, that was more than enough.

Holzman did write over a half-dozen books about basketball. But, unlike many famous coaches, none were on leadership. Red never thought being a winning basketball coach made him an authority on how to run a successful business. He was the first to admit that, had he not been blessed with great players, no one would have read any of his books.

Much like the man himself, Holzman's legacy carries on in its own quiet way. It can be seen watching the Golden State Warriors, winners of three recent NBA championships (2015, 2017, and 2018.) They epitomize his mantra: hit the open man.

Red did not have the advanced technology that exists today. In 1970, there were no cameras tracking every angle of the game, resulting in a myriad of statistics that today's NBA teams' analytic managers use to produce detailed postgame reports. The report for each Warriors game lists both teams' passing totals at the very top. The reason for this is simple.: If the Warriors pass the ball 300 or more times in a game—roughly three passes for each possession—they invariably win. The Warriors, like the championship Knicks teams, are built around a core of talented players who can all shoot, pass, and dribble the ball. For the Warriors, everything that the phrase "hit the open man" implies has been simplified by their coach, Steve Kerr, into one easy to remember number: 300. It's no coincidence that Kerr's most productive seasons as a player were spent with a Chicago Bulls team coached by Phil Jackson.

In 2015, Phil Jackson came out of retirement to become president of the Knicks. His goal was clear: to turn the team back into champions. Jackson's five-year, $60 million contract only added to the pressures he faced. But being a great coach does not necessarily translate into being a great basketball executive, and Jackson was fired after only three seasons. His demise can be traced, in part, to his failure to follow one of the most important lessons Holzman taught him.

Red defined a great player as one who elevates his teammates' performance. When coaching the Chicago Bulls, Jackson had said those exact words to Michael Jordan. In New York, as team president, Jackson re-signed the Knicks' high-scoring All-Star forward Carmelo Anthony to a long-term, no-trade contract hoping he would accept the triangle offense and meet Holzman's definition of greatness. Unfortunately Anthony didn't, and there was little Jackson could do to change that. When he decided to trade Anthony, his options limited by the no-trade contract and being goaded on by the local media, Jackson tweeted regarding Anthony, ". . . one doesn't change the spots on a leopard." This violated Holzman's rule: never publicly say anything that could potentially be misconstrued by the headline-hungry New York press, and misunderstood by your players. Jackson told me, "I learned a lot from Red. I was ineffective in using it in my final stint in New York."

Even if Jackson's time as Knicks president did not end well, he remains appreciative of his long-time coach. "He [Holzman] told me I would be a coach. He said, 'You see the game.'" When Jackson won with the Red Auerbach Trophy as the NBA Coach of the Year, he made it clear, for him, it would always be the Red Holzman Trophy.

"Jackson," Holzman said, "was one of my favorite people. I guess it's because I 'discovered' him in the boondocks of the country. He was a strange combination: the hipster son of a minister. He played both parts well."

Another of Holzman's coaching protégés, Butch Beard, now heads the woman's basketball team at Simmons College of Kentucky in Louisville. At Simmons, a NCAA Division II school far removed from March Madness and the billion-dollar business that is college basketball at the elite Division I programs, education is the focus. The Simmons sports program exists to encourage men and women who might otherwise fall through the cracks and fail to complete their college educations. Beard had been coaching men's teams all his life and initially found coaching women a challenge. In the beginning, it was sometimes difficult to get his female players to just say good morning to him. But, by the end of his first season, Beard proudly told me he was "the first male they felt comfortable enough to talk with."

If it were not for Holzman, it is doubtful Beard would ever have become a coach. "I'm the luckiest human in the world," Beard told me, "to have run into Red at that point in my career. If the Knicks hadn't picked me up, my career is completely different."

One night in the spring of 2018, shortly after Beard finished his first season coaching the women's team at Simmons, Dick Barnett was speaking to an auditorium full of young men and women in Connecticut on behalf of the Stamford Peace Youth Foundation. A nonprofit organization, the foundation utilizes basketball to attract and engage young people to use the academic support and enrichment programs they also offer. After his basketball career ended, Barnett earned his PhD at Fordham and taught sports management at St. John's. In the auditorium in Stamford, following a screening of the documentary *When the Garden Was Eden*, about the Knicks teams of the late 1960s and early '70s, Barnett stood and spoke for half an hour about the importance of education. In his version of "see the ball," he repeated over and over again, "You have to live your dream every day."

On that stage in Stamford, because of the respect Barnett had garnered as an essential member of those great Knicks teams, and for what he subsequently achieved in the field of education, he commanded great respect. At eighty-one, he had traveled a long way from the Gary, Indiana, slum, where he had grown up. And his journey wasn't over. That July, he traveled to Cuba as a basketball ambassador for the NBA.

"I'm now doing what I always dreamed of doing," Barnett told me.

Holzman, who had lived his dream of a life in basketball, sensed Barnett's potential decades before. In 1971, he wrote, "Dick Barnett is one of the most knowledgeable men in the National Basketball Association. He's probably the smartest player in the league."

That same year, 1971, Holzman traded Cazzie Russell, establishing Bill Bradley as his starter at small forward and ending four-season of battle between the two players. "But," Bradley told me, "there was always that tension." In 2010, at the 40th anniversary celebration of the Knicks' 1970 championship, Russell asked Bradley if he could speak with him. Bradley agreed, and Russell said, "I'm a Christian preacher now, and I can't preach my best sermon if there is anything heavy on my heart. So, Bill, if I ever said or did anything in those years that offended you, will you forgive me?"

Bradley responded similarly, asking Russell to forgive him for anything he might have said or done all those years before. "We both said yes, and we hugged," Bradley said. "And with that, forty years of tension was gone. The night before, when we all got together, there was still that tension. And I give him so much credit for taking that step. For me, it released something that had been there for forty years. That is a story about the power of forgiveness."

Holzman authored the opening chapter of that story, one he would have been pleased to see conclude with such serenity.

Bradley understood better than most that Holzman's circum-
spect approach with the press was intentional. In his book, *Life
on the Run*, Bradley wrote, "Holzman's 'cooperation' exasperates
some reporters, but it works beautifully. He has mastered probably the most tricky aspect of being a New York coach. He will
probably never be a celebrity. But then, he only wants to be the
Knick coach."

In the acknowledgements to his autobiography, Earl Monroe
thanks Gene Shue, his Baltimore coach, "who allowed me to be
me," and Red Holzman, "who taught me to be me." In Baltimore,
Monroe freelanced more, but never won a championship. In
New York, as Red had surmised, Monroe freelanced less, hit the
open man more, and helped the Knicks win a championship. By
the time he retired, Monroe was the last of the old guard. And,
to Holzman's deep appreciation, Monroe went out preaching the
importance of team pride to his restless teammates.

When Holzman died, stored away, out of sight, in his
Cedarhurst home were hundreds of photographs accumulated
over the course of five decades: Holzman and his Rochester teammates, Holzman with Nat Holman and Les Harrison, Holzman
and Ben Kerner, Holzman and Selma with Academy Award–
winning actor Dustin Hoffman, Holzman and New York City
Mayor John Lindsay, Holzman and Reed, Holzman and Reed
and Frazier, Holzman and Bradley, Holzman and his championship teams, Holzman and Martina Navratilova, even Holzman
and Auerbach. But the only photo of any of Red's players actually hanging in his home was a candid photo of himself and Earl
Monroe joyfully embracing one another.

Don May, a benchwarmer on the Knicks' first championship
team, may have upset Holzman with his shot selection while

playing HORSE, but, in a handwritten note May sent me, he was most appreciative of his former coach. "I learned so much from him," May wrote, "especially defense, that it kept me in the NBA for seven years."

When Red was coaching the Knicks, a Brooklyn teenager who sat up in the nosebleed section of the Garden, not only attended most home games but often arrived way before game time. Red's secretary, Gwynne Bloomfield, often noticed him while she was at courtside setting up the press table before games. One day, Holzman asked Bloomfield, "Who is that kid?" Bloomfield informed Red that he was a very dedicated Knicks fan. From then on, if Holzman had an extra ticket closer to the court, he gave it to the young man who, coincidently, grew up to become a talented filmmaker. Decades later, in his book, *Best Seat in the House: A Basketball Memoir*, Spike Lee referred to Holzman as "*Our* Red."

And Gwynne Bloomfield also noticed that when Red Auerbach was in New York he sometimes stopped by Holzman's office for a chat. Surprisingly, away from the cameras—their mongoose-and-cobra-like rivalry momentarily an afterthought—they were just a couple of Brooklyn guys smoking cigars.

In 1982, several months after Holzman was fired, the Knicks traded Micheal Ray Richardson to the Golden State Warriors for Bernard King. Richardson didn't last long in Oakland and, a few months later, was traded to the New Jersey Nets. After a brief renaissance with the Nets, Richardson, after failing a third drug test, was banned from the NBA for life. But, much to his credit, Richardson faced his demons and had a productive playing career in Europe before retiring at the age of forty-seven. He later returned to the United States and successfully coached in the CBA. Red would have no doubt smiled hearing Richardson yelling at his players from the bench, imploring them, as he once had Richardson, to be "thinking" out there.

Like Richardson, Bob Pettit's view of Holzman mellowed with the passage of time. In *Basketball: A Love Story*, Pettit said, "Red was a great guy and a really good coach. He had an impossible situation with us in St. Louis. We just didn't have the team, and Ben Kerner was a volatile owner. If you didn't produce, he just got rid of you."

But, thanks in part to Kerner, and with an assist from Fuzzy Levane, Holzman ended up back in New York. And, as anyone who was lucky enough to have seen the Knicks play during the late 1960s and early '70s, Red's legacy remains a beautiful memory. As Joe Lapchick, the Knicks' most successful coach prior to Holzman, said during the 1969–70 season, "I just sit at the games and want to rip out the mooring of my seat at some of the plays they make. You really have to know and understand basketball to enjoy some of the things they are doing out there. They are not just playing one-on-one basketball. The ball handling, and the way they are always looking for the open man, are just beautiful to watch."

In *Basketball: A Love Story*, Walt Frazier and Earl Monroe summed up how a team of diverse personalities came to play with such cohesion. "We had harmony because Red Holzman demanded that," Frazier said. "Red was color-blind. That's how he conducted himself, and that's why he had the respect of the team."

Monroe added, "I think his [Holzman's] real skill was communication. A lot of times there's a barrier between player, coach, management, but he seemed to melt that barrier. He didn't show you up, he didn't talk about you in the papers, and he was a player himself so he understood being a jock and being in the locker room. He was a guy you wanted to play for, and his relationship with his players, top to bottom, was always very even."

* * *

What, then, is Holzman's legacy to a new generation of coaches?

Never overreact. This, despite the fact, as Bill Parcells, the New York Giants Hall of Fame football coach, once said, "In this town, it's either euphoria or disaster."

Be firm, but fair. Focus on defense. Set a few important rules, but don't overcoach. Have a sense of humor. As Holzman told Phil Jackson, "It's not rocket science, Phil. It's not rocket science."

It feels appropriate to conclude with Red's ultimate legacy: find yourself a spouse who loves basketball as much as you do and rejoice when he or she steals the show. Although Holzman was the sole interviewee in 1978, Selma, as this excerpt shows, chimed in as necessary:

Steiner: When did you get married, after college?

Holzman: I got married when I was in the Navy in nineteen . . . That was thirty-five years ago, so what would that make it, 1942?

Steiner: Sounds right to me. '42, '43.

Holzman: Sounds like '42. I think huh? November of—

Woman's voice (Mrs. Holzman): Well, weren't you there?

Holzman: [Laugh] November of '42, right?

Woman's voice: Uh-huh.

Holzman: Was it? It was '42, not '43.

Woman's voice: Yes, '42. '42. [Laugh]

Steiner: Did you go out with other girls when you were in college?

Holzman: Oh, never.

Woman's voice: That's a bad question.

Holzman: Never

Steiner: [Laugh] I'm asking it because you're here.

Woman's voice: [Laugh]

Holzman: Never. Never. I think this is a good session, no?

Steiner: Well, we have a few more minutes on the tape, can we just do a few more?

Holzman: Okay.

AN ORDINARY MAN'S LEGACY

Red Holzman was humble, but he was no Moses.

He did steer the Knicks to the only two championships in their seventy-three years of existence. And with each passing season that accomplishment only grows in significance. As a result, it's easy to understand why Dave Checketts called Holzman "the most important man in the history of the New York Knicks franchise."

It was that success which drove the NBA further down a golden road that has, in recent years, produced billion-dollar television contracts. In this regard, Holzman even left an annuity: Phil Jackson. Although his time as president of the Knicks did not end well, how much value did Jackson's coaching add to Michael Jordan's Chicago Bulls—the team that turned the NBA into a global phenomenon? What about his time with the Lakers, where Kobe Bryant and Shaquille O'Neal had already been teammates for three years before Jackson joined, then leading them to three straight championships?

But Holzman's most enduring legacy is to basketball fans.

It lives on in the greatest moment in Rochester professional sports history, when Red dribbled out the clock at the end of Game Seven of the 1951 Finals to bring the Royals their only championship in franchise history.

It lives on in the basketball fans who personally thanked Red—long after he stopped coaching—for the joy they felt watching the Knicks hit the open man.

And it lives on in me, Brooklyn born and bred, and proud to bring Red Holzman's legacy to a new generation of basketball fans.

ACKNOWLEDGMENTS

In March 2017, Dave Stallworth, one of the key bench players on the Knicks' 1970 championship team, passed away. His death brought back my childhood memories of listening to Marv Albert doing the play-by-play of the great Knicks teams of the late 1960s and early '70s when the chants of the Garden crowd, "DE-FENSE, DE-FENSE," resonated across the East River to the Brooklyn apartment where I grew up. Reading Stallworth's obituary, I thought of Holzman. Biographies of other famous basketball coaches had recently been published. Why not one about Holzman, the only man to ever coach the Knicks, a franchise that dates back to the NBA's founding in 1946, to a championship? Wouldn't the story of his coaching success, hidden beneath his modest demeanor, resonate with a new generation of basketball fans? Many thanks to my editor, Jason Katzman, for agreeing with me.

In addition, knowing how the apple has not fallen far from the tree, my sincere thanks to Gail Holzman and her husband

Charlie, who were kind enough to sit down with me for an interview. My thanks to Senator Bill Bradley, Richard Barnett, PhD, Dave Checketts, Butch Beard, the late Cal Ramsey, Ira Berkow, and Jon Segal for also granting me in-person interviews. Berkow and Segal, in particular, went above and beyond the call of duty.

Similarly, when I met with Senator Bradley, he asked me if I had spoken to Phil Jackson. I hadn't, and wasn't sure I would. Jackson had recently been fired as president of the Knicks, and I had my doubts whether he wanted to relive his time in New York. But Bradley's voice went up just a bit when he said, "Oh, I think you'll be hearing from Phil." About a week later, I received an email from Jackson indicating that Bradley had contacted him on my behalf. It read, in part, "I was Red's whipping boy, so I have a lot of stories."

I am appreciative of all those individuals, like Jackson, who took the time to speak with me by phone: Marv Albert, the late Dave Anderson, Dick Van Arsdale, Manny Azenberg, Jim Barnett, Dolly Berkow, Al Bianchi, Gwynne Bloomfield-Pike, Bill Calhoun, Jim Cleamons, Barry Clemens, Jerry Colangelo, Bob Cousy, Joey Crawford, Dennis D'Agostino, Jim Drucker, Johnny Egan, Walt Frazier, Mike Glenn, Robert Goldaper, Cliff Hagan, Bob Harrison, Bill Hosket, Barry Kramer, Jack Levitt, Francis Murphy, Bill Raftery, Willis Reed, Micheal Ray Richardson, Mike Riordan, Ed Rush, Cazzie Russell, Mary Saul, Frank Selvy, Mike Shatzkin, Norm Stewart, Donnie Walsh, John Warren, Michael Whelan, Pat Williams, and Mike Woodson. Thanks to Don May for his note about Holzman, and to Jane Gross and Edward Hershey for their emails.

Thanks to Barry Martin, who helped me track down Holzman's surviving Rochester Royals teammates and sent me his copies of the *Rochester Democrat and Chronicle*; Professor William Gibbons, who assisted me in reviewing the Nat Holzman archives at CCNY and told me about Holzman's Dorot transcript; Anne-Marie Belifante of the Dorot Jewish Division of the New York Public Library for making the transcript of Red Holzman's interviews available; Ken Mattucci and Andrew Lazirko for allowing me access to the video archives of MSG Network; Dan Schoenberg and Scott Weiss for arranging my interview with Walt Frazier; the NBA's Joe Borgia for answering my question regarding technical foul rules in the 1950s; George Kalinsky for allowing me to use his photographs; Harvey Araton for his guidance; and Ray Lebov and his invaluable Association of Professional Basketball Research web site. Thanks to John Feinstein for his emails regarding Red Auerbach's World War II service. Thanks to my writing mentor, Anne Neumann, and my local literary heroes, David Anderson and Jim Hockenberry.

And as always, thanks to my wife, Nurit, the sauce, source, and love of my life.

SELMA HOLZMAN'S CHICKEN-IN-THE-POT RECIPE

Willis Reed told me he still has fond memories of Selma's chicken soup. She had it delivered to him each winter when he got his annual flu. After coming across Selma's recipe on page 210 of the Knicks' 1998–99 media guide, I deemed it worthy of inclusion.

> Buy a chicken, three-and-a-half to four pounds. It should be a big chicken. It should serve four, but in our house it serves two because we're big eaters. Have the butcher cut it into eighths. Boil some water. Put the chicken in a bowl and pour the boiling water over it. Strain it and clean the remaining refuse off the chicken.
>
> Put the chicken in a pot of cold water that barely covers the chicken. Add two table spoons of salt and bring the

water to a boil. Skim off the fat. Put in four or five carrots and four celery stalks with greens on top. Add two onions, a parsnip and a root. The root is very important. A turnip is optional. So is a bay leaf.

Now, cook on a soft boil, half-covered so the steam comes out. Cook about an hour and then add some dills and few stems of parsley. Very important. You might have to add a little more water if it is thick soup and the water has boiled down. Cook another half-hour. The dill and parsley should give it a nice aroma and the chicken should be meaty.

SOURCES

Interviews

Family: Gail and Charlie Papelian

Rochester: Dave Anderson, Bill Calhoun, Mary Saul

Milwaukee and/or St. Louis: Bill Calhoun, Cliff Hagan, Bob Harrison, Jack Levitt, Frank Selvy, Norm Stewart

Puerto Rico: Gail Papelian, Bill Raftery, Ed Rush

New York: Marv Albert, Dick Van Arsdale, Manny Azenberg, Dick Barnett, Jim Barnett, Butch Beard, Ira Berkow, Dolly Berkow, Al Bianchi, Gwynne Bloomfield-Pike, Senator Bill Bradley, Dave Checketts, Jim Cleamons, Barry Clemens, Jerry Colangelo, Bob Cousy, Joey Crawford, Dennis D'Agostino, Jim Drucker, Johnny Egan, Walt Frazier, Mike Glenn, Robert Goldaper, Jane Gross (by email), Bill Hosket, Phil Jackson, George Kalinsky, Barry Kramer, Francis Murphy, Cal Ramsey, Bill Raftery, Willis Reed, Micheal Ray Richardson, Mike Riordan,

Ed Rush, Cazzie Russell, Jon Segal, Donnie Walsh, John Warren, Michael Whelan, Pat Williams, Mike Woodson.

Interview Transcripts

Red Holzman interviewed by Stephen Steiner: William E. Weiner Oral History, Library of the American Jewish Committee, March 21, April 4, and April 20, 1978: Dorot Jewish Division of the New York Public Library, Fifth Avenue and 42nd Street, New York City.

Archives

National Basketball Hall of Fame, Springfield, MA: Red Holzman clip file

Newspapers

New York Times, Rochester Democrat and Chronicle, and *St. Louis Post-Dispatch*

Magazine Articles

Frank, Stanley. "Basketball's Nat Holman." *Collier's,* February 18, 1950, page 19, 65–67

Film and Tapes

Game Seven of the 1970 NBA Finals, Knicks vs. Lakers

Red Holzman documentary, MSG Network

Red Holzman interview with Sal Marchiano, March 27, 1980

Red Holzman interview with Marv Albert, MSG Network

BIBLIOGRAPHY

Alfieri, Gus. *Lapchick*. Guilford, CT: The Lyons Press, 2006.

Araton, Harvey. *When the Garden Was Eden*. New York: Harper, 2011.

Auerbach, Red and John Feinstein. *Let Me Tell You A Story*. New York: Little, Brown, 2004.

Axthlem, Pete. *The City Game*. New York: Harper's Magazine Press, 1970.

Barnett, Dick. *Inside Basketball*. Chicago: Henry Regnery Co., 1971.

Beard, Butch. *Basic Basketball*. New York: Michael Kesend Publishing, 1985.

Berkow, Ira. *To the Hoop*. New York: Basic Books, 1997.

_____. *Full Swing*. Chicago: Ivan R. Dee, 2006.

Berger, Phil. *Miracle on 33rd Street*. New York: Simon & Schuster, 1970.

Bjarkman, Peter. *The Biographical History of Basketball*. Chicago: Masters Press, 2000.

Bradley, Bill. *Life on the Run.* New York: Quadrangle/New York Times Books, 1976.

Colangelo, Jerry. *How You Play the Game.* New York: AMA Publications, 1999.

DeBusschere, Dave. *The Open Man.* New York: Random House, 1970.

D'Agostino, Dennis. *Garden Glory: An Oral History of the New York Knicks.* Chicago: Triumph Books, 2003.

Davis, Seth. *Wooden: A Coach's Life.* New York: St. Martin's Griffin, 2014.

Dorfman, H. A. *Coaching the Mental Game.* Guilford, CT: Lyons Press, 2003.

Federman, Wayne. *Pete Maravich.* Carol Stream, Illinois: Tyndale House, 2006.

Frazier, Walt. *The Game Within the Game.* New York: Hyperion, 2006.

FreeDarko. *The Undisputed Guide to Pro Basketball History.* New York: Bloomsbury, 2010.

Hahn, Alan. *100 Things Knicks Fans Should Know & Do Before They Die.* Chicago: Triumph Books, 2012.

Halberstam, David. *The Breaks of the Game.* New York: Alfred A. Knopf, 1981.

Haywood, Spencer. *The Rise, The Fall, The Recovery.* New York: Amistad, 1992.

Holman, Nat. *Championship Basketball.* New York: Ziff-Davis Publishing, 1942.

Holzman, Red and Harvey Frommer. *Red on Red.* New York: Bantam, 1987.

Holzman, Red and Leonard Lewin. *Holzman's Basketball: Winning Strategies and Techniques.* New York: Macmillan, 1973.

_____. *My Unforgettable Season*. New York: Tom Doherty Associates, 1993.

Isaacs, Neil. *Vintage NBA: The Pioneer Era 1946–1956*. Indianapolis, IN: Masters Press, 1996.

Jackson, Phil. *Maverick*. Chicago, Illinois: Playboy Press, 1975.

Jackson, Phil and Hugh Delehanty. *Eleven Rings*. New York: Penguin, 2014.

Koppett, Leonard. *24 Seconds to Shoot*. New York: Total/Sports Illustrated, 1999.

Lee, Spike. *Best Seat in the House*. New York: Crown Publishing, 1997.

Levine, Peter. *Ellis Island to Ebbets Field*. New York: Oxford University Press, 1992.

MacMullan, Jackie. *Basketball: A Love Story*. New York: Crown Publishing, 2018.

Marecek, Greg. *Full Court: The Untold Story of the St. Louis Hawks*. St. Louis, MO: Reedy Press, LLC, 2006.

Martin, Barry. *Bob Davies: A Basketball Legend*. Rochester, NY: RIT Press, 2016.

McIntosh, Jack. *Frank Selvy: Coal Miner's Son*. Anderson, SC: PIP Marketing Signs, 2016.

McPhee, John. *A Sense of Where You Are*. New York: Farrar, Strauss & Giroux, 1965.

Miller, Larry. *Driven: An Autobiography*. Salt Lake City, Utah: Deseret Book Co., 2010.

Monroe, Earl and Quincy Troupe. *Earl the Pearl: My Story*. New York: Rodale, 2013.

Peterson, Robert, *Cages to Jumpshots: Pro Basketball's Early Years*. New York: Oxford University Press, 1990.

Pettit, Bob. *The Drive Within Me.* Englewood Cliffs, NJ: Prentice-Hall, 1966.

Pluto, Terry. *Tall Tales.* New York: Simon & Schuster, 1982.

Pomerantz, Gary. *The Last Pass.* New York: Penguin, 2018.

Reed, Willis. *A Will to Win: The Comeback Year.* Englewood, NJ: Prentice Hall, 1973.

Robertson, Oscar. *The Big O.* Emmaus, PA: Rodale, 2003.

Rosen, Charley. *The Chosen Game.* Lincoln, NE: University of Nebraska Press, 2017

_____. *Scandals of '51.* New York: Seven Stories Press, 1999.

_____. *Sugar.* Lincoln, NE: University of Nebraska Press, 2018.

Salzberg, Charles. *From Set Shot to Slam Dunk.* New York, Dutton, 1987.

Shatskin, Mike. *The View from Section 111.* New York: Prentice-Hall, 1970.

Stark, Douglas. *When Basketball Was Jewish.* Lincoln, NE: University of Nebraska Press, 2017

Ward, F.T. *Basketball.* Annapolis, Maryland: US Naval Institute, 1943.

New York Knicks Media Guides: 1991–92; 1998–99

New York Knicks Official Guide and Record Book, 1970–71

NOTES
———

Epigraph

"I never really did anything": "The Ordinary Man," *New York Times*, April 19, 1969.

Preface

"In the clamor": "Red Holzman: Cliches in a Crisis," *New York Times*, April 18, 1974. Phone interview with Manny Azenberg.

Prologue

The Chuck Cooper story comes from a July 27, 2017, phone interview with Bill Calhoun. The "pathologically modest" quote is from an MSG film on Red Holzman. The other quotes are from the *New York Times*. "Who cares about": "In a Game of Individuals, They Are a Community," January 25, 1970; "There is not one player": Ibid; "He may well be": "Knicks Quiet Leader," May 12, 1973; "We were a great team": "Former Players and Peers Fondly Recall Holzman, A Friend and a Professional," November 15, 1998.

Chapter One: "You should have known my father."

The Holzman quotes in this chapter without a stated source are from a transcript of the three 1978 interviews for the William E. Weiner Oral History, Library of the American Jewish Committee which are stored with the Dorot Jewish Division of the New York Public Library. They are subsequently referred to in the text as either the Dorot interviews or as the 1978 interviews. Additional information, where noted, comes from Holzman's autobiography, *Red on Red*. Family ages, the year his parents immigrated and from where, Abraham's income, and details about the other residents of their building come from the 1940 US census. Story of the two kids on the bicycle: Interview with Gail Papelian, April 23, 2018. The account of Moe Goldman's first professional game is from an interview he gave for the book, *From Set Shot to Slam Dunk*. Information and quotes pertaining to James Naismith comes from Robert Peterson's *Cages to Jump Shots: Pro Basketball's Early Years*; "passing the ball from one player to another," p. 64. Details and quotes regarding Red Sarachek come from his *New York Times* obituary, November 19, 2005. Details of Holzman's high school games are from the *New York Times*. Information about Red Auerbach comes from *Let Me Tell You A Story* by Red Auerbach and John Feinstein.

Chapter Two: "You even saw the library once in a while."

Additional sources for this chapter were from the *Baltimore Sun*; Holtzman's 1978 interviews with the Dorot; the *New York Times*; CCNY's 1941 and 1942 *Microcosm*; interviews with Jim Drucker and Mike Shatzkin; and Stanley Frank's February 18, 1950 *Collier's* article on Nat Holzman.

Chapter Three: "The best thing I ever did in my life."

Navy-LIU game: *New York Times*, Feb. 16, 1943; Selma story: phone interview with Dolly Berkow.

Chapter Four: "Like being in heaven."

Details of Holzman's playing schedule in independent leagues immediately after the war: "Marksman, Playmaker, Passer—That's Holzman, Royals' 5-year Veteran of Pro Cage Warfare" by George Beahon, *Rochester Democrat & Chronicle*, March 5, 1950. The primary sources for this chapter are Barry S. Martin's biography, *Bob Davies: A Basketball Legend*, Robert W. Peterson's *Cages to Jump Shots*, Leonard Koppett's *24 Seconds to Shoot*, *The Democrat & Chronicle*, Holzman's autobiography, and the Dorot interviews.

Synagogue Story: phone interview with Manny Azenberg, April 11, 2018.

Chapter Five: "The end of the world."

Holzman coaching the Hawks: *Full Court* by Greg Maracek; *The Drive Within* by Bob Pettit; The *St. Louis Post-Dispatch*, 1955–1957, *From Set Shot to Slam Dunk* by Charles Salzberg; *Tall Tales* by Terry Pluto; *Miracle on 33rd Street*, by Phil Berger; Interviews with Jack Levitt, Norm Stewart, Cliff Hagan, Bob Harrison,

Frank Selvy, Bill Calhoun, and Charlie Papelian. Auerbach coaching the Celtics: *Let Me Tell You A Story*.

Chapter Six: "Kid, you're going to do pretty well in this game."

Earl the Pearl by Earl Monroe; *When the Garden Was Eden* by Harvey Araton; Carl Braun testing Holzman: *Miracle on 33rd Street* by Phil Berger; phone interview with Johnny Egan, April 19, 2018; Holzman scouting Rosen: *The Chosen Game* by Charley Rosen. Phone interview with Willis Reed, April 4, 2018. *How You Play the Game* by Jerry Colangelo and phone interview with Jerry Colangelo, February 4, 2018.

Chapter Seven: "I coach without a clipboard."

Interview with Gail and Charlie Papelian, April 23, 2018; Van Arsdale riff: *Miracle on 33rd Street*, by Phil Berger pp. 141-42; phone interview with Bill Raftery, November 1, 2017; *Life on the Run* by Bill Bradley, pp. 62–63; *Red on Red*, pp. 58–62. Phone interview with Phil Jackson, September 28, 2017, *Maverick* and *Eleven Rings* by Phil Jackson. Selma quote on Jackson: interview with Bill Raftery, November 1, 2017. Phone interview with Ed Rush, September 12, 2018. Phone interview with Jerry Colangelo, February 4, 2018.

Chapter Eight: "See the ball."

Phone interview with Barry Clemens, August 11, 2017; phone interview with Phil Jackson, September 28, 2017; *Maverick* by Phil Jackson; *Red on Red*; phone interview with Willis Reed, April 4, 2018; in-person interview with Dick Barnett, May 2, 2018; phone interview with Walt Frazier, December 17, 2018. John

Rudd quote, *New York Times*, November 14, 1978; unspoken interaction between Frazier and Bradley: interview with Bradley, September 14, 2017.

Chapter Nine: "Hit the open man."

Details of the Knicks 1969 preseason camp: *The Open Man* by Dave DeBusschere. Frazier as "key man": phone interview with Marv Albert, June 15, 2018. Interviews with Willis Reed, Cazzie Russell, Mike Riordan, Bill Hosket, Phil Jackson, John Warren, and Robert Goldaper.

Chapter Ten: "Did I Scintillate You With My Retorts?"

HORSE riff: interview with Bill Hosket; Earl Monroe insights: Monroe's biography, *Earl the Pearl*, Sargent Shriver riff: interview with Ira Berkow. Leornard Koppett on Holzman: *New York Times*, May 12, 1973.

Chapter Eleven: "Never let a bald barber cut your hair."

Drinks following the final game of the 1976-77 season: interview with Phil Jackson, September 28, 2017. Quotes regarding coaching: third Dorot interview, April 20, 1978.

Phone interviews with Jim Barnett and Ed Rush, September 12, 2018. Spencer Haywood's New York Knicks years: *Spencer Haywood: The Rise, the Fall, the Recovery* by Spencer Haywood; Women reporters in the locker room: email from Jane Gross, September 14, 2018.

Jack Ramsay's frustration with Holzman's firing: *The Breaks of the Game*, p. 379

Holzman on Walton: *The Breaks of the Game*, p. 130.

Chapter Twelve: "I don't care if they're red, black, or green."

Interview with Butch Beard, December 29, 2017; "Sports of the Times: Holzman's Legacy of Absolute Loyalty" by Harvey Araton, *New York Times*, November 16, 1998.

Chapter Thirteen: "You never think it will happen, and then it does."

Holzman's regrets regarding returning to coaching: interview with Michael Whelan, December 20, 2017. Holzman-Jackson discussions regarding assistant coaching: email from Jackson, May 23, 2018. Holzman's use of index cards for team practices: interview with Butch Beard.

Chapter Fourteen: "You don't call anymore."

Phone Interview with Dolly Berkow, June 12, 2018; interview with Cal Ramsey, April 12, 2018; email from Phil Jackson, August 15, 2018; Jackson Zen quote regarding Holzman: "Mind, Spirit and a Yen to Coach," *New York Times*, January 10, 1998; follow-up phone call with Ira Berkow, August 23, 2018; Selma's death: "Selma Holzman is Remembered," by Ira Berkow, *New York Times*, July 31, 1998. Riffs on Boswell and Murphy calling Holzman: D'Agostino article, "Remembering Red," December, 1998; interview with Dave Checketts, September 25, 2017. Phone interview with Bill Raftery. Holzman on airplane noise: interview with Jon Segal, May 2, 2018. "You never heard . . ." and visiting Levane in the hospital, Araton, *When the Garden Was Eden*, pp. 25, 34

Epilogue: One Night in Stamford

Golden State Warrior's focus on passing: "When they come to pass," by Sam Amick, *USA Today*, May 14, 2018; in-person interviews with Bill Bradley, Butch Beard, and Dick Barnett.

Afterword: An Ordinary Man's Legacy

Checketts quote about Red is from Alan Hahn's *100 Things Knicks Fans Should Know & Do Before They Die.*